SUDAN, SOUTH SUDAN, AND DARFUR

WHAT EVERYONE NEEDS TO KNOW

SUDAN, SOUTH SUDAN, AND DARFUR

WHAT EVERYONE NEEDS TO KNOW

ANDREW S. NATSIOS

OXFORD
UNIVERSITY PRESS

OXFORD
UNIVERSITY PRESS

Oxford University Press, Inc., publishes works that further
Oxford University's objective of excellence
in research, scholarship, and education.

Oxford   New York
Auckland   Cape Town   Dar es Salaam   Hong Kong   Karachi
Kuala Lumpur   Madrid   Melbourne   Mexico City   Nairobi
New Delhi   Shanghai   Taipei   Toronto

With offices in
Argentina   Austria   Brazil   Chile   Czech Republic   France   Greece
Guatemala   Hungary   Italy   Japan   Poland   Portugal   Singapore
South Korea   Switzerland   Thailand   Turkey   Ukraine   Vietnam

Published by Oxford University Press, Inc.
198 Madison Avenue, New York, NY 10016

www.oup.com

Oxford is a registered trademark of Oxford University Press

Library of Congress Cataloging-in-Publication Data
Natsios, Andrew S.
Sudan, South Sudan, and Darfur : what everyone needs to
know / Andrew S. Natsios.
p. cm.
Includes bibliographical references.
ISBN 978-0-19-976420-4 — ISBN 978-0-19-976419-8 (pbk.)
1. Sudan—History—1956-   2. Sudan—Politics and government.
3. Darfur (Sudan)—History.   4. South Sudan—History.
5. Sudan—Race relations.   I. Title.
DT157.66.N37 2012
962.404—dc23   2011037951

1 3 5 7 9 8 6 4 2
Printed in the United States of America
on acid-free paper

This book is dedicated to the memory of two of the great
humanitarian figures of our time who pioneered the creation
of Operation Lifeline Sudan and the humanitarian aid
program early in the Second Sudanese Civil War
Fred Cuny (1944–1995)
and
Julia Taft (1942–2008)

CONTENTS

7 The Three Rebellions of Darfur   117

8 The Third Darfur Rebellion Continued   144

GLOSSARY

Abbala Rizaiqat—The camel-herding Arab Rizaiqat tribe that resides in the deserts of northern Darfur. Together with the Baqqara Rizaiqat, they form the second largest tribe in Darfur.

Abyei Border Commission (ABC)—Designated under the Comprehensive Peace Agreement to establish a proper border demarcation of the Abyei region and to resolve some of the outstanding land title disputes between the Dinka and Misiriyya tribes.

African Union (AU)—A regional multilateral organization that promotes cooperation among the independent nations of Africa. The organization's primary objectives are political and socioeconomic integration; peace and security; and democratic institutions, good governance, and human rights. It is the successor to the Organization for African Unity.

Ansar Army ("The Defenders of Islam")—The Islamic army led by the Sudanese Islamic mystic called the Mahdi in the late 1800s and his successors in the twentieth century.

Anyanya rebellion—The common term used by southerners to describe the first civil war between the North and South from 1955 to 1972.

Arab Gathering—In Arabic called the Tajamu al Arabi, a pan-Arab supremacist group formed in the 1980s with the backing of the Libyan government and then backed in the 1990s by the Sudanese government, and one of several sources of the Janjawiid militia.

Arab Triangle—A geographic region of northern Sudan in the Nile River Valley marked by Port Sudan in the east, Dongola in the north, and Sennar in the south.

Azande—An African tribe that had for several centuries a highly developed system of governance; they live primarily in the northeastern part of the Democratic Republic of the Congo, southwestern Sudan, and the southeastern part of the Central African Republic.

Baqqara Rizaiqat—The cattle-herding Arab Rizaiqat tribe that resides in the plains of southern Darfur. Together with the Abbala Rizaiqat, the groups form the second largest tribe in Darfur.

Comprehensive Peace Agreement (CPA)—The political power and oil-revenue-sharing agreement signed between the Sudan People's Liberation Movement and the Government of Sudan (GOS) in January 2005, marking the end of the Second Civil War in Sudan.

Democratic Unionist Party (DUP)—A political party in Sudan based in the Islamic Sufi orders and led by the al-Mirghani family. This party has traditionally supported close Sudanese ties with Egypt and at one point after independence advocated union with Egypt.

Dinka—The largest tribe in Sudan and the dominant tribe in South Sudan, numbering between 3 to 4 million at the turn of the twenty-first century. John Garang and Salva Kiir are both Dinkas.

First Civil War—The first civil war (also called the Anyanya war) between the North and South started in 1955 months before independence and ended with the Addis Ababa Agreement of 1972.

Funj—A federation of tribes that formed the Funj Sultanate in eastern Sudan along the Ethiopian and Eritrean borders that existed before the colonization of Sudan in 1821.

Fur—The largest tribe in Darfur (approximately 1–2 million), after whom the three westernmost provinces of Sudan (Darfur) are named. Existing for more than three centuries prior to the conquest of Sudan in 1821, the Fur Sultanate was one of the most powerful sultanates in Sudan, with a highly developed political and economic system.

Government of National Unity (GNU)—The interim Khartoum government formed under the 2005 Comprehensive Peace Agreement, which included both northern and southern participation and ended when the South became independent July 9, 2011.

Government of Southern Sudan (GOSS)—The semiautonomous government entity based in Juba under the Comprehensive Peace Agreement created in 2005, which ceased to exist on July 9, 2011, the date of Southern independence, when the Republic of South Sudan was officially created as an independent and sovereign state.

Government of Sudan (GOS)—The national government of the Sudanese state, based in Khartoum, officially called the Islamic Republic of Sudan as of the date of southern Sudanese independence.

Intergovernmental Authority on Development (IGAD)—an East African multilateral organization that promotes cooperation among member states in the following areas: food security and environmental protection; peace, security, and humanitarian affairs; and economic cooperation and integration. This organization supersedes the Intergovernmental Authority on Drought and Development, its predecessor organization, which acted as the official convener and mediator of the North–South peace negotiations that led to the Comprehensive Peace Agreement.

Internally displaced person (IDP)—"Persons or groups of persons who have been forced or obliged to flee or to leave their homes or places of habitual residence, in particular as a result of or in order to avoid the effects of armed conflict, situations of generalized violence, violations of human rights or natural or human-made disasters, and who have not crossed an internationally recognized State border" (according to the Guiding Principles on Internal Displacement of the UN Commission on Human Rights).

International Committee of the Red Cross (ICRC)—An independent and neutral international organization founded in 1863 that works worldwide to provide humanitarian help for people affected by conflict and armed violence, to promote the laws that protect victims of war, and to enforce the Geneva Conventions.

International Criminal Court (ICC)—Governed by the "Rome Statute"; the first permanent, treaty-based international criminal court, established, theoretically, to end impunity for the perpetrators of genocide, war crimes, and other gross violations of human rights. Sudanese leader Omar al-Bashir (among other Sudanese) was indicted by the court for crimes against humanity, war crimes, and genocide in March 2009.

Islamic Legion—A pan-Arab military force created by the Libyan government under Muammar Gaddafi in 1972. Darfur Arabs provided the Islamic Legion with recruits and a launching point for military operations against Chad and were a source of troops for the Janjawiid militia in Darfur during the second and third rebellions.

Jama'at 'al-Islamiyah—A violent offshoot of the Muslim Brotherhood of Egypt; assassinated Egypt's third president, Anwar el-Sadat, and attempted to assassinate the fourth president, Hosni Mubarak.

Janjawiid—An ally of the Government of Sudan, this militia was formed out of the Arab Gathering and Islamic Legion. In Arabic *janjawiid* means "devil on horseback," as its members committed many of the atrocities during the third Darfur rebellion, when they raided and burned Darfuri towns, raped women, and killed young men who might join the rebellion.

Joint Integrated Units (JIU)—Created under the Comprehensive Peace Agreement (CPA) to integrate the northern and southern armies into an interim, unified unit that would meet security needs in the South. However, the two forces were never fully integrated.

Magdum—A prime minister or viceroy of the Fur Sultanate.

Masalit—An African tribe of approximately 250,000 members residing in Darfur, primarily in western Darfur along the border with Chad. The Masalit sultans are rulers of the tribe.

Mengistu Haile Mariam—The Marxist dictator of Ethiopia while it was a client state of the USSR during the Cold War. During his rule from 1973 until 1991, he was an adversary of the Government of Sudan in northern Sudan and one of the earliest and strongest supporters of the Sudan People's Liberation Army.

Misiriyya—One of the largest Arab tribes in northern Sudan.

Muslim Brotherhood—The world's oldest, largest, and most influential Islamic transnational movement, founded in the 1940s in Egypt; Hassan al-Turabi was one of the founders of the Sudanese branch of the Muslim Brotherhood in the 1950s, which eventually evolved into the Islamic Charter Front in the 1960s and then later into the National Islamist Front (NIF).

National Congress Party (NCP)—An outgrowth of the National Islamic Front, this political party was formally founded by Omar al-Bashir in 1998. It remains the governing party of Sudan as of 2011.

National Islamic Front (NIF)—Fundamentalist Islamic political party founded and led by Hassan al-Turabi. After the political falling-out between Turabi and Omar al-Bashir in 1998, the two leaders formed separate political parties; Bashir formed the National Congress Party and Turabi formed the Popular Congress Party.

National Intelligence Security Service (NISS)—The largest and most powerful of the secret police apparatus of the Government of Sudan in Khartoum.

Nazir—An Arab prince.

Nongovernmental organization (NGO)—A legally constituted organization that operates independently from any government. The term is usually applied to organizations that run humanitarian and development programs.

Nuer—Predominantly comprised of cattle herders, this Nilotic tribe is the second largest in South Sudan, with approximately 840,000 tribespeople. The most influential Nuer in Sudan is Riak Machar, the vice president of the Republic of South Sudan and leader of the South Sudan Independence Movement, formed in 1991 with the support of the northern government.

Operation Lifeline Sudan (OLS)—A formal organized consortium of UN humanitarian agencies and approximately thirty-five NGOs established to coordinate humanitarian assistance in South Sudan following the famine of 1988 until 2005.

Paramount chief—The "chief above all chiefs" or king in a particular Southern tribe.

Popular Arab and Islamic Congress (PAIC)—The international Islamist organization created by Hassan al-Turabi in order to challenge the legitimacy of the Arab League and the Organization of the Islamic Conference—two other more traditional Arab and Islamic organizations—as the legitimate representatives of Islam and faithful Muslims.

Popular Defense Force (PDF) (formerly the Murahalin Militia, founded by Prime Minister Sadiq al-Mahdi)—An Arab militia group created under the National Islamic Front (NIF) and Turabi in the 1980s as an alternative force to the regular Sudanese armed forces. This group, which is a predecessor of the Janjawiid, is responsible for many attacks against southern villages and civilians, and committed many of the worst atrocities in the Second Civil War between the North and South.

Republic of South Sudan—The legal name for the world's newest country after South Sudan became officially independent on July 9, 2011.

Refugee—A person who, "owing to a well-founded fear of being persecuted for reasons of race, religion, nationality, membership of a particular social group, or political opinion, is outside the country of his nationality, and is unable to or, owing to such fear, is unwilling to avail himself of the protection of that country" (according to the UN Convention Related to the Status of Refugees).

Revolutionary Command Council (RCC)—The top governing body of the Sudanese state after Omar al-Bashir's coup of June 30, 1989. Membership initially consisted entirely of the military officers who led the coup itself.

Second Civil War—Began in 1983 and was led by Dr. John Garang, ending with the Comprehensive Peace Agreement (CPA) signed in January 1905. The eventual outcome of the CPA was Southern independence on July 9, 2011, when the South officially became a sovereign state.

Sheikh—Literally "a venerable man of more than fifty years of age," this Arabic title of respect is applied to a political and religious leader in an Islamic society.

Shilluk—One of the largest tribes in South Sudan, located along the Nile River close to the North–South border; has traditionally maintained better relations with Arabs than any other Southern tribe. The Shilluk have been led traditionally by a king called the *reth*.

Sudanese Armed Forces (SAF)—The military forces of the Government of Sudan (GOS) in Khartoum.

Sudan People's Liberation Army (SPLA)—The Southern Sudanese rebel army that fought against the GOS in the Second Civil War from 1983 to 2005. After John Garang's death in 2005, Salva Kiir Mayardit became the commander of the SPLA forces.

Sudan People's Liberation Movement (SPLM)—The dominant political movement and civilian organization in Southern Sudan, created by John Garang as a parallel organization to the SPLA.

SPLM and SPLA (North)—The Northern Sudanese political party formed from the parts of Garang's movement that came from and remained part of Northern Sudan—led by Yasir Arman, Abdul Azziz al Hilu, and Malak Agar—even after Southern independence.

Sultan—The Arabic title conferred on political leaders by the caliph, the titular head of the Muslim community.

The Three Tribes—The three Arab tribes—the Ja'aliyiin, Shaiqiyya, and Danagla—inhabiting the northern Nile River Valley that have dominated the economic, political, intellectual, and military power in Sudan since independence in 1956, and in some respects even earlier.

Umma Party—An Islamic centrist political party led by Sadiq al-Mahdi for thirty years starting in the mid-1960s. This is the successor party of the Islamic Ansar movement, and its base of support was located in Kordofan and Darfur provinces.

United Nations International Children's Emergency Fund (UNICEF)—As a permanent agency within the UN system, this organization provides long-term humanitarian and developmental assistance to children and mothers in developing countries.

United States Agency for International Development (USAID)— The U.S. federal government agency that has been primarily responsible for administering U.S. economic development and humanitarian assistance worldwide since the early 1960s.

World Food Program—The UN agency responsible for administering food aid programs, particularly in humanitarian crises.

Zaghawa—One of the most militarily powerful rebel tribes in Darfur, numbering several hundred thousand; joined the Fur and Masalit in revolt during the third rebellion. Members of this tribe also reside in Chad and Libya.

INTRODUCTION

My first meeting with a Sudanese national was with Dr. John Garang, then commander of the Sudanese People's Liberation Army (SPLA), founded to fight against the Sudanese state—located in the country's north, with its capital in Khartoum—and to advance the rights of the southern part of the country (henceforth "North" and "South"). It was June 1989. By this point, Garang and the SPLA had been in open war against the Arab-dominated government in Khartoum, then led by Prime Minister Sadiq al-Mahdi, for six years. This was during the second of two major North–South conflicts, which for purposes of clarity I will call the "First Civil War," which occurred from 1955 to 1972, and the "Second Civil War," which started in 1983 and lasted for twenty-two years—until the South achieved its independence from the North in a referendum. Sadiq al-Mahdi, or Sadiq, as he is known in Sudan, is the great-grandson of the Mahdi, or "Guided One," an Islamic mystic and political leader whose troops overcame the Egyptian forces under the command of British general Charles Gordon during the siege of Khartoum in 1885, when the Mahdi finally drove the Egyptians and British out of Sudan. Gordon was beheaded.

Garang, an African and a Christian, asked to meet with me in Washington, D.C. I had just joined the administration of President George H.W. Bush as director of the Office of Foreign

Disaster Assistance (OFDA), part of the U.S. Agency for International Development (USAID), which leads U.S. government humanitarian relief efforts in crises around the world. And southern Sudan was in crisis: a famine had already killed 250,000 people. My predecessor as director of OFDA, Julia Taft, had mobilized a massive humanitarian aid effort, working with international and private aid agencies. "Dr. John"—as Garang was known—wanted to explain the South's perspective and to remind me how crucial humanitarian assistance was to his people, who for many years had been victims of starvation, atrocities, and epidemics caused by Northern tactics during the war. I learned a great deal that day. Garang was a very gifted and dedicated teacher, and I will always be indebted to him. Much of the story that follows involves Garang and the process that has now led to Sudan's division into two separate sovereign states, as of July 9, 2011.

I made several other Sudanese friends in my early years of involvement with Sudan, but they will remain anonymous in this book because they are Northern Arabs and devout Muslims who would be at risk of reprisals from the Bashir government if I mentioned their names. They are well-educated, sophisticated members of the Khartoum elite who believe in democracy and human rights and oppose much of what the Bashir government is doing, and have educated me over the years on the dynamics of Northern Sudanese society and politics. I am indebted to them as well.

Three months after my meeting with Garang, I took the first of dozens of trips to Sudan and began a long engagement with the country and its people. From 2001 to 2006 I served as administrator of USAID and oversaw the U.S. government's reconstruction efforts in southern Sudan and the American government's humanitarian aid efforts during the rebellion in Darfur, a region in western Sudan, and consisting of three states—West Darfur, North Darfur, and South Darfur—in which nearly 300,000 people lost their lives and which involved atrocities against the civilian population on a grand scale. In October 2006, President George W. Bush appointed me as his special envoy to Sudan to lead diplomatic efforts to end the bloodshed in Darfur and to support the implementation of a North–South peace agreement.

Sudan is situated in eastern Africa, nestled in a vast and intricate network of rivers—including the White and Blue Nile—and their tributaries, as well as along the fault line between Black Africa and Arab Africa. Indeed, one of the greatest unresolved issues in the region's politics has involved Islam. With the exception of the Communist Party and the Sudanese People's Liberation Movement (SPLM; the political arm of Garang's army), most major Northern Sudanese political parties claim their roots in and legitimacy from the Quran and Islamic teaching. They cover a broad range of opinion on public policy issues, from the more moderate Republican Brothers to the Umma Party, led by Sadiq al-Mahdi, who is at heart a modernist, and who during the Cold War was pro-Western and anti-Communist. He remains very much in the Islamic democratic tradition (though his government— he has twice served as prime minister— committed atrocities against the southern people on a scale comparable, as we will see, to what happened in the 1990s under the Bashir government).

Among these parties are a subset—called Salafists—that accepts only the Quran, and the three generations of Islamic scholarship following that of the Prophet Muhammad, as authentic, rejecting all subsequent scholarship as a corruption. The terms "Islamic" and "Islamists" should not be confused. Islamists are part of the Salafist tradition and have been associated with the Egyptian-based Muslim Brotherhood (though many Salafists reject the Brotherhood's political agenda, both in and outside Sudan). For the past half century, the best known and most dominant Sudanese Islamist has been Hassan al-Turabi, whose views and actions, as we will see in some detail, have deeply influenced Sudan's modern history.

Some might interpret my treatment of both Islamic and Islamist movements as an attack on Islam. Of course, it is not. There is nothing inherently undemocratic about Islam; in fact, many elements of the Prophet's teaching could form the basis for a robust democratic political tradition. For a set of peculiar reasons beyond the scope of this book, that is not how political Islam has evolved in recent decades, including in Sudan.

A second unresolved issue has been the relationship of the periphery of Sudan to the Arab Triangle, which is located at the center of the country, demarcated by Port Sudan on the Red Sea, Dongala on the Nile River to the north, and Sennar to the south. Khartoum, North Khartoum, and Omdurman lie at the center of the Arab Triangle; known as the three cities, they form one large metropolis. Three tribes of the Northern Nile River Valley in the Arab Triangle—the Ja'aliyiin, the Shaiqiyya, and the Danagla—have dominated Sudan since colonization by Egypt in 1821. Their dominance has led to the virtual exclusion of other tribes and regions from political, economic, and military power. This does not mean that all of the members of the three tribes are oppressors, or that they all agree with one other on all issues. Many from the Sudanese Northern Nile River elite have devoted their lives to human rights and good governance, and risked their lives fighting the abuses of power by successive Sudanese governments. But the concentration of power in these three tribes and their some-times ruthless efforts to keep that power has nonetheless led to constant strife and human rights abuses on a epic scale.

This book is part of the "What Everyone Needs to Know" series of Oxford University Press. Because of the nature of the series, I have had to abbreviate the country's long and rich history. Most of the book (chapters 4–11) describes Sudanese history since the Second Civil War began in 1983, which I know best from personal experience. As will become evident to some readers, I am indebted to several scholars for their research and writing about earlier (and sometimes current) Sudanese history: Douglas Johnston, the late Robert Collins,

Millard Burr, Alex deWaal, Julie Flint, Francis Deng, and M. W. Daly. I would like to thank several Georgetown University graduate students who helped with research and fact-checking, and in gathering together photographs, maps, and charts: Kelly Doley, Zach Pusch, Zach Scott, Matthew Sinn, and David Trichler. My hardworking teaching assistant, Mark Skeith, did yeoman's work editing the manuscript, formatting, and arranging the bibliography. I would also like to thank Mike Abramowitz, Kate Almquist, Brian D'Silva, Kate Farnsworth, Julie Flint, Alan Goulty, Dan Large, Jason Matus, John Voll, and Roger Winter, for reading the manuscript and offering many useful suggestions to improve it. My literary agent, Leona Schecter, has been a thoughtful critic and made valuable suggestions, as has my daughter Emily, who is an editor herself. Tim Bent, executive editor at Oxford University Press, has greatly improved the clarity of my prose and the flow of the book with his sharp editing pen. My wife of thirty-six years, Elizabeth, has been a constant encouragement to me, helping me stay on schedule as I wrote and edited this book the summers of 2010 and 2011 at our summer home on an island off the coast of Maine. The many people who have given me advice on this manuscript may not agree with some of my perspectives on Sudan; I am finally responsible for the analysis contained in the book.

The Sudanese people—Northerners and Southerners alike—are admired throughout African and the Arab worlds for their gentleness, hospitality, and resourcefulness. They do not deserve the leaders or governments that have ruled them, or the staggering suffering they have been forced to endure with each successive year since independence. My hope—all of our hopes—is that the resolution of the North–South issue through the creation of the Republic of South Sudan as an independent sovereign state will create enough stability that the two new countries—the Islamic Republic of Sudan and the Republic of South Sudan—can focus their energies and resources on their own development and not on each other.

CHRONOLOGY

1821   The Ottoman Turkish Viceroy of Egypt sends his armies to invade and conquer Sudan.

1881–85   The Mahdi, a Sudanese Islamic mystic, rebels against the Ottoman-Egyptian rule, eventually driving them out, and declares an Islamic state.

1892–94   Famine, conflict, and epidemics kill half of Sudan's population.

1899   The British and Egyptian governments return to crush the Mahdist state, establishing an Anglo-Egyptian Condominium to govern Sudan jointly.

1916   The last ruling sultan of the Fur, Ali-Dinar, is killed in a battle with Anglo-Egyptian forces, consolidating the Condominium's control of the country.

1955   Northern Sudanese officials take over administration of the South after Southern Sudanese mutiny.

1956   Sudan becomes independent. The first North–South civil war ensues.

1958   General Aboud overthrows the democratically elected government.

1964   Aboud is deposed through a popular uprising. Democratic elections are held, and new government takes power.

1965 Hassan al Turabi forms the Islamic Charter Front, an outgrowth of the Muslim Brotherhood, eventually the National Islamic Front.

1969 General Numayri takes power in a coup.

1972 Numayri signs the Addis Ababa Agreement, ending the first North–South civil war.

1974 Chevron oil exploration in Sudan begins.

1983 Numayri declares an "Islamic revolution," abrogates key provisions of the Addis Ababa Peace Agreement, causing an uprising in South Sudan.

1983 Second North–South civil war begins. Dr. John Garang leads Sudan People's Liberation Movement/Army (SPLM/A).

1983–84 Famine kills an estimated 200,000 people across the North.

1985 Numayri overthrown in a popular uprising; Sudanese military takes control for one year.

1986 Sadiq al-Mahdi, great-grandson of the Mahdi, is elected prime minister.

1987 First Darfur rebellion takes place between the Fur tribe and Arab tribes allied with the Sudan government.

1988–89 Famine in the South kills an estimated 250,000.

1989 Operation Lifeline Sudan is established by the United Nations to provide access for humanitarian relief operations during the second North–South civil war. Coup led by Brigadier-General Omar al-Bashir overthrows the al-Mahdi government and establishes an Islamist state. First Darfur rebellion ends through a negotiated peace agreement.

1991 Provinces become known as states.

1995 Assassination attempt against President Mubarak of Egypt in Addis Ababa, Ethiopia. UN Security Council imposes international sanctions on Khartoum. Second Darfur rebellion begins between the Masalit tribe and Arab tribes allied with Khartoum.

1996 Government of Sudan evicts most radical Islamist groups and leaders, including Osama bin Laden.

1999 Second Darfur rebellion ends through a combination of repression and a political settlement. Oil first pumped into new pipeline to Port Sudan. Omar al-Bashir and Hassan al-Turabi locked in power struggle to control Sudanese government. Bashir deposes Turabi, dissolves national assembly, and declares state of emergency.

2000 Publication of *The Black Book*, detailing Darfur's marginalization by the government and domination by the Northern Nile River Arab elites.

2001 U.S. government negotiates Nuba Mountains ceasefire agreement to grant humanitarian access to areas aligned with the SPLM/A.

2002 The Government of Sudan and SPLM/A sign an agreement in Machakos, Kenya, with a framework of broad principles, including self-determination for the South, as a basis for negotiating a peace agreement.

2003 Third Darfur rebellion begins with an alliance of Fur, Masalit, and Zaghawa pitted against the Sudanese government and its allies among the Northern Darfur Arab tribes. Sudan army initiates counter-insurgency campaign to crush the rebellion, resulting in 300,000 deaths, 1.8 million people displaced, and 2,800 villages destroyed.

2004 N'djamena Humanitarian Ceasefire Agreement signed between Government of Sudan and Darfur rebel movements. A UN Commission of Inquiry is established to investigate the question of genocide in Darfur.

2005 Comprehensive Peace Agreement is signed by the Government of Sudan and SPLM/A, ending the Second Civil War. Dr. John Garang becomes president of the Government of Southern Sudan and first vice president of the Government of National Unity in Khartoum. Garang killed in helicopter crash. Salva Kiir, vice president of the Government of Southern Sudan, becomes new president of the interim Government of South Sudan.

2006 The Darfur Peace Agreement is signed in Abuja, Nigeria, to resolve the third Darfur rebellion, but two major rebel factions refuse to sign. Eastern Sudan Peace Agreement signed between the Government of Sudan and the Eastern Front, ending the rebellion in eastern Red Sea State.

2007 Second Darfur Peace Conference, held in Sirte, Libya, ends in no agreement. UN/AU peacekeeping troops begin arriving in Darfur.

2008 Darfur rebel commander Khalil Ibrahim leads attack on Khartoum to unseat the Bashir government and is repulsed by forces from the NISS (secret police). Start of negotiations in Doha, Qatar, between the Sudanese government and various rebel groups.

2009 The International Criminal Court indicts President Bashir for crimes against humanity and war crimes.

2010 National elections held in Sudan; Bashir is elected with 68 percent of the vote, Salva Kiir elected president of the Government of Southern Sudan with 92 percent of the vote, and new national and Southern assemblies elected. The International Criminal Court adds the charge of "genocide" to Bashir's indictment.

2011 Southern Sudanese people vote 98.6 percent in favor of the South becoming an independent state in a referendum deemed free and fair by the international community.

Internal coup may have taken place in Khartoum; Bashir pushes out the civilians in his own government and military takes control.

Formal Declaration of Independence ceremony held in Juba on July 9, establishing the Republic of South Sudan as an independent, sovereign state.

New civil war begins in the North in the Nuba Mountains and Blue Nile State.

The Doha Document for Peace in Darfur is signed by the Government of Sudan and a Darfur rebel movement.

New Coalition that unites all Northern rebel groups—three from Darfur, South Kordofan, Blue Nile, and Red Sea states—announces its intention to remove Bashir and his party from power.

SUDAN, SOUTH SUDAN, AND DARFUR

WHAT EVERYONE NEEDS TO KNOW

1

THE PLACE AND SIGNIFICANCE OF SUDAN

Why should anyone care about Sudan?

For more than two centuries, Sudan has attracted an unusual
level of attention beyond its own borders. This international
interest converged in the last decade of the twentieth century
and the first decade of the twenty-first century as four
independent factors met, which raised the stakes and the visibility of both Sudan's remarkable potential and its troubling
dysfunctions.

First, the brutality of two internal conflicts created an international movement for outside intervention: the twenty-
two-year civil war between the North and South (1983–2005),
which led to the death of 2.5 million people and displaced
4 million more, and the third Darfur rebellion (the first Darfur
rebellion took place between 1986 and 1989, the second,
1995–1999, and the third 2003–present), characterized as
"genocide," separate from the North–South civil war but
related to it. Second, the discovery and rising production of
oil in Sudan after 1998 attracted the attention of energy markets. Third, by the mid-1990s Arab and African leaders grew
increasingly alarmed by the Sudanese government's plan to
use the country as a base for projecting an apocalyptic Islamist revolution abroad. Finally, Sudan became a haven for

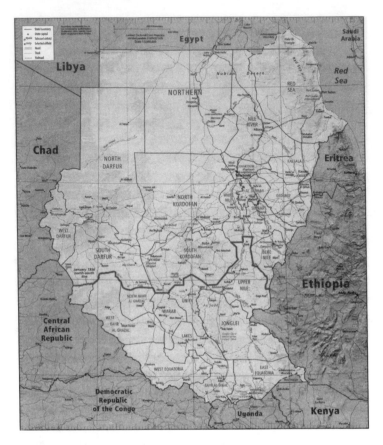

Map of Sudan, circa 1959. (Library of Congress)

international terrorist groups that committed violent attacks against Arab, African, and Western countries.

Let us now review each of these four factors in more depth. The first factor that attracted so much international interest was the third Darfur rebellion that began in 2003. This long-neglected western region has been intermittently at war since 1985 and claimed the lives of 300,000 Darfuris in its most recent phase. Peace in Darfur has been an aberration, conflict the rule. This rebellion led to an ongoing humanitarian emergency, costing Western governments about $1 billion annually at the peak of the crisis to sustain the 1.8 million people driven into sixty-five international displaced persons (IDP) camps scattered across Darfur. The Sudanese government committed widespread atrocities in Darfur as part of its counterinsurgency strategy, which involved a massive ethnic cleansing campaign to displace the tribes that started the rebellion and has motivated an international advocacy campaign to compel Western governments and international organizations to address the violence. The crisis has led to the deployment of 26,000 United Nations/African Union (UN/AU) peacekeeping troops and police—the largest in UN history to a single conflict—to Darfur, which cost $2 billion to maintain in 2007 alone. (The AU, a successor to the Organization for African Unity, seeks to create a more integrated Africa on the model of the European Union, though they are a very long way from achieving that.)

The third Darfur rebellion has recently obscured the far more lethal North–South wars, spanning twenty-two years in their most recent conflict (two North–South civil wars have taken place—the first between 1955 and 1972 and the second, 1983–2005), which has cost the lives of 2.5 million southerners—eight times the number who died in the current Darfur rebellion. The North–South war was brought to an end in 2005 by the North–South peace agreement—called the Comprehensive Peace Agreement (CPA)—which the Bush administration played a central role in fashioning, along with Great Britain, Norway, and neighboring African states. In January 2011, southern Sudan voted in a historic referendum—required by the CPA—to become an independent country, and the Sudanese government led by its president, Omar al-Bashir, agreed to recognize this secession, which formally took place July 9, 2001.

Second, Sudan's vast natural resources (most of which are in South Sudan), particularly oil and minerals, have attracted the interest of extractive industries and governments in need

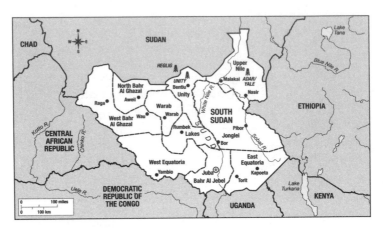

South Sudan.

of natural resources for their growing economies such as India and China. More than 75 percent of Sudan's oil production (43 percent of which was, until southern independence, jointly controlled by the Sudanese government and the Chinese, 39 percent by Malaysian, and 8 percent by Indian government–owned oil and gas companies) is located in the South, and its reserves are believed by some oil experts to hold 2 to 3 billion barrels. Mining companies have been rushing to explore reportedly large deposits of gold, diamond, uranium, copper, and coltan (a mineral used in electronic products), also located in the South.

Sudan's natural resources are not limited to oil and mineral wealth. Some argue that all of Africa and even the Arab world could be fed by farming from southern Sudan's luxuriant soils, plentiful rainfall, and seemingly limitless river system with its great irrigation potential.

A comprehensive USAID (United States Agency for International Development—the international development agency of the U.S. government I led between 2001 and 2005) wildlife study of the Sudd—the largest wetland in Africa, located in the southeast corner of the country—was conducted with *National Geographic* support by naturalist J. Michael Fay and southern Sudan scholar Malik Farjan. Their study discovered a teeming population that had been unknown by the outside world of between 1 and 2 million—including white eared kob antelope, elephants, giraffes, gazelles, antelopes, hippopotamus, ostrich, reedbucks, tiang, lion, and oryx—animal herds rivaled in size in Africa only by those of the Serengeti and Kalahari. These wild herds are matched by those of the South's domesticated cattle, which are estimated at 8–10 million animals, the highest people-to-cattle ratio in Africa.

For Egypt, Sudan's immediate northern neighbor, the country's most precious resource may not be its oil, mineral wealth, or farmland but its water; the headwaters of the Nile are located there. Egypt has traditionally sent some of its most seasoned and able diplomats to Sudan and Ethiopia because the Nile River waters (from the White Nile, which begins in Uganda, and the Blue Nile, which begins in Ethiopia; they merge in front of the Presidential Palace in Khartoum)

South Sudan cattle camp. (Henrik Stabell/NPA)

profoundly affect Egypt. Without the Nile, Egypt would be unable to sustain its 80 million people. Egyptian government agencies predict that Nile water flows will be insufficient to meet the country's agricultural, industrial, and human needs by 2017. Egyptian focus on events in Sudan grows more intense and more concerned every year. One of the many causes of Sudan's North–South wars was southern opposition to Khartoum's Jonglei Canal project, which would have increased the volume of Nile waters by 5 to 7 percent but in the process shrank Sudd wetlands by 40 percent. This project, which the North–South wars effectively ended, would have destroyed the rich southern fishing grounds, endangered the domesticated cattle herds of the south, as well as the wild animal population of the marshlands, and changed the southern climate. It is unlikely that any southern government will support a new canal project, which is why until recently Egypt has been reluctant to support an independent southern Sudan. Egypt's economic and strategic interests are inextricably linked to Sudan, and thus Egypt has often played over two centuries an active and even aggressive role in Sudan's internal affairs.

The third factor engaging the outside world's interest has been the ongoing conflict between the religious visions of Christianity and Islam. Sudan has been a religious battleground for generations, and any attempt to ignore or deny this yields an incomplete and distorted picture of the country. The conflict of visions between Islam and Christianity are matched by the tensions within Islam itself. Sufist orders dominate the Islamic religious practice of rural areas of the Northern Sudan, while the more formal Islam imported from Egypt dominates the Arab triangle and dismisses the Sufist orders as a corrupted and heretical form of Islam.

In historic Sudan before the South's secession, approximately 70 percent of the people confessed Sunni Islam, 20 percent Christianity, and 10 percent traditional tribal religions. Since 1956, four governments whose ideology has been based on various schools of Islamic teaching have taken power: two democratically, in 1964 and 1986; one through the gradual conversion of General Jaafar al-Numayri from Arab socialism to an Islamist political agenda in 1976; and one with the 1989 coup d'état that brought the longest sitting Islamist government in Sudanese history under the leadership of Omar al-Bashir. All four governments undertook violent military campaigns against the southern Sudanese people, persecuting local Christian populations and expelling missionaries. This persecution has had profound consequences for southern Sudan because it has accelerated the growth of the indigenous churches and led to one of the largest and fastest conversion of indigenous people to Christianity in modern history.

It was the last of these four governments—inspired by the most prominent Islamist prophet and political leader Hassan al-Turabi and formally led by Omar al-Bashir—that has raised the unwanted visibility of Sudan to the outside world. Hassan al-Turabi used the Bashir government to reshape Sudanese society and government to conform to his Islamist vision and simultaneously laid plans for his expansionary grand strategy. His sermons, calling for a world Islamic uprising, were recorded and distributed by his acolytes and broadcast in mosques across North Africa. Turabi's intention was to use Sudan as a base for the radical Islamization of Africa, alarming neighboring African states, such as Eritrea, Ethiopia, Kenya, and Uganda, all of which saw Turabi's regime as a threat to their internal stability, since they all have considerable Muslim minority populations (who are Sufist Muslims) who have generally lived in harmony with their Christian neighbors.

Fourth and finally, the Sudanese government caught the attention of the United States and Western Europe when it invited dozens of Islamist groups that had been involved in bombings and assassination attempts to move their headquarters and training schools to Sudan, including al-Qaeda led by Osama bin Laden. The Sudanese government gave these groups unrestricted access and entry into Sudan and sanctuary for their operations.

Thus, within only a few years, Sudan attracted the attention of the outside world because of repeated humanitarian catastrophes; the discovery of vast economic riches; the mobilization of a religious jihad to project the Sudanese Islamist revolution into the heart of Africa and overthrow moderate Arab governments everywhere; and because of an invitation Hassan al Turabi made to a man—Osma bin Laden—who was later to become the most wanted war criminal in the world. These four factors are what has drawn such wide international interest in Sudan.

Why has the Sudanese State been so unstable since independence in 1956?

Powerful centrifugal forces have been pulling the country apart since its formal creation in 1956. The first and most apparent force is geography. Before the South's secession, Sudan was the size of the U.S. mainland east of the Mississippi River and about the size of continental western Europe. It constituted 2 percent of the land surface of Earth and was the tenth largest country in the world, at 1 million square miles. The Sahara Desert lies in the north, the semi-arid Sahelian region in the middle of the country, and of course the vast Nile River watershed in the South. The historic Sudan—as we might term it before South Sudan seceded in July 2011—is ringed by mountains on its eastern and southern borders, the Red Sea Hills along the seacoast to the northeast, the Imatong Mountains to the south, and the Ethiopian highlands along the eastern border. All of these limited foreign penetration of the country before the advent of modern transportation. To the north, the Sahara Desert and the Nile River cataracts limited river access from Egypt.

A vast plain rolls through the center of Sudan, punctuated by small hills and mountains, including the Nuba and Moro mountains (where some of the worst atrocities of the North–South civil wars were committed by Khartoum) and the Jebel Marra massif in the center of Darfur. For four centuries, Jebel Marra was the mountain fortress of the Fur sultanate; it now serves as the redoubt of the Darfuri rebels from the Fur tribe, who have held out against Khartoum's attacks for almost a decade. Along the southern border with Kenya lie the Imatong Mountains, where John Garang—the leader of the South for twenty-two years during the second civil war—died in a helicopter crash in 2005. In the northwest corner of the country—the north Darfur and the Northern states—half a mile below the surface of the Sahara Desert lies the Great Nubian Sandstone Aquifer, a prehistoric water deposit that extends into Libya and Egypt and is equivalent in size to Germany.

Haboobs—deadly sandstorms sometimes lasting days—sweep with little warning across the Sudanic plain and can suddenly drop the usual 130-degree temperatures in the Sahara by 40 to 50 degrees. These *haboobs* in some ways mirror Sudan's history, in which sporadic and unexpected upheavals sweep violently across its vast human landscape.

The country's geography has made it difficult for any government to tie it together through transportation or administrative infrastructure, though most governments have never much tried, as they have been more concerned with maintaining control over the country from the so-called Arab Triangle (the geographic region marked by Port Sudan, Dongola, and Sennar) and alternately neglecting or suppressing the periphery. This pattern of focus and neglect has a long and sordid history, as we shall soon see.

The plain in the center of the country, woven together by an extensive river system, make it ideal for cattle herding. Both the animal-herding Nilotic tribes in the South—the Dinka, the Shilluk, and the Nuer—and the Arab Misiriyya and Rizaiqat tribes of the North sustain themselves on their

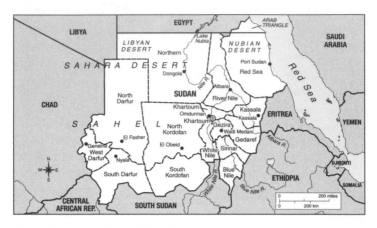

North Sudan and Arab Triangle.

cattle. The herding tribes of Sudan have developed basic, diffused, and decentralized systems of traditional governance and social organization. Thus, at least in the Savanna regions of the country, geography has over millennia led to the development of an economic order that has resisted highly developed, centralized, and complex political structures—a condition that has contributed to Sudan's modern governance problems.

Tribe, religion, language, and race form a second set of powerful centrifugal forces. There are 597 tribes and sub-tribes, which speak 133 languages and even more dialects, though many of these ethnic groups consist of no more than a few thousand people each. For example, a number of the largest tribes, such as the Dinka of the South—with twenty-five subtribes, the largest ethnic group in Sudan—speak so many distinctive dialects that many are incomprehensible to each other. Rivalries and tensions among the Dinka subtribes remain a historical reality in southern Sudan, as do tensions among the Arab tribes such as the Misiriyya and Rizaiqat of the North, and thus it is something of an oxymoron to write about "tribal identity."

Race has contributed to disunity, though peoples' race does not necessarily correlate to their tribe. Southerners from the Nilotic tribes, for example, are of one racial group but divided into tribes and subtribes, some of which have historically competed and even clashed with each other. Racial consciousness in Sudan is intense yet contrived. Most northern Nile River Arabs are not genetically Arabs but instead Arabized Africans, mostly from the Nubian tribes of the Northern Nile River valley who adopted Arab culture and language. Self-identified Arabs in historic Sudan before the South's secession made up a minority of the country's population at 45 percent, while self-identified Africans made up 55 percent. Other Arabs outside Sudan consider northern Sudanese not Arabs but Africans aspiring to change their race, and they are often treated with disdain. This has made some Nile River Arabs insecure about their adopted cultural inheritance, sometimes leading them to be more Arab than the Arabs themselves, and may partially explain why successive Khartoum governments have behaved so brutally toward the non-Arab populations of the country.

In Sudan, race and culture have affected the meaning and use of common words in Arabic. Southerners refer to northern Arabs as Jallaba, which means Arab trader in classical Arabic but in the South and many areas of the North has over time begun to carry with it an implication of conniving or untrustworthy behavior. The word for low-caste black slaves in Arabic, *a'bid*, is used by some northern Arabs to describe southerners. White people are called *hawajas* (meaning "master" in Arabic), which has its own implications from Sudan's earlier history.

The task of building a unified nation out of this confusion fell to three Arab tribes (referred to henceforth as the Three Tribes) in the Nile Valley, the Ja'aliyiin, the Shaiqiyya, and the Danagla—comprising 5.4 percent of the population of the historic Sudan—that have dominated the country since independence. These tribes allied themselves with the colonial powers and thus established their power base almost two centuries ago. Since 1956, they have held the majority (roughly 70 percent) of the cabinet posts in successive governments, senior officer positions in the Sudan armed forces, control of big business and markets, university posts, and civil service jobs. The Three Tribes' solution to the centrifugal forces bearing on Sudan has been a campaign of forced Islamization and Arabization in the South and Arabization of the non-Arab Muslim people in the North, all of which has only served to alienate the 55 percent of the population of the old Sudan that was African and the third of the country that was non-Muslim. With southern independence, the proportionate ethnic makeup of the North will change: now the Arabs will rise to 55 percent of the North.

A logical, if parochial, extension of this Arabization policy has been the development of the Arab Triangle, where the flow of oil revenue into the Sudanese government treasury has been disproportionately invested since 1998, giving it the same appearance as the booming oil states of the Gulf. The Sudanese periphery, however, is mired in poverty and underdevelopment. This parochial policy, more than any other single factor, has fueled successive revolts; the most visible of these have been among the southern Sudanese, Darfur in the west, the Nuban tribes of the Nuba Mountains, the Funj of Blue Nile State, and the Beja people of Red Sea State along the coast. Thus efforts by successive Khartoum governments to pursue an aggressive Arabization and Islamization policy have had the opposite effect of what was intended: instead of unifying the country and creating a true nation-state, this policy has divided Sudan; caused repetitive revolts; led to a terrible loss of human life, widespread suffering, and the embitterment of the population; and accelerated the very centrifugal forces it sought to restrain.

The political history of Sudan is a story of rebellions, insurrections, and civil wars, layered on top of each other. The two North–South civil wars—of 1956–1972 and of

1983–2005—pitted the southern tribes against the central government in their attempt to create a multi-ethnic, multi-religious, secular state and a new political culture for the country or, failing that, secede and form an independent state. The South was united from 1956 to its independence in 2011 in one matter: its abhorrence of the successive Khartoum governments' policy of forced Arabization and Islamization. The three Darfur conflicts—of 1987, 1995, and 2003—were rebellions by the three Darfur states against the neglect and oppression of the central government; they were not attempts to create an independent state but to force Khartoum to invest in the development of the region and give the people some control over their own futures.

2

THE BIRTH OF
MODERN SUDAN

How has Sudan's early history affected its current problems?

To answer this question, we need to follow Sudan's history, principally that of the last two centuries. European fascination with Sudan dates from attempts in the eighteenth century to find the source of the Nile, one of the longest rivers in the world, which flows south to north through Sudan, dividing the country into two parts, east and west. Egyptian, Turkish, and British adventurers and traders in the nineteenth century created Sudan out of hundreds of Arab and African tribes in the region and several sultanates and kingdoms, setting the stage for the unstable Sudanese state that existed from 1956 through 2011.

First Period of Modern Sudan's History (1821–1881):
Turco-Egyptian rule

Many historians date the beginning of modern Sudan to the 1821 Turco-Egyptian invasion, but at least four developed and organized states (among others) had already existed before then: the Fur and Funj sultanates and the Azande and Shilluk kingdoms. The Fur sultanate, encompassing present-day Darfur and the western region of Northern Kordofan State, as well as parts of the Central African Republic and Chad, developed over a period of three hundred years, beginning in the sixteenth century, and expanded through the dominant leadership of the Fur tribe. The present-day descendants of the Fur sultans contend that Islam was adopted as the state religion by a reigning sultan in the sixteenth century when a Moorish prince, expelled from Spain by King Ferdinand and Queen Isabella in 1492, traveled along the trade routes of North Africa. He eventually settled in the Fur sultanate, met the sultan, converted him to Islam, married his daughter, and introduced Arabic as a language. For several centuries thereafter, both Arabic and Fur, an African language, were spoken in the sultan's court. Sufist Islam dominated the religious observances of the Darfur population for five centuries.

The Fur sultanate's original capital rested on an ancient volcanic mountain known as the Jebel Marra and smaller hills surrounding it. The mountain is situated in the geographic center of Darfur and is the only watershed in the Sahel between the Ethiopian escarpment to the east and the Niger River to the west. Because of the area's microclimate, rich soils, and plentiful water resources from its deep volcanic lakes, the Jebel Marra has always been much richer agriculturally than any area within hundreds of miles. (Flying over the Jebel Marra by helicopter in 2004 during the earlier years of the third rebellion there, I noticed that the homes were constructed of fired brick with steel roofs—rather than mud brick with grass roofs, like most other homes in the region—a sure sign of greater prosperity.) The sultans later moved their capital to El Fasher, where they built a palace surrounded by rich gardens, fish ponds, and exotic orchards. The Fur sultans of the Keira dynasty were the wealthiest merchants of their empire and ruled through a highly developed governance system that withstood periodic invasion, drought, and famine until cataclysmic events of the nineteenth century weakened the sultanate and led to its eventual collapse in 1916. During the centuries-long sultanate, the Fur empire expanded, absorbing smaller tribes, converting them to Islam, and teaching them the Fur language.

The Funj Sultanate—centered in what is now the Blue Nile region, bordering present-day Ethiopia in eastern Sudan down to the rain forests in the South—was not a single tribe but a federation of sultanates that all spoke African languages and embraced Sufist Islam. The Funj empire dates its founding to 1504, when Amara Dunqas created the "Black Sultanate" and gradually absorbed smaller neighboring tribes. The ruling Funj sultan was called the *mek* (there is still a Funj mek, but he has been stripped of most of his power by successive Khartoum governments). The sultanate's power peaked in the mid-seventeenth century.

The Azande kingdom in Equatoria, the southernmost state of the Republic of South Sudan, followed the same pattern of expansion as the Funj and Fur sultanates, conquering and assimilating dozens of other smaller tribes over a period of 150 years prior to the foreign invasions of the nineteenth century. The Azande kingdom was governed by the Avongara ruling clan, from which the noble families of the kingdom came, as well as the Azande king. As Islam had not yet made its way this far south, the tribes' local traditional religion predominated. The local economy was based on settled agriculture with large farming estates in some areas.

These four sultanates or kingdoms governed the various regions of Sudan and expanded beyond their current boundaries: the Fur sultanate into present-day Chad and Kordofan; the Funj sultanate from the Ethiopian border to southern Kordofan; the Shilluk kingdom in the center; and the Azande kingdom into the Congo and Uganda. Within these kingdoms' territories, smaller chiefs and less-developed local systems of authority survived by accepting the sultan's or king's authority.

It was within this political context that an Egyptian army, under the command of an ethnic Albanian, brought the Ottoman Turkish Empire to Sudan in 1821, thus beginning the first period of modern Sudanese history. Muhammad Ali, the Ottoman Turkish viceroy to Egypt, had by 1820 established his complete and autonomous control over the country. Thus Egypt, virtually an independent colony of the Ottoman Empire, in turn conquered Sudan. The Turco-Egyptian army led by Muhammad Ali's third son, Isma'il Kamil Pasha, swept through Nile Valley in northern Sudan. Only the Shaiqiyya tribe resisted the invading army, and it was easily overcome by superior Egyptian fire power. Isma'il Kamil Pasha was so impressed by the Shaiqiyya's fighting ability, however, that he enlisted their horsemen into his army. As they proved their loyalty to Muhammad Ali's forces, their influence spread through the new governance system, and they eventually became the tax collectors for the Turco-Egyptian colonial empire. Their influence remains to this day, as one of the Three Tribes that has dominated the Sudanese state since its creation in 1956: Ali Osman Taha, the vice president who negotiated the North–South Peace Agreement called the Comprehensive Peace Agreement (henceforth the CPA) is a Shaiqiyya. The Ja'aliyyin tribe—the second of the Three Tribes, from which Omar al-Bashir, the current president of Sudan, and descends –chose not to resist and swore allegiance to the Turco-Egyptian invaders.

As the new overlords imposed draconic discipline and confiscatory taxes on the local population, the Ja'aliyyin were the first of many tribes to revolt, burning Isma'il Kamil Pasha and his retainers to death while they slept. Soon thereafter, the Nile Valley rose up against the invaders. The Shaiqiyya tribal cavalry remained loyal to the Turco-Egyptian army, now under siege by the Ja'aliyyin and other tribes of the valley, and rescued their overlords from defeat.

Muhammad Ali, enraged by his son's murder, unleashed his army across the region, which left in its wake utter devastation. The local governing class of Sudanese tribal elites did not recover from this campaign sufficiently to challenge the Turco-Egyptian administration for another sixty years. While the successive governors sent by Egypt over the next thirty years to run Sudan were wiser and more restrained than the initial conquering force—resettling farmers driven from their land by the war, modestly reducing oppressive taxes, and taking into account the opinions of the local elites—their legacy was not a particularly constructive one. The Turco-Egyptian administration imposed a degree of order and stability, but at a high price. The economy was based on a complex system of heavy taxation, as well as two powerful and lucrative enterprises: the slave and ivory trades. The slave trade took an annual human harvest of as many as 30,000 people captive among the non-Muslim, African population in southern Sudan. Men were typically shipped to Egypt, to populate the slave army of the Ottoman Turkish viceroys, and the women and children were sold as laborers and servants. Some regions of the South were virtually depopulated by the slave trade during the nineteenth century. This trade, however, was not new: Egyptian traders had taken slaves from the Funj kingdom centuries before the colonization of Sudan. What was different was the scale.

The other legacy of the Egyptian colonial period was the development of the Nile Valley and the comparative neglect of the other areas, which became a resource to be exploited rather than a region to be developed. Thus, a pattern of development was set in place a century before Sudanese independence.

During this period, the Egyptians also imported to Sudan the Islam of the formal scholars from Egyptian Islamic schools, such as the al-Azhar. This type of Islam remains dominant today among elites in the Nile Valley and forms the basis of the Islamist Salafism of Hassan al-Turabi. The historic tensions remain to this day between the teaching/scholarly tradition of Islam brought from Egypt and Sufi orders, a form of mystical Islam with a panoply of Sufi saints, contemplative prayer, miracles, and mystical practices emphasizing the present experience of Allah for the individual believer, which had deep roots in Sudanese society well before the Turco-Egyptian invasions, with broad support in rural Sudanese villages. The Egyptian Islamic scholars viewed the Sufi orders as purveyors of a corrupted form of Islam. Two of the major political parties in modern Sudan and the families that dominate them—the Umma Party, led by the al-Mahdi family, which opposed the Turco-Egyptian conquerors, and the Democratic Unionist Party (DUP), led by the al-Mirghani family, which maintained warm relations with the Egyptians—arose out of these two conflicting Islamic traditions in nineteenth-century Sudan.

In the early 1860s the Ottoman viceroy, the Khedive Isma'il Pasha of Egypt, a westernized Eastern potentate, introduced technology to Sudan: steamboats on the Nile, railroads, a telegraph system, government schools, and a post office. His attempts to abolish the slave trade under pressure from the British were unsuccessful. In fact, slavery in some more limited forms continued in Sudan until the CPA of 2005 finally put a de facto stop to the practice of raiding the South for slaves. William Wilberforce, an evangelical Protestant member of the British Parliament, led the antislavery movement in Great Britain and sponsored an 1807 law that forbade the slave trade in the British Empire (but continued to allow slavery) and another in 1833 that made slavery itself illegal. In 1849, the first British Christian missionary society office for the abolition of slavery was opened in Khartoum. (Thus the campaign led by Western churches to stop slavery in Sudan in the 1990s, as well as to protect both the southern Sudanese and Darfuris from their own government, had antecedents in the evangelical Protestant campaign in Britain to abolish slavery in Sudan in the nineteenth century.)

The Khedive Isma'il Pasha attempted to enlarge the Egyptian empire in Sudan by pressing south and west with a massive and very costly invasion force. He hoped to extend commerce along the Nile with the African kingdoms and to abolish the slave trade, but this campaign brought his government to near bankruptcy and led to intervention by

European powers. Further hampering the Khedive's cause, the Egyptian army was consumed by the malarial swamps of the Sudd, as well as the resolute southern Sudanese tribal resistance. With his removal as viceroy by the Ottoman sultan in 1879 under European pressure, the Turco-Egyptian imperial presence in Sudan drew to an inglorious close. By 1882 the exhausted Egyptian empire in Sudan recruited British officers to lead their troops before the most powerful movement in modern Sudanese history conquered the country: the Mahdiya.

The Second Period of Modern Sudanese History (1882–1898): The Mahdiya

While on Aba Island in the White Nile, south of Khartoum, in March 1881, Muhammad Ahmad bin Abdallah, the son of a boat builder from the northern province of Sudan, which runs along Egypt's southern border, experienced several ecstatic visions of the Prophet Muhammad. In one such vision, Mohammed chose him, as the long-awaited Mahdi (literally "the guided one"), who would lead an army of believers to usher in a new age of Islamic justice and devotion. Thus began the second period of modern Sudanese history, one dominated by the Mahdi's political movement (called the Mahdiya), which was a violent reaction to foreign presence in Sudan and to the perceived corruption of Islam under the Turco-Egyptian rule.

While Muhammad Ahmad impressed the poor Muslims of rural Sudan, the educated elite in Khartoum took a very different view. The Egyptian Ulema in Khartoum ridiculed his claim to be the Mahdi, arguing that he did not conform to the requirements of the Hadith (the sayings of the Prophet Muhammad). Some of the great Sudanese sheikhs from the Sufi orders dismissed him; others decided to go into exile in Egypt. The Mahdi's mystical experience on Aba Island in 1881 represents one of the seminal moments of modern Sudanese history.

The Mahdi recruited an army of believers—the British estimated the force at 200,000 men strong at its peak, likely an exaggeration—to rid the country of the hated foreigners: Turks, Egyptians, and British. Three groups were drawn into the Mahdi's army: (1) the rural poor, whose spiritual leaders were the members of the Sufi orders (the Mahdi himself had been a Sufi sheikh of the Samaniyya Brotherhood but later insisted his followers abandon the Sufi orders just as he had when he declared himself the Mahdi), and despised the more legalistic Islam of the Al-Azhar University introduced by the Egyptians to Sudan; (2) the slave traders, whose businesses had been damaged by the Westerners brought in by the Isma'il Pasha to suppress the slave trade; and (3) the Baqqara Arab cattle herders, whose livelihoods were being decimated by the confiscatory colonial tax system. As nomads, the Baqqara Arabs had mastered the use of weapons to defend their herds and to raid those of other tribes; it was their militia that became the assault troops of the Mahdi's Ansar ("Defenders of Islam") Army.

We see in the Baqqara militia recruited into the Ansar Army in 1881 and in the Shaiqiyya cavalry recruited into the Turco-Egyptian military in 1821 the roots of the use of tribal militias by Sudanese governments to prosecute the North–South war in the 1980s and 1990s. This was also evident in the conflict in Darfur beginning in 2003, when the Bashir government organized the Arab Janjawiid militia to defeat the rebellion there. When the Three Tribes have feared defeat in the wars of Sudan's periphery in the modern period, they have often recruited tribal militias to do their dirty work.

You can see why. The Mahdi's Ansar Army, equipped with no more than spears and swords, swept across the Sudanic plain as a whirlwind of unstoppable, chaotic ferocity, cleansing the country of the hated invaders. In battle after battle, his forces overcame the modern weapons of the demoralized Turco-Egyptian army. At the battle of Shaykan, south of El Obeid, capital of Kordofan Province, the Mahdi's forces virtually destroyed an expeditionary force of 10,000 troops sent by the Egyptians and British to stop the rebellion. The British, French, and Ottoman Turks did not fear that the Mahdi would attempt to expand his power beyond Sudan through conquest, but rather that he would serve as a fiery inspiration for Islamic revolutions among long-oppressed Arab societies and thus destabilize their colonial empires. In 1884, in a final effort to save the last remaining colonial presence from the Ansar zealots, William Gladstone, the British prime minister, dispatched General Charles George Gordon to Khartoum as the governor general, though nominally under the authority of the Turco-Egyptian administration. Gordon—charismatic, eccentric, a militant opponent of slavery, and a devout evangelical Christian—had led the British army to victory against the Taiping Rebellion in China and served briefly as governor general of Sudan under his friend and admirer Isma'il Pasha in 1877. (Today, Chinese diplomats annually visit the Mahdi's tomb in Omdurman to emphasize their common cause with the Sudanese against Western—British—oppression, as they argued General Gordon had both Chinese and Sudanese blood on his hands.)

Gordon's arrival in Khartoum in 1884 and subsequent leadership of the colony was described by Alan Moorehead in *The White Nile*, his celebrated history of nineteenth-century Sudan: "He promotes captains to majors, doles out special rations for the feast days, rewards the more daring soldiers with double pay, imprisons criminals and settles disputes with an air of absolute authority that no one can deny."

One of the most dramatic and colorful moments in nineteenth-century Sudanese history unfolded as Gordon organized his doomed defense of Khartoum—the last remaining colonial stronghold that had not fallen to the Mahdi's forces. While the Ansar Army surrounded him and the city, he waited for relief from a British-Egyptian expeditionary force slowly moving down the Nile, but these reinforcements were harassed at every turn by the Mahdi's forces.

Gordon's unyielding defense of Khartoum lifted the spirits of a demoralized city, whose inhabitants were calmed each night when his silhouette could be seen at the window of the governor general's palace. This was the same palace that Sudanese presidents would occupy after independence in 1956; it had been erected earlier by the Egyptians and Turks on the bank of the Nile near the confluence of the White and Blue Niles. On January 25, 1885, the Mahdi's forces successfully scaled the walls of the city and overwhelmed Gordon's forces. While the Mahdi had given orders to spare Gordon, the Mahdi's forces killed him on the steps of the palace before they received this message; his beheaded corpse was paraded through the Ansar Army.

As the Mahdi's army advanced to the west, he consolidated his power through an alliance with the Fur sultanate by marrying a Fur princess as one of his four wives. Thus, Fur blood flows in the blood of the Mahdi's descendants, which may explain the continuing support in Darfur of the party they formed—along with the fact that his successor was from Darfur. Six months after his final victory, he developed typhus and died within a few days, leaving his inner circle of followers to fight over succession. The succession battle divided the tribes of the Nile River Valley in the east from the Baqqara Rizaiqat Arabs from Darfur in the west.

In one of the few instances of the Three Tribes losing out to the tribes of the periphery, Khalifa Abdallahi, a Darfuri Baqqara, succeeded the Mahdi as the leader of the Mahdist state. Once he had consolidated power and put down several challenges to his authority, the Abdallahi dispatched the Ansar Army to conquer southern Sudan and southern Egypt, both of which ended in decisive defeats for his forces. His armies enjoyed greater success in defeating the massive force of the Ethiopian Emperor John IV (the Ethiopian emperors and nobility from the highlands were Orthodox Christians and felt threatened by expanding Islamic power)—more by accident than by military skill: a stray bullet killed the emperor during the battle, plunging the Ethiopian army into chaos just as they were overwhelming the Ansar. In 1888 the Fur sultanate, which had governed Darfur for three centuries, allied with the Masalit tribe and revolted against their historic rivals, the khalifa's Baqqara tribe, now in control of the Mahdist state.

Thus, the same alliance of linguistically African tribes (with the later addition of the Zaghawa) in Darfur that had revolted against the central Mahdist state in 1888 also revolted against the central government in 2003, leading to the present-day Darfur crisis. The first seven years of Abdallahi's reign placed enormous strain on the people, as his armies (and his armed adversaries) had to be fed: the rural poor peasantry were recruited at gunpoint into the army, which left fewer adults to grow food. This stress, compounded by droughts in 1889 and 1890 in northern Sudan, caused major crop losses, followed successively by catastrophic epidemics and famines. Some accounts record that these catastrophes reduced the population of the North by half. Nearly five million Sudanese died in fighting, famines, and epidemics during the Mahdist rule.

The Mahdist state ruled Sudan from Gordon's defeat and death in 1885 to its own defeat in 1898 at the hands of the British Expeditionary Force led by Lord Horatio Herbert Kitchener. The British government dispatched Kitchener to prevent the French, the Germans, and the Italians from establishing a colonial foothold in Sudan; they feared it could threaten the waters of the Nile and control over the Suez Canal, which was critical to British commerce. The British army had another motive: avenging the death of Gordon, who had been a favorite general of Queen Victoria and the British public. Lord Kitchener's army comprised 26,000 well-trained troops, armed with forty-four field artillery guns, twenty machine guns, and ten gunboats mounted with an additional thirty-six guns and twenty-four machine guns. The British forces were arrayed against the Khalifa's 50,000 troops, only a quarter of whom had old-fashioned Remington rifles; the rest were armed with spears and swords.

Winston Churchill, a young cavalry officer under Lord Kitchener's command, later recorded events in his book *The River War*. He participated in one of the last cavalry charges in Western history. British gatling guns and field artillery wiped out the Khalifa's Ansar Army just as the Mahdi's Ansar Army armed with swords and spears had done to the Egyptian-British force thirteen years earlier. The Ansar lost 11,000 soldiers, with 16,000 wounded, while the British forces suffered fewer than 250 casualties. The Battle of Omdurman

The Madhi's Mausoleum in Omdurman. (Courtesy of Valerie P. Reynolds)

brought the Mahdist state to an end. Its energies constantly sapped first by its failed attempts to expand its empire, second by drought, famine, and epidemic, and third by the serial revolts of the Sudanese periphery against the center, it finally fell to modern British weaponry.

How did the Mahdiya affect modern Sudanese history?

The Mahdi and the state of his successor left several legacies. First, he created an Islamic political movement rooted in a purist and puritanical interpretation of the Quran, one that sought to cleanse the country of foreign influence. This movement would make periodic reappearances through Sudanese history, with violent consequences for the Sudanese people. Second, he created a powerful political dynasty whose descendants created a formal political party, the Umma, in 1945, with a political base in Darfur and Kordofan, which would later win national elections in 1966 and 1986 and put Sadiq al-Mahdi, great-grandson of the Mahdi, into power twice. Third, he started the long line of (failed) attempts to control Sudan's periphery through manipulation, repression, and conquest. Fourth, the Mahdi's successors continued the Three Tribes' long effort to Islamize and Arabize the South. The mausoleum of the Mahdi and his successors in Omdurman remains a holy site for many Sudanese and the physical manifestation of one of the most influential movements in its modern history.

3

THE RULE OF THE ANGLO-
EGYPTIAN CONDOMINIUM

*How did the British and Egyptian colonial period set the stage
for later Sudanese conflicts after independence?*

The British and Egyptian rule continued and accelerated the
discontinuities of nineteenth century development in Sudan.
The disparity between the development of the Nile River
Valley and the neglect of the periphery, if anything, grew
more extreme during this period. To protect the South from
the slave traders, the British isolated it from the North and in
so doing slowed down its development, so that by
independence in 1956 one part of the country was relatively
well developed and the other was one of the least developed
parts of the British global empire.

*The Third Period of Modern Sudan (1898–1956):
The Anglo-Egyptian Condominium*

The defeat of the Ansar Army and destruction of the Mahdist
state in 1898 began the third period of modern Sudanese
history, in which the Anglo-Egyptian Condominium, or joint
rule by British and Egyptian officials, governed Sudan. In
practice, this meant that British officials served at the top of
the local administration, Egyptians served as mid-
ranking officers, and a newly emerging class of educated

Sudanese from the Nile River Valley filled lower-level government positions. Under the Anglo-Egyptian Treaty of 1899, the British recognized the Egyptian legal claim to Sudan but administered Sudan on behalf of the king of Egypt. During this nearly sixty-year period, which ended with Sudan's independence in 1956, this joint role only became less ambiguous as Egyptian influence waned and the British more firmly established their authority. In 1924, the British expelled Egyptian officials and troops from the country after the assassination of the British governor general, Lee Stark, by an Egyptian nationalist. The British made no further reference to the diplomatic fiction of Egyptian sovereignty until 1936, when they negotiated a new treaty of military cooperation with Egypt, thus affirming Egypt's claims to Sudan. However, this did not diminish effective British administrative and policy-making authority in Sudan.

The British maintained order in Sudan through the military suppression of any armed opposition. British intelligence showed that the Fur sultan, Ali Dinar, who in 1898 had reestablished the historic Fur sultanate, had decided to answer the Ottoman Turkish sultan's call for a jihad against the Western Alliance (Great Britain, France, and Russia) in World War I (the Ottoman Turks were part of the Triple Alliance in the war, allied with Germany and the Austro-Hungarian Empire). The British army put down the Fur jihad with brutal efficiency. Some Fur historians claim the British fabricated this rumor to provide an excuse in 1915 to destroy the Fur sultanate and formally merge Darfur into Sudan. However, the historical evidence for the sultan's support for the Central Powers against Britain is persuasive. When mass nationalist demonstrations by the rising Nile River Arab professional class against the British in 1924 triggered a violent mutiny at the Sudanese Military Staff College, the British responded by annihilating all of the rebels with their field artillery in the ensuing battle.

British rule ushered in a period of relative stability, as its hand in running the country was remarkably light—as long as no one challenged its ultimate authority or control—with no more than 400 political officers total during the entire sixty years of Condominium rule. They were able to do this through a policy they termed "indirect rule," later promulgated formally as the policy of "Native Administration," in which a thin layer of educated British administrators exercised authority through the traditional tribal chiefs, sheikhs, and clan elders, whose influence they strengthened, cultivated, and facilitated. This model of governing Sudan was very different from the rest of the British Empire, where tens of thousands of British families would settle in their colonies to govern, engage in large-scale farming, and start businesses. This did not happen in Sudan. Unlike all other British colonies that reported in London to the Colonial Office, British officials in Sudan reported to the Foreign Office. The British governing system in Sudan took Englishmen from aristocratic lineage who had attended proper British schools and recruited them into the Sudanese political service to rule through the local Sudanese aristocracy: one inherited nobility ruling through another. While Arabic was the language of government and business in northern Sudan, English was the language of the thin layer of local tribal elders and officials governing the South, as well as the language of instruction in scattered Christian missionary schools. British political officers learned Arabic if they served in the North and the local tribal languages of southern Sudan when they were assigned there.

In his remarkable and evocative autobiography, *Life of My Choice*, the late Wilfred Thesiger, one of the last of the great British explorers and travel writers (from a distinguished noble family himself—his uncle was the viceroy of the British Raj in India), recounts his experiences as one of these political officers in 1935–1940 stationed in Darfur and then the Upper Nile in southern Sudan. His workday consisted of settling tribal disputes, trying locals accused of capital offenses, and hunting lions who had killed tribespeople. When the NGOs and Western government aid agencies responded to the great famine of 1988–1989 by delivering humanitarian aid to remote areas of the South, some of the older southerners welcomed them, thinking they were the British political service returning. While I was U.S. presidential envoy to Sudan in 2007, I traveled to Nyala, Darfur, to meet Ahmed Adam Rijal, the *magdum* (the traditional Fur viceroy or prime minister, though now with little formal authority, as it had been stripped from him by the Khartoum regime) of the Fur sultanate. Widely respected for his independence and integrity, he was then in his eighties. We talked about the rebellion in Darfur, and I asked for his help in trying to bring peace to the region, which he tried earnestly to do. He recounted fond memories of being educated by the British at boarding school and playing polo with members of the British Imperial Political Service before taking his position in the sultanate hierarchy, which at that point was part of the British political order.

The new class of educated Nile River Arab professional elites saw the British "Native Administration" policy of indirect rule through the tribal nobility for what it was—a subtle way of consolidating power and disempowering them. The rising tide of Sudanese nationalism would manifest itself though this new class of professionals in the later years of British rule, though it never developed a popular base. Only the great religious parties carrying Islam as their banner were able to mobilize the rural population. Many of these professional Sudanese attended Gordon Memorial College, which had been built by Lord Kitchener in Khartoum between 1899 and 1902 to honor the memory of General Gordon and to train the clerks and lower-level staff of the colonial administration. In 1936 major educational reforms added technical schools to the college, including a medical school. By 1951 it evolved into the University College of Khartoum and then, after independence, the University of Khartoum.

In the 1940s and 1950s, it became a center of nationalist sentiment. Over time, the college developed a reputation as one of the finest schools of higher education in Africa, until its decline in the 1990s due to its gradual politicization under the Bashir government.

It took the British nearly thirty years to assert effective governmental authority over the South. Only after the Nile waterways had been dredged through the great Sudd marshland could such authority be established. Officials traveled up and down the Nile by steamboat with a judge and jail on board to try those accused of capital offenses. The British pursued a policy of benign neglect in southern Sudan, isolating it from the North, both to prevent Arab slave traders from harvesting their human quarry in the South and to create a buffer zone containing the expansion of Islam into Africa, which the British feared would be destabilize their empire.

The slave trade and slavery as a social institution were so pervasive in the nineteenth century that General Gordon believed two-thirds of all Sudanese were slaves and therefore trying to abolish the trade entirely would cost the colony two-thirds of its revenue. Other historians report more conservative figures of 20–30 percent of the population being slaves at the time of the British reconquest in 1898. In 1910, when the British military commander and governor general of Sudan, General Reginald Wingate arrived in the South with his army, he expelled northern Arab troops, merchants, and government administrators from the South.

The British left the Islamic authorities in place in the North, strengthening the Egyptian Islamic presence in order to weaken the influence of the Mahdist elites, whom they feared. While doing so, however, they also cultivated the late Mahdi's son, Sayyid Abd al-Rahman al-Mahdi, and his extensive family by directing contracts to him for meat, wood, and fuel, thus enriching them and winning their loyalty.

The British encouraged Christian missionaries to establish a presence in the South, avoiding sectarian conflict by assigning regions to particular denominations. Roman Catholic missionaries from an Italian order, the Comboni Fathers, began work in Sudan in 1842; to this day they have a reputation for running the finest schools in the country. (Even now, elite families among the Three Tribes try to get their children into Comboni high schools.) They established their mission in Rumbek and the Upper Nile. British and American Presbyterians missionaries began their work in 1899. British Anglicans settled their headquarters in Omdurman but had missions in the South and North. The Pentecostal Church of Sudan, now one of the fastest growing in the South, was started by Swedish missionaries.

The large and powerful southern Nilotic tribes of cattle-herders—the Dinka, the Shilluk, and the Nuer—had established loosely organized traditional hierarchies of chiefs. The British believed that these threatened their control, so they imposed their own system of appointed chiefs through whom they could govern. The governance systems of these tribes were thus artificial, lacking deep historical and cultural roots.

The peace brought by the British Empire—Pax Britannica—did have several salutary consequences in Sudan. For one thing, the colony enjoyed relative prosperity, particularly in the years prior to the Great Depression. This was partly due to a prolonged period of political stability enforced by the British military, which pushed rising nationalist aspirations among the growing class of Sudanese professionals underground. By 1903, British diplomatic and military power settled power disputes over Sudan's borders—with the notable exception of Darfur—thus demarcating the modern Sudanese state. In 1919, the British signed an agreement with the French that established the border between French Equatorial Africa (currently Chad and the Central African Republic) and Sudan.

This prosperity was also due partly to the great Gezira irrigation scheme, on which British engineers began construction just before World War I. The project covered nearly 10 million acres of land at its peak, making it one of the largest irrigation projects in the world. Located in a triangle between the Blue and White Nile Rivers south of Khartoum, it employed 400,000 seasonal wage laborers and another 90,000 smallholder farmers, who were principally growing cotton for export—the alluvial soils of the Nile are ideally suited for its cultivation. In 1925, the British constructed a dam across the Blue Nile at Sennar, which created a reservoir for irrigating the Gezira project and generating electricity for Khartoum; it's still in use to this day. The Great Depression brought this prosperity to a temporary end; recovery came partially in 1934 and only fully after World War II.

The Condominium period also allowed a multiethnic business community to develop, which General Gordon had encouraged in the nineteenth century. It was composed of Armenian (5,000), Iraqi Jews (400), and Lebanese-Syrian Christian (20,000) merchants and businessmen, who ran much of Sudan's commercial economy. There were also 17,000 Greeks, who established a foothold in the region fairly early on. When Theodore Roosevelt went big game hunting in southern Sudan, in 1909–1910, he traveled to Juba, where he stayed at the home of one of these Greek commercial families. The house was painstakingly restored after the 2005 peace agreement by the new owners, a Greek-Sudanese businessman, and turned into a restaurant called Notos. (Efforts were being made in 2010 to reclaim the Greek Orthodox Church in Juba.) The railroad Lord Kitchener built from Egypt to Sudan, as well as the construction of Port Sudan, made access to the country much easier and effectively ended its geographic isolation—at least for the Nile River Valley.

Whatever its exploitative designs, the British Empire did make permanent and positive contributions to the creation of modern Sudan—in building institutions and infrastructure, stimulating commercial development, and promoting education and good governance. All of this activity

Port Sudan, built by the British to connect the Gezira irrigation system to world markets. (Wikipedia Creative Commons)

was heavily concentrated in the Nile River Valley, however. Southern Sudan, as well as Darfur and Kordofan to the west, remained undeveloped, with few schools, roads, or public services and therefore little chance for economic growth. This developmental disparity between the North and the South was to haunt Sudan for its entire twentieth century history, exacerbated by successive Khartoum governments after independence.

The Arabs of the North would later argue that it was British colonial policy that set the political stage for the nearly continuous state of civil war between the North and the South after independence. The British did this by introducing Christianity in the South, containing the expansion of Islam, expelling Arabs, encouraging Western dress among local officials, and using English rather than Arabic as the southern lingua franca.

Leading southern intellectuals take a very different view. They would argue that the South had successfully resisted Arab and Islamic encroachments into southern Sudan long before the British colonial presence. The British simply isolated the region in order to reduce the risk of conflict and did little to develop the South until very late in Sudan's colonial history. Indeed, there is little evidence that Muslim missionaries or Arab traders had any success in spreading Islam to the South before the British arrived. For the southerners, the Arabs and their religion were associated with the slave trade and with repeated invasions, which threatened their semi-nomadic way of life and traditional culture. The British policy of benign neglect retarded the modernization and development of the South and created great disparities of development across the country. Southern intellectuals saw the British as their protectors against the Islamizing and Arabizing proclivities of the Northern Nile River Arabs and the brutality of their slave trade.

How did Sudan achieve its independence?

The chaos produced by World War II inspired an entire generation of African and Arab nationalists to seek independence. The professional elites in the French, British, and Dutch colonial empires witnessed the Nazi conquest of continental Europe and the siege of Britain with astonishment; the invincibility of their formerly colonial overlords had disappeared. This perception of vulnerability helped to accelerate independence movements following the war, including those in Sudan.

Britain supported nascent Sudanese aspirations for independence so as to ensure the allegiance of the growing professional class of Nile River Arabs and to forestall a union between Egypt and Sudan that would threaten British interests in the region and potentially their control over the Suez Canal.

The Sudanese independence movement was characterized by three contentious issues, the first of which was the relationship between Egypt and Sudan. The Umma Party, led by the Mahdi's descendants, argued for a completely independent Sudan, while the Khatmiyya, the base of indigenous support for Egypt for more than a century, advocated union with Egypt, with the support first of Egypt's King Farouk and later, indirectly, of President Abdel Nasser.

The second issue was the status of the South. Most southerners were unprepared for rapid independence, but the few who were demanded a say in the status of the South in an independent Sudan. The two northern religious parties either tried to minimize the southerners' influence in the independence movement or excluded them entirely from the process because they were neither Muslims nor Arabs.

The third issue was the relationship between the state and religion: there were non-Muslims in the South, as well as Communists, socialists, and secularists in the North supporting a secular Sudan. But the major religious parties of the North insisted on the formation of an explicitly Islamic state.

These three issues have haunted Sudanese politics ever since. Only with the CPA, signed in January 2005, and the referendum for southern independence held in January 2011, where the South voted overwhelmingly for independence, has the third issue been addressed. Nonetheless, the matter of Islam's relationship to the Sudanese state remains a source of contention in northern politics. Sudan's independence did not end Egyptian meddling in the internal affairs of the country, as we shall see later.

British and Egyptian rivalry over Sudan's future led to a bidding war between the two colonial powers to win the loyalty of the Nile River Arab professional class; this had the inadvertent consequence of accelerating the timetable for independence well before important issues had actually been settled. On November 16, 1950, King Farouk declared before the Egyptian Parliament his intention to abrogate the 1899 Condominium Agreement with Great Britain and the 1936

Anglo-Egyptian Treaty, which had established a joint British-Egyptian claim on Sudanese territory. Shortly thereafter, Farouk announced the unification of Egypt and Sudan under the Egyptian monarchy, and then approved a new constitution for this new unified country, which existed on paper only so long as British control over Sudan remained unimpaired. On none of these matters had the king's government consulted any Sudanese, northern or southern.

Two years later, in 1952, the Free Officers' coup in Egypt, organized by Nasser, a colonel, with General Muhammad Naguib as its titular leader, unseated Farouk and established an Arab socialist regime that espoused a pan-Arab secular ideology, calling for the unification of Arab countries into one new grand Arab state. The new Egyptian government announced a new Sudan policy: Egypt abandoned any sovereign claims to Sudan and supported Sudan's complete independence from Great Britain. This was more of a tactical maneuver than a true policy change, as Egypt continued to encourage nationalists in Sudan to support the union of the two countries, but it did put the British on the defensive on the independence question. No Egyptian leader, regardless of ideology, can ignore the all-consuming importance of the Nile River (and thus of Sudan) to Egypt's survival, so Nasser's embrace of Sudanese independence, while rhetorically in support of Egypt's pan-Arab ideology, was primarily based on Egyptian national self-interest.

The southern Sudanese question weighed on the British during the Condominium period, but it was never answered with any coherent strategy. The British found it easier to recruit their colonial troops, constabulary, and provincial officials from the sedentary farmers of the Equatoria province rather than from the Nilotic herder tribes, which were more difficult to recruit, given that they annually followed their cows toward the savannah north of Equatoria in search of grazing land and water. These Nilotic tribes, particularly the Dinka and Nuer, were also among the largest in all of Sudan, let alone the South. With their more informal tribal hierarchies, they were elusive and difficult to control. So the British inadvertently created a nascent political class that was unrepresentative of the South as a whole—nearly all its members were from Equatoria. When John Garang, himself a Dinka, began the second revolt in 1983, the Dinka and Nuer, who represent more than 50 percent of the present-day population of the South, were completely dominant yet also the most alienated from the Sudanese political system. Only later, when he tried to broaden the movement, did Garang recruit Equatorians into his rebel army. Many Equatorians now serve in senior positions in the Republic of South Sudan or the ruling party. For example, Ann Ito, a rising political figure in the South with a Ph.D. from Kansas State University in entomology is the second in command of the SPLM (the southern ruling party), and Major General James Wani Igga is speaker of the National Assembly of the Republic of South Sudan.

This British failure to prepare for independence was compounded by another and perhaps even more serious matter. Before the education reforms of 1937, the only schools in the South during the Condominium were those established by Christian missionaries; there were precious few schools in the most underdeveloped, least-educated regions of Sudan. Few roads were built in the South during the Condominium, and the only large-scale development scheme—the aforementioned Zande project—was ultimately a failure, unlike the successful Gezira project in the North.

On June 12 and 13, 1947, a crucial conference was held in Juba, capital of southern Sudan, at which seventeen southern and three northern representatives met to decide the future of the South. The meeting was dominated by the charismatic judge Muhammad Salih al-Shingeiti, the first Sudanese justice of the High Court and an Arab from the Nile River Valley. He convinced the conference to maintain a unified Sudan and to have the South participate in a National Assembly, which the authorities in Khartoum had already decided was to be created. Prior to the conference, the British political service in the South had strenuously objected to the creation of a legislative assembly for the entire country without any safeguards for southern participation. The British feared that any National Assembly would be dominated by the Nile River Arabs. The Juba Conference itself was hardly representative of southern opinion, given who was chosen to attend and who did the choosing.

Shortly after the Free Officers' coup ousted King Farouk, the new Egyptian government secretly made a deal with some of the northern Sudanese political parties, guaranteeing self-determination within three years. The agreement was made public on January 10, 1953, and—quite intentionally—failed to indicate whether Sudan would be a sovereign and independent state or united with Egypt. By the end of the year, free and fair elections were held across the country, a new National Assembly was elected to prepare for decolonization, and a Sudanization Commission was created—with northerners chosen for its most important posts. The new National Assembly voted against union with Egypt following independence.

4

FOURTH PERIOD OF MODERN
SUDAN (1956–2005)

How did the first North–South civil war begin?

Between October 18 and 21, 1954, southern leaders organized a second Juba Conference, this time with no northern sanction or delegates present to guide the results. The conference voted for independence from Egypt (which affirmed the National Assembly's vote against union), but only if the South was given autonomy in a federal system. Were such autonomy not afforded, the southerners insisted on self-determination, including the possibility of independence from the North. Thus, at this second Juba Conference, the nascent southern leadership proposed two of the central features of the CPA that was approved in 2005: an autonomous South within Sudan and, failing that, self-determination leading to possible independence. It would take fifty-one long and bloody years, 4 million deaths, and systematic campaigns by successive northern governments to emasculate southern tribal culture before the last decision of the second Juba Conference was realized: an independent South.

Fourth Period of Modern Sudan (1956–2005):
Independent Sudan

As more northern officials, merchants, and military officers streamed south to take the place of the departing British—800 posts were given to northerners, while only eight went to southerners—disaffection and anger spread. In July 1955, spontaneous riots broke out in Yambio, the western Equatorian capital, and police intervened by firing into the crowd, killing eight. One month later, a mutiny took place in Torit among the Second Company of the old colonial Equatorial Corps: southern troops rushed the weapons depot, seized rifles, and murdered northerner officials and merchants as well as their families. The riots spread to Wau and Malakal, though there is no evidence that any of these outbreaks were planned or organized. More than 300 people, two-thirds of them northerners, were killed during the violence. The Arabs blamed Christian missionaries, though an investigative commission later found no evidence of their involvement. British officials, still nominally in charge in Sudan, helped the Sudanese army restore order and capture some of the mutineers, while reports circulated of northern army retaliation against the civilian population. Fearing reprisals, some southern leaders left for Uganda, where they were given sanctuary.

The departure of the British was greeted with jubilation in the North and foreboding in the South, where the British were popular. In his autobiography, Joseph Lagu, later the commander of the southern rebel army during the first civil war, recalls witnessing as a 25-year-old the departure of the British in 1955 and the arrival of the Nile River Arabs.

We felt this [Arab] occupation indicated a possible renewal of the slave trade after the British left. The southern Sudanese had always regarded the British as their deliverers and protectors, while they viewed the northerners as slave traders and tormentors. The sudden departure of the British was a shock to most of us... fear and suspicion hovered over the south. It was not a true independence for the south, but the start of another colonialism by the north, their traditional enemy (*The Sudan: Odyssey Through a State from Ruin to Hope*; memoir of Joseph Lagu, p. 60).

The uprising in the South convinced the British government to accelerate its departure, since officials there still had responsibility with little corresponding control. On January 1, 1956, the British hastily departed, and the Sudanese state was born—with an unstable, unprepared government in charge of a country that was still taking shape. The temporary constitution drafted by British scholars left unresolved the critical issues of federalism and the role of Islam. After independence, more and more educated southern leaders, fearing arrest, fled to Uganda or into the bush. Thus, the prelude to the first civil war began five months before Sudanese independence had even become a formal reality.

In the first democratic elections in an independent Sudan in 1958 (the 1953 parliamentary elections had taken place while Sudan was under the Condominium), the two major Islamic parties—bitter rivals though they continued to be—won 89 of 173 seats in the National Assembly. The second democratically elected Parliament of newly independent Sudan took office with the prime minister and cabinet, amid high public expectations.

They were soon disappointed. What followed were two years of weak and ineffective government, petty squabbling, economic recession, and Byzantine political intrigue. The civilian transition government—a coalition of the two major Islamic parties—was overthrown on November 17, 1958, by a bloodless coup led by Major General Ibrahim Abbud, commander-in-chief of the Sudanese military. The officers who led the coup were nearly all from the Three Tribes, while the foot soldiers came from the outlying provinces of the periphery, a pattern of tribal-military power that continues to this day. These officers also shared one other characteristic: they belonged to the political party that supported union with Egypt and had roots in the Khatmiyya sect.

General Abbud's military government brought temporary economic prosperity and relief from the messy business of democratic party politics, for with it came an injection of foreign aid into the country from donor governments and World Bank loans, modest infrastructure development in the North, and the building of schools in the South (with funding from USAID). When I first visited Sudan in 1989 as a USAID officer, I remember seeing in many southern garrison cities the shells of bombed-out buildings that had been constructed with multicolored square stone blocks, a distinctive trademark of General Abbud's schools. In many areas, these blocks were the only evidence of development in the South and they were funded through foreign aid.

Abbud's military council believed that the only way to unify the country was to extend Arab culture and Islam to the South, which they proceeded to do. Southerners complained that the Abbud schools were a disguised effort to Arabize and Islamize the South. Under the Missionary Societies Act of 1962, the military government restricted the activities and presence of Christian missionaries in the South. Two years later, Khartoum expelled them altogether. During this period, the North took control of all missionary schools, changed the Sabbath in the South from Sunday to Friday, established Quranic institutes that taught Islam to new converts, changed the language of instruction from English to Arabic, and promulgated Islamic instruction.

The small southern elite, many of whom had been educated by missionaries and had fond memories of their schools, did not react well to the Abbud policy. Conversions to Christianity in the South accelerated rapidly after the expulsion of the missionaries and the imposition of the Arabization and Islamization policy.

The attraction of Christianity among southerners may be attributed to four factors. First, the traditional religious beliefs of the southern tribes were monotheistic, in that they believed in a Supreme Being. Given their relatively similar theological disposition, it did not take a major conceptual leap for southerners to accept a single Christian God.

Second, Western missionaries in the South had comported themselves well and brought basic education and rudimentary medical care, whereas earlier contact had mostly been with Arabs, who had often been violent and predatory.

Third, the narrative of a martyred prophet, sentenced by a hated imperial power and executed by crucifixion, only to rise triumphantly from the dead, appealed to southerners, who had suffered for so long from the slave trade and wars of conquest.

Fourth, southerners associated Islam with Arabs and Arabs with the terrible violence of the slave trade. Unlike West Africa, where indigenous African slavery existed before American and European slave traders raided the coastal areas, the southern Sudanese Nilotic tribes had no preexisting human chattel culture. By the time the British arrived in southern Sudan in the nineteenth century, the British Parliament had already abolished the slave trade. To the southerners, slavery was exclusively associated with the Arabs. Had the northern Arabs pursued a policy of Islamization without Arabization, while respecting the southern tribal cultures and not engaging in the slave trade, Islam might well have spread across the South well before Christian missionaries arrived.

Southerners fled to Uganda and the Congo in increasing numbers, and their leaders formed competing political organizations to promote the simmering southern insurgency that southern political leaders called the Anyanya Civil War, a name taken from the Madi word *inya nya*, meaning "snake poison," and the Moru word *manya nya*, meaning a "soldier ant." By 1964, the first (Anyanya) civil war could count 5,000 irregular troops, who did cause some trouble, increase insecurity in the South, and harass northern administrators, but they did not represent a real threat to northern administrative control of the South.

General Abbud's military rule came to an unceremonious end after student disturbances arose at the University of Khartoum, followed by mass demonstrations led by the professional elite against the regime, which in turn drew support from the trade unions and the Communist and Umma parties. Wishing to avoid civilian bloodshed, Abbud dissolved the governing military council on October 26, 1964, and turned power over to a broad civilian coalition government. This popular uprising against an unpopular dictatorship came to be known as the "October Revolution" and established in Sudanese politics the precedent of the Khartoum professional elites, labor unions, and students bringing down dictatorships through mass, if mostly peaceful, demonstrations. This precedent was not lost on the later dictatorship of Omar al-Bashir, who developed an elaborate security apparatus (described later) to prevent such events after he took power in 1989.

Two months later, in December 1964, a crowd of southerners living in Khartoum gathered to welcome back Clement Mboro—the minister of the interior and the first southerner ever appointed to a senior cabinet post in the Sudanese government—from a visit to the South. His flight was delayed for some reason; rumors spread that he had been assassinated. Southerners went on a rampage across Khartoum, killing Arabs. The military was called in to restore order, and a hundred people lay dead in the streets in the aftermath of what was later considered a race riot and called "Black Sunday." (In August 2005, similar riots took place in Khartoum after the death of Dr. John Garang described in later chapters.) Mboro was alive and well; he died of natural causes in 2006.

Black Sunday convinced the new government that the "Southern Problem"—the term used by the Nile River Arabs to describe the issues associated with the South—had to be addressed. This led to a three-month peacemaking conference between southern and northern leaders. Endless debate, southern factional bickering, and northern manipulation led to its failure. The Anyanya Revolt continued. Three months after the conference ended, two incidents occurred in the South that accelerated the departure of southerners for neighboring countries. When a Sudanese soldier was killed in Juba in an altercation with a civilian, the Sudanese Armed Forces (SAF) garrison, with the tacit approval of their officers, went on a rampage, killing 1,400 southern civilians. A few days later at a wedding, the Sudanese army garrison from Wau surrounded the ceremony, opened fire, and systematically executed seventy-six men from the southern elite in attendance. More southerners fled to neighboring countries. The number of recruits in Anyanya militias continued to increase.

The first leadership of the South in the First Civil War was hampered by several constraints. No single figure emerged with the moral authority, experience, intellectual capacity, or fighting ability to lead southern forces in the civil war. The poisonous southern tribal rivalries were reflected in the factional intrigue among Anyanya commanders and politicians, who were unable to form a unified military command structure or political organization, advance a single political ideology, or develop a coherent plan to defeat the North. The division between the military commanders in the bush and southern exiled political figures—whom the commanders often dismissed as armchair rebels—weakened the effectiveness of the southern forces. (The Darfur rebellion that began in 2003 suffered from all of the same problems.) Meanwhile, the northern army added fire to the civil war by continuing to commit atrocities against the civilian population; the weaknesses of the northern army ensured that they would be unable to secure the South; and the political instability in Khartoum made a diplomatic settlement ever more remote. One ineffective and short-lived Khartoum government followed another between 1965 and 1969. All of them pursued the same policy of Arabization and Islamization.

Anyanya took a decidedly new turn in late 1967, when Joseph Lagu, an Equatorian, succeeded in unifying the militias under his command through an alliance with the Israeli government, which provided him with training in military operations along with modern weapons systems and funding. Beginning in 1969, he and other commanders traveled to Israel, marking the beginning of Israeli support for the Anyanya revolt. The divisions and infighting within the civilian factions of the southern leadership disgusted Lagu, and as he grew stronger, he refused to deal with the southern political leaders.

Economic mismanagement and the paralysis of successive civilian democratic governments in Khartoum led to the military once again intervening as it had in 1958 under General Abbud. On May 25, 1969, Colonel Jaafar al-Numayri toppled the government, taking power in a bloodless coup modeled after the Egyptian revolution that had brought Abdel Nasser to power in 1952. Numayri called his military coalition the Committee of Free Officers—the same name used by Nasser's military coalition in Egypt—and embraced the same secular, socialist, pan-Arab ideology. Egypt had a firm junior ally in Numayri's new government, which held power from 1969 to 1985.

How did Colonel Numayri govern Sudan for so long?

Colonel Numayri had risen through the military ranks from a modest family and without inherited claim to political or religious leadership. He was therefore unencumbered by the demands of the Islamic political teaching that formed the basis of the two most powerful political parties in Sudan— the Umma (Mahdiyya) and the DUP (Khatmiyya), both led by the descendants of their founders. The first seven years of Numayri's rule proved to be the most promising for a resolution of the "Southern Problem." Soon after taking power, he announced that the civil war would be resolved through political negotiation, not military victory, and proceeded to devise a new system of decentralized self-government in the South. Political intrigue in Khartoum delayed his action on this new policy.

Numayri joined Egypt and Libya in a short-lived Arab Socialist Union. While he nationalized hundreds of private businesses, banks, and other parts of the Sudanese economy and improved relations with Soviet Bloc countries, his political maneuvers were not sufficient to ensure the loyalty of the Sudanese Communists. He soon faced challenges from the right- and left-wing political forces in Sudan. After Sadiq al-Mahdi, the great-grandson of the Mahdi, was arrested and jailed, his half-brother and rival, the imam al-Hadi al-Mahdi, assumed leadership of the pro-Western and anti-Communist Umma Party. This party was increasingly alarmed by Numayri's socialist policies and by the number of Communists he had enlisted in his government from among the Sudanese army officer corps, which had long been an organizing center for Communist recruitment. The imam mobilized the Ansar Army, which had evolved over time into a religious militia of the Umma Party, and held mass demonstrations against the regime, which brutally suppressed them. The Ansar forces then barricaded themselves behind their military fortifications on Aba Island for their last stand—the same island where their spiritual founder, the Mahdi, had had his ecstatic visions of the Prophet in 1881. Numayri dispatched the army, which killed some 12,000 Ansar soldiers in the ensuing bloodbath on the island, and then the imam as he was trying to escape the country. This ended the conservative counterreaction to the Numayri regime—at least temporarily.

Following the Ansar massacre, Numayri purged his government of Communists, whom he realized were unreliable allies. In July 1971, the Communists attempted a coup to unseat him. Over the next three days, he was able to resist the coup with support from Colonel Gaddafi of Libya and President Sadat of Egypt, who had taken over after Abdel Nasser's death in 1970. Numayri then proceeded to arrest and execute dozens of Communist leaders, while also detaining 3,000 of the Communist rank and file for questioning. Numayri did not have deep public support. In the first two years he faced a total of nine overthrow attempts, of which the two mentioned above were only the most visible.

Numayri's popularity among the public grew, however, after his successful prevention of the Communist takeover—a coup attempt that had frightened conservative Sudanese society. At this point he decided that he needed to broaden his base of political support within Sudan, and the logical manner for doing so was to act on his earlier promise to resolve the "Southern Problem" through a political settlement. By ending the increasingly violent civil war, he would earn the support of the South—at least in theory. The war was not going well for Numayri, in any case. The unified military command under Joseph Lagu and his 13,000 southern troops equipped with Israeli training and weapons had given the southerners what they did not have before: an armed force that matched the North's. Numayri turned to the Soviet Union and the Egyptians for help. The Soviets sent advanced weapons systems, including helicopter gunships, and the Egyptians sent two commando units. The southerners defeated both, scoring repeated victories in 1970 and early 1971, and effectively fighting the northern army to a standstill. While Lagu's attempts to take SAF-controlled southern garrison cities were repulsed, the North was incapable of defeating southern forces in the countryside, a pattern that would repeat itself in the Second Civil War. Thus by early 1971, it became increasingly apparent that a military solution to the "Southern Problem" was unlikely.

Numayri had hanged his minister of southern affairs, Joseph Garang (no relation to John Garang), a Communist who had supported the coup attempt against him, and in July 1971 replaced him with the southerner Abel Alier, a Dinka, lawyer, and ideological moderate. A skillful negotiator, Alier accepted the position on the condition that he could quietly begin talks with southern political leaders about a peace settlement. He had developed extensive contacts with southern Christian church leaders and their denominational counterparts in European churches. These church leaders helped facilitate the peace process and reported to Alier that the southerners would agree to conduct negotiations within the context of a united Sudan and not insist on independence. This was enough of a guarantee for Numayri to support an accelerated peace process.

At the first meeting, which had been held in January 1971 in Addis Ababa, Ethiopia, Numayri had declared a unilateral cease-fire in military operations; in response, Lagu had attempted to constrain his commanders from taking offensive action. Attending the conference with Lagu was a young Anyanya officer named John Garang. A second meeting was held a year later in February, again in Addis Ababa, and an agreement was reached on February 27, 1972. Talks nearly broke down over one central issue: whether the South would be allowed to retain its army. This was only resolved through the mediation of Haile Selassie, emperor of Ethiopia. The Sudanese army would remain united, but with a southern command composed of equal proportions of southerners and northerners.

The agreement created a federal Sudanese state in which the South would be governed by a legislative assembly and a council of ministers. The southern government would be run by southerners appointed by Numayri with the advice and consent of the high executive council. English was to be the official language of the South and the language of instruction in schools. Because Numayri was a secularist, the issue of Islamic law was not yet the stumbling block to peace that it eventually became in the Second Civil War. On March 27, 1972, the Addis Ababa Agreement was signed by Lagu for the South and Mansur Khalid (who switched sides and later joined John Garang during the Second Civil War) on behalf of Numayri. Peace was at hand, or so people thought.

Lagu's support for the agreement proved critically important, for many of his commanders and southern politicians in exile had expected it to support southern independence and became disenchanted when it didn't; some threatened a new revolt. Other African states, while sympathetic to the southern cause in the first civil war, were concerned about the separatist tendencies of the Southern rebellion because they faced their own internal civil wars and separatist movements. Nigeria had been torn apart by the Biafran civil war in the late 1960s. Ethiopia faced a decades-long independence movement in Eritrea and a war with Somalia in the 1970s over the status of the ethnic Somali population in its southeastern region. Zaire was threatened by the separatists in Katanga province, among others. For African nations to support southern Sudanese independence would create a dangerous precedent. Since the 1960s, U.S. State Department policy had opposed any separatist movements in Africa (this policy only changed in 1991 with the Eritrean independence referendum). However much southerners may have wished for independence, the diplomatic deck was stacked against them.

President Numayri quickly embraced the Addis Ababa Agreement and campaigned for the deal at rallies across the country, which allowed him to portray himself—accurately for the moment—as the great Sudanese peacemaker, a title none of his predecessors could claim. When Lagu arrived in Khartoum, he was warmly received by Numayri and given the rank of major general in the Sudanese army, a promotion that some in the South thought smacked of a political deal: Lagu's support for the agreement in exchange for a senior military rank in a Sudanese army with authority in the South. Numayri named Abel Alier as the new vice president for the South without consulting any southerners, infuriating Lagu and other Anyanya leaders who saw Alier as a front for the Three Tribes and an accommodationist. (It is interesting that in 2010, as Sudan prepared for the independence vote, President Bashir announced that Abel Alier had been appointed as his advisor to try to convince the southerners to vote against secession, while Salva Kiir, the southern president, countered with the appointment of Joseph Lagu as his advisor to support secession.)

In the years following the Addis Ababa accords, Numayri embarked on a series of large-scale development schemes, nearly all of which were in the North: a new highway system in the Arab Triangle, telecommunications, and improvements in the railroad system. In 1973, after the massive increase in oil revenues to Arab states following the rise in global oil prices, the Gulf States decided to invest in Sudanese agriculture in order to reduce their dependence on Western food imports. They envisioned Sudan as the breadbasket of the Arab world, a vision that was apparently not shared by the local market economy or the Sudanese state. The same year, under pressure from the IMF and World Bank, Numayri began selling off or returning to their private owners the enterprises he had nationalized when he first took power. Money poured into the country and produced a temporary economic boom. But the projects themselves, despite heavy Gulf investment, began to fail, and the income they were supposed to generate did not materialize. Eventually, Khartoum was left with huge public and private debts, amounting to $13 billion by 1990.

Also in 1973, Numayri drafted a secular constitution that, on its face, appeared to be a reasonable replacement for the temporary document drafted by the British at independence. The constitution theoretically settled the long-running dispute over race and religion that had haunted Sudanese politics for a century. It declared Sudan to be both Arab and African, creating a secular state that implicitly would not impose Islamic law on nonbelievers. The Islamic parties of Sudan—despite their rivalry—were united in their opposition to Numayri and to his constitution.

Why did Numayri embrace an Islamic political vision for Sudan?

After his first six years of rule, Numayri could point to some major accomplishments. He had ended the first civil war through a political settlement, while maintaining the unity of the country and conceding very little to the southerners. He undertook a number of large infrastructure schemes, adopted a new secular constitution, and opened international aid spigots so that development funds could pour into the country.

His accomplishments, however, were never enough to create a stable and loyal popular base of support for his government. What's more, they came at a steep price. He centralized autocratic power in his own hands, using brute force to suppress opposition on both the left and the right. As described earlier, he decapitated the underground Sudanese Communist organizational structure after the abortive coup of 1971, which alienated the Soviet Union, its allies in Ethiopia, and segments of the Sudanese military. The Alba Island massacre of the Ansar Army, the killing of Imam al-Hadi and driving of Sadiq al-Mahdi into exile, the adoption of the secular constitution of 1973, and his personal disinterest in Islam—he seldom attended prayers, and he drank alcohol— alienated the conservative Islamic political parties. The Addis Ababa peace agreement caused resentment in Darfur and led to an unsuccessful coup attempt in 1975 by Darfuri officers in the Sudanese army who resented the South getting autonomy when their region had not. In short, with each passing year and with each new initiative, his list of enemies grew longer and stronger.

On July 2, 1976, a coup unfolded at the Khartoum airport as he was returning to Sudan from a trip to the United States. The coup leaders had intended to kill the Sudanese government officials assembled at the airport to greet Numayri's plane, but his plane arrived early, throwing off the timing of the plot. Numayri and the officials escaped unharmed, mobilized the army, and within three days crushed the revolt with a heavy loss of life. The coup leaders were an unholy alliance of all the enemies Numayri had collected over the preceding seven years of his presidency. The Soviet Union, Colonel Gaddafi's Libyan government, Sadiq al Mahdi, and Mengistu Haile Mariam's Ethiopian government had provided the weapons, funding, and base of operations to support the coup. The ground troops came from two sources: first, Sadiq al-Mahdi's Ansar Army from Darfur, and second, the Arab Legion (also called the Islamic Legion), recruited and organized by Gaddafi—and trained and armed by the Soviet Union—to spearhead Gaddafi's grand strategy for expanding Libyan (and Arab) influence in the region. These Legion recruits mainly came from the Baqqara Rizaiqat tribe from Darfur, Arab cattle herders whose way of life was slowly disappearing as the Sahara Desert moved southward, rainfall declined, and other herders encroached on their traditional grazing areas. (The Khartoum government later turned to the same Arab Legion in the 2003 Darfur rebellion to conduct an ethnic cleansing campaign against the rebellious African tribes.)

Numayri addressed his political dilemma and growing internal opposition by making a dramatic course correction—adopting an Islamic political agenda for Sudan. Beginning in the summer of 1977, he released political prisoners, stopped the persecution of the Ansar, and announced a broad amnesty that even covered Hassan al-Turabi's followers in the NIF. He reconciled with Sadiq al-Mahdi, whom he had sentenced to death in absentia following the failed coup. At a reconciliation meeting with the Islamic parties in July 1977, he secretly promised to renegotiate key provisions of the Addis Agreement, which Hassan al-Turabi and his allies had despised: regional autonomy for the South, an independent military structure for the absorbed southern troops, a secular constitution for Sudan, and English rather than Arabic as the language of the South. The roots of the second civil war that would unfold later may be found in this fateful meeting, which reflected the discontinuities in Sudanese politics. If Numayri intended to embrace the Islamic parties and thus theoretically widen his base of support, he would have to abrogate the hard-won peace agreement with the South. Sadiq returned home from this meeting skeptical of Numayri's promises.

Numayri's reconciliation efforts also included the return of Hassan al-Turabi from exile to be his new attorney general. Turabi used his new position to advance his own agenda: the rebuilding of the NIF cadres that had been decimated by Numayri and the implementation of his plan to replace the secular legal code used in the Sudanese judiciary with Sharia (or Islamic) law, thus abrogating one of the central provisions of the new constitution. Turabi's policies would have profound consequences over the course of the next thirty-five years of Sudanese history. In Turabi's proposed legal code the use of *Hadood* (the amputation of a hand and foot from opposite sides of the body), stoning and cruxification as forms of execution were codified as part of Sharia law.

Turabi's return had revolutionary consequences. Some saw him as a modern-day Mahdi, who would sweep away the old, corrupt Arab socialist order that Numayri had brought to Sudan from Egypt, just as the Mahdi had swept away the corrupt Egyptian administration a century before. Sadiq al-Mahdi may have been the genetic and institutional heir to the Mahdi's throne, but he lacked the crusading fire of his great-grandfather and believed in a Quranic interpretation of Islam informed by successive centuries of Islamic scholarship, which Turabi adamantly rejected as corrupt. While theologically Turabi's roots were in Salafist Islam, in other ways he was the true heir to the Mahdi's jihad.

Numayri was torn between his loyalty to his new found Islamist allies and his long history with the Egyptian government, which had saved him in one coup attempt and whose example he had consistently followed throughout his political career. In 1976, the year after his shift toward Islam, his friend and ally Anwar el-Sadat became the first Arab leader to travel to Jerusalem to speak to the Israeli Knesset. This began a peace process that resulted in the Camp David Accords, effectively ending the state of war between Israel and Egypt. Sadat's effort enraged much of the Arab world. The Muslim Brotherhood, founded and centered in Egypt, was at the forefront of opposition to Sadat's peace overtures. Egypt was expelled from the Arab League, whose headquarters were moved to Libya. Numayri was alone among Arab leaders to endorse the Camp David Accords (out of loyalty to Sadat, but also perhaps because he feared Israeli interference in Sudan's affairs, as during the first civil war). In 1981, when a more radical offshoot of the Muslim Brotherhood—Turabi's true philosophical godfathers—assassinated Sadat in retaliation for his peace agreement with Israel, Numayri was the only Arab head of state to attend his funeral.

5

FOURTH PERIOD (CONTINUED): THE SECOND CIVIL WAR AND THE TURABIST STATE

Why and how did the Second Civil War start in the South?

Southerners hoping for an immediate peace dividend following the Addis Ababa Agreement were disappointed. Some of this disappointment stemmed from wildly unrealistic expectations. Even under the most favorable circumstances, development is a long, complex, and arduous process. The South's physical isolation, high illiteracy rates, and lack of both infrastructure and institutional capacity would have slowed the process down to a crawl no matter who was in charge in the North. While Numayri wanted the war in the South to end, he wanted it on his terms. He had no intention of giving up indirect control over budgets, appointments, natural resources, policy, or military forces deployed in the South. Most important, he did not want anything done to accelerate the separatist sentiments he suspected lurked in most southerners' hearts.

During the eleven-year period of the Addis Ababa peace, Numayri interfered in every election for president of the High Executive Council—the top policy-making body of the new southern Regional Government. He had orchestrated the election of Abel Alier as the first president of this council, a widely unpopular maneuver, given that Alier was seen as a northern collaborator by southerners, particularly the Anyanya leaders. Alier's greatest rival during these eleven years was Joseph Lagu, who resented being subordinated to a man who had never fought in the civil war or even served in the civilian wing of the rebel movement. Both the Alier and Lagu factions sought Numayri's personal support to oust the other. Thus southern infighting and factionalism strengthened Numayri's hand and weakened the South's semiautonomous status, exacerbating widespread suspicion in the South that the Addis Ababa Agreement was a sham, a cynical effort to end the fighting while maintaining Khartoum's control.

How did the discovery of oil change Sudanese politics?

The exploration for oil was begun in 1964 by the Italian gas and oil company Agip. Initially it proved unsuccessful. In 1974, Chevron (with Shell Oil later taking a 25 percent position in the effort) began exploration in Red Sea State, in the North; Muglad, which is in the disputed region of Abyei; and Malakal, in the South. In 1976, Chevron discovered the Suakin Red Sea gas deposit; in 1978 commercially exploitable oil deposits were found near Bentiu and Heglig; and in 1981 the Unity Field north of Bentiu was discovered. In 1984, a year after the Second Civil War began, rebel forces attacked the Chevron oil fields, kidnapping and killing three expatriate workers. The arrogant and dismissive reaction from the Sudanese oil minister to Chevron's request for security and protection, as well as the company's own internal risk assessment, led Chevron to decide to suspend operations, which it did not restart until 1988.

Between 1974 and 1992 Chevron and Shell Oil invested nearly a billion dollars prospecting for oil in Sudan. Some experts at the time claimed that unexplored reserves could constitute as much as 10 billion barrels, with known reserves

at a half billion barrels (current estimates are much more conservative—2 to 3 billion barrels). The southern government in
Juba insisted that a newly proposed oil refinery be built in the
South, connecting oil deposits located there to a planned oil
pipeline that would run to Port Sudan and international markets. Numayri, once again without consulting the southerners, approved the construction of the oil refinery in the North,
and the otherwise divided government officials (all from the
Three Tribes) united behind his decision. Southern students
took to the streets in mass protests after the decision was
announced.

The 1978 oil discovery complicated another simmering
dispute—the demarcation of the North–South Border—that
had been resolved on paper (but which Khartoum cynically
ignored in practice) by the 1972 Addis Ababa Agreement. The
border debate centered on the grazing rights of Misiriyya
Arabs, who lived in Kordofan State, and those of the Dinka,
who lived in the adjacent Bahr al-Ghazal State and whose
kings (called paramount chiefs) had governed from Abyei for
centuries. The Addis agreement had called for the return of
certain areas of the northern states to the South. The discovery
of oil ensured that none of this would happen. The National
Assembly considered a bill—initiated by Turabi, as newly appointed minister of justice (or attorney general)—that would
have moved all the disputed areas clearly into the northern
provinces. This infuriated the entire southern delegation. For
the moment, Numayri sided with the South and put the
inflammatory bill aside.

What event precipitated the Second Civil War?

The border demarcation controversies that threatened peace
after the Addis Ababa Agreement in the 1970s remained
unresolved thirty years later at the time of southern
independence in 2011. The North and South border became
an even more contentious issue at independence because it

would no longer be an internal border but an international one between independent and sovereign states.

Long before the Addis Ababa Agreement had been signed in 1971, various southern factions had debated a demarcation issue of a different sort: whether the South should be treated as one province or broken into smaller provinces, each with a separate local assembly and government. This might seem a minor administrative question, but Numayri used the dispute to abrogate the Addis Ababa Agreement in 1983, as follows. As we've seen, one of the ongoing tensions in southern Sudan was the tensions between the Dinkas and the Equatorian tribes, which were disproportionately employed by the British during the colonial period. Many Equatorians feared that the far more numerous Dinka would dominate any political or military arrangements in the South, and so supported an effort to partition the South into separate Equatorian states. Joseph Lagu, of the Madi Tribe from Equatoria, supported the subdivision. However, Dinka leaders, including Abel Alier, argued that this would allow Khartoum to play one region off against another, weakening the South's political influence.

On June 5, 1983, President Numayri announced his promulgation of Republican Order Number One, which broke the South into three provinces with separate capitals, replaced the southern Regional Assembly in Juba with three much weaker legislative bodies with no independent fiscal authority, rescinded the required election of governors (so that they would now be appointed by him alone), eliminated the separate southern army units and their proportional representation in the SAF in the South, and substituted Arabic for English as the official language. With one signature, Numayri swept away what remained of the Addis Ababa Agreement and seized complete control of the state apparatus of southern Sudan. He had kept his promise to Turabi and Sadiq al-Mahdi at Port Sudan five years earlier. The Addis Ababa Agreement was dead.

Republican Order Number One was followed in September 1983 by what are commonly called the September Laws, imposing Sharia law on all peoples and provinces of Sudan and spurring support for the nascent second civil war. The government-controlled news media was filled with reports of floggings for alcohol possession and sex crimes, cross-amputations for larceny and other crimes, and public executions by stoning for capital crimes. The first cross-amputations were held at the stadium in Khartoum, and Numayri ordered government ministers to attend. Turabi, who had pressed for imposition of Sharia, fainted while watching the first amputation.

Three weeks before Republican Order Number One, what has been called the Bor mutiny had already triggered the second civil war, which then drew additional momentum from both the Order and the September Laws. The mutiny occurred as Numayri began redeploying southern troops at the end of 1982 to the North—once again in direct violation of the Addis Ababa Agreement—away from their homes and kinsmen. These troops feared they would be unable to protect their homeland from the northern Army, which southerners continued to see as an occupying force. Numayri had thought the transfer of southern military units to the North would reduce the risk of a full-scale civil war. He badly miscalculated; his order precipitated what he sought to avoid. While some southern units, including the Abyei Battalion, bitterly protested but carried out their orders, the Bor Battalion refused. That act of resistance spread and developed into a full-scale civil war, mainly due to the efforts of a leader named John Garang.

Who was John Garang?

Any description of the Second Civil War must begin with the figure most closely associated with it: John Garang de Mabior. Garang was born in 1945 to a Twic Dinka family of cattle herders in Bor County in Upper Nile State—the state was served by the missionary-run Bor primary school. Many of the war's early leaders attended this famous missionary school, principally because it was one of the few schools in the region.

Garang's uncle, who worked in the school, arranged for Garang to attend after his parents died when he was ten. He later traveled to Tanzania as a refugee early in the Anyanya civil war, where he attended high school. For a year after graduation, he taught mathematics at a high school at Mount Kenya. From there he received a Thomas Watson Fellowship to Grinnell College in Iowa, a small liberal arts college founded by New England Congregationalists in the nineteenth century that became the center of the Social Gospel movement in American Protestantism, which emphasized the social justice commands of the Gospel. For a small school, Grinnell graduated a remarkable number of senior government officials (including Harry Hopkins, who served in the Franklin Roosevelt administration and helped create the New Deal).

At Grinnell, Garang reportedly took economic development courses that examined the prevailing schools of thought at the time, which likely included dependency theory. This particular theory was to have a profound effect on his understanding of what ailed Sudan. Dependency theory argued that rich northern countries (meaning, essentially, Europe and the United States), mostly former colonial powers, were extracting natural resources and raw agricultural products from poor developing countries at depressed prices, trapping them in a state of permanent underdevelopment, while big northern factories were able to process the raw material and take large profits. Any poor countries that resisted this "world system" would be marginalized by the North or, in some cases, subjected to military threats or invasion. The theory contained a certain Marxist determinism and has been since discredited as lacking explanatory power for the causes of underdevelopment in poor countries—particularly given the fact that it does not explain the course of globalization; the deindustrialization of Western economies; the rise of China, India, Indonesia, and Brazil, among others, as industrial powers; and the nationalization of oil companies by developing countries. But given Sudan's history as well as its ongoing political and economic crises, dependency theory presented Garang with a remarkably prescient explanation for his country's structural dysfunctions.

Garang's experience in the United States was trans-formational. He saw how a society could be organized: as a multiparty democracy, with independent legal institutions enforcing the rule of law, protections for human rights and religious freedom, a free media, separation of powers among the three branches of the state and national governments, a system of social services for the poor, and a vibrant private market economy. He studied in the United States in the aftermath of the civil rights revolution and thus saw how

Dr. John Garang, leader of the South during the Second Civil War.

reform could transform a society suffering from deeply rooted prejudice.

Garang graduated with a bachelor's degree in economics in 1969, returned to Sudan, and promptly joined the Anyanya civil war with the rank of major as an adjutant to Joseph Lagu, whom he eventually accompanied to the Addis Ababa peace negotiations. Garang observed all the mistakes the South made in these negotiations in dealing with the North, which, as he once told me (in 2002), he was determined to avoid in any future negotiations. When the Anyanya troops were integrated into the Sudan army, Garang, perhaps the best-educated southern officer at the time, was promoted to lieutenant colonel and sent to Fort Benning, Georgia, to attend military school. He convinced his commanders in Khartoum to let him continue his education in the United States, and in 1981, along with five other southern Sudanese officers, he went on to get a Ph.D. in agricultural economics at Iowa State College, where his dissertation focused on the Jonglei Canal project. He concluded that the project would damage livelihoods in the South and opposed its construction. When he returned to Khartoum, his Sudanese commanders gave him the task of creating a military library for the Sudanese army; he also took a position teaching agricultural economics at the University of Khartoum. While he labored in these jobs for two years, he quietly organized a network of southern officers angry with the unfolding events in the South.

Garang was remarkably well positioned for the movement he was about to lead. One of the great weaknesses of the southern Anyanya movement in the first civil war had been the ongoing division and acrimony between its military and political wings. Garang bridged all these divides: he was an intellectual who understood development economics and had a clear vision of what he wanted Sudan to become; he was a politician who had for ten years observed and studied the operation of the American political system and news media and ways to use both for his own purposes; and he was a

Nile River at Bor County, Jonglei State, South Sudan, where the
Second Civil War began. (Henrik Stabell/NPA)

military commander who had been trained at Fort Benning,
home of the U.S. Army Infantry School just as the lessons of
the Vietnam War and the strategy of its Communist insurgency were being woven into the course of study. Khartoum
had inadvertently prepared the ideal figure to lead a civil war
against itself. And that is exactly what Garang did.

What was Garang's role in the Second Civil War?

Garang had been commander of the 105th Battalion of Bor in
the SAF while he fought briefly in the First Civil War, so he
knew the unit well. While legend has it that President
Numayri sent Garang to quell the Bor mutiny and, along the
way, Garang switched sides and led the civil war, the reality
is very different. Garang and his network of southern officers
had been planning the Second Civil War for some time. When
the order from Khartoum was given in January 1983 to move
southern units northward, their commanders refused to
comply, as the Addis Ababa Agreement had made it clear that

they would only serve in the South. The SAF was sent in May 1983 to end the civil war, but Major Kerubino Kuanyin Bol (later infamous for repeatedly switching sides during the Second Civil War and for his human rights abuses) had recently taken command of the 105th and pushed back the SAF forces. It was Kerubino who fired the first shot of the Second Civil War. After the assaults, Kerubino and his forces, joined by Garang, withdrew to Ethiopia, where they were offered refuge by the Ethiopian government. In all, about 3,000 southern troops deserted the SAF and joined the civil war, along with other southern militia groups (loosely called the "Anyanya II"). Together, this force grew to 10,000 troops within two years, with another 20,000 being trained in Ethiopia.

On July 31, 1983, Garang announced, as their new commander-in-chief, the creation of both the unified Sudanese People's Liberation Army (SPLA) and the Sudanese People's Liberation Movement (SPLM) as its civilian arm. The Southern Manifesto soon followed, which described the weaknesses of the Addis Ababa Agreement and the failures of the government in Juba that resulted from the Addis Ababa agreement. The language of the rebellion was overtly Marxist—the term "liberation struggle" and "Manifesto" came from the *Communist Manifesto*—but this is not surprising, since the Ethiopian government, the Soviet Union's principal client-ally in Africa, was funding, training, and arming the SPLA. At the time of the Bor mutiny, Ethiopian support was one of the few options available for Garang.

By the end of 1985, Garang was in control of most of the South, with the exception of the garrison towns and cities, which 60,000 SAF troops occupied.

What was Garang's vision for Sudan?

Garang constructed his movement on three central positions that he consistently took throughout the Second Civil War.

First, he argued that the Nile River Arabs were sucking the resources from the periphery of the country inward to fund a higher level of development, education, and standard of living in the Arab Triangle. One statistic, more than almost any other, supports his argument: in the early 1990s, the greater Khartoum area consumed 87 percent of all electrical power in Sudan, while most regional cities and rural areas were not even on the electrical grid. He likely drew this construct from dependency theory by viewing Sudan in the context of the center versus the periphery. (Garang helped change the meaning of *jallaba*, "trader," referring to the Arabs, to imply an untrustworthy trader who takes advantage of his customers.) Later in the war, this "center versus the periphery" analysis fueled rebellions among the Beja people in Red Sea State, an incipient rebellion of the Nubian people in the far North in 2006 and 2007, the tribes of the Nuba Mountains, the Funj in the Blue Nile region, and among the Darfuris to the west, all of whom lived in an state of underdevelopment equivalent to that of the South. Garang tied together this regional dissatisfaction and formed a powerful alliance for reform. For their part, successive Khartoum regimes fueled the resentment driving the alliance with their short-sighted focus on the Arab Triangle and their policy of forced Islamization and Arabization.

Second, Garang argued that Sudan could only exist as a multiethnic, secular state and not as an Arab Islamist state, given its multiple ethnic, racial, and religious composition. As we have seen, this theme permeated Sudanese political debate well before Garang entered the drama, but he gave it a broader and more appealing meaning by tying it to principles of democracy and human rights.

Third, Garang advocated a reformed but united Sudanese state, just as Joseph Lagu and Abel Alier had during the Addis Ababa negotiations that ended the First Civil War. Mirroring that civil war, however, the rank-and-file officers and foot soldiers of the SPLA supported complete independence, making the argument for unity the most problematic element of Garang's vision. Just as Haile Selassie had faced a separatist rebel movement in Eritrea before and during the Addis Ababa Agreement negotiations, Mengistu, the Ethiopian Marxist dictator, now faced not only the Eritrean separatists but also separatist rebel movements among ethnic Somalis, Oromos, and Tigrayans. An independent South might have by example encouraged those separatist movements and thus set a dangerous precedent for Ethiopia, so Garang had little choice but to argue against southern independence if he wanted Ethiopian support.

As the Second Civil War progressed and spread to other regions of the country, Garang evolved from a Bor County Dinka to the leader of a the southern Sudanese civil war and then to a national figure who spoke for an increasing number of people in the North and South who wanted Sudan to turn away from its repressive and violent past and toward a "New Sudan" (another SPLM term, which increasingly took on a national meaning). Garang broadcast from SPLA Radio on the border with Ethiopia to the entire Sudanese nation and developed a constituency for his views among progressive northerners, including some from the Three Tribes. Most northern Arabs would not likely have ever voted in a free and fair national election for a Christian southerner, with one exception: John Garang.

However well prepared Garang was for the role he took in the Second Civil War, and however appealing his message seemed to the Sudanese people, his leadership faced challenges from within the South itself. Most of the early rebel leadership were Twic Dinka from Bor, which meant that Garang's tribal base was very narrow and did not even encompass the border Dinka tribe, let alone the Nuer, Shilluk, or Equatorian tribes. Many of the older veterans of the First Civil War resented the idea of a younger man, with only eight months of combat experience, taking leadership of the Second Civil War. He was also widely criticized by older Anyanya leaders who were disappointed with the Addis Ababa Agreement, which supported Sudanese state unity, when they had overwhelmingly wanted complete independence. There was grumbling among SPLA commanders well into the war, and some overtly opposed Garang's leadership.

Both the Ethiopian government's support and the movement's early Marxist rhetoric, arguments, and symbolism led Western critics to dismiss Garang's movement as a Communist front, an accusation that continued to follow him until the collapse of the Soviet Bloc and the fall of Mengistu from power in 1990 and 1991. Until the coup of 1989, which brought Omar al-Bashir to power, the Sudanese government remained a key U.S. ally in Africa—as a counterweight to Soviet-allied Ethiopia—and its largest sub-Saharan aid recipient. (Some scholars have argued that Numayri held power for so long because of American aid, a claim I think is exaggerated and overstates the importance of foreign aid.) With the end of the Cold War and collapse of the Soviet Union, Garang could project his central messages to the Sudanese people without suspicion of external ideological baggage.

The SPLA's unity of leadership and effort came at a steep price, as the SPLA used repressive tactics to enforce it. They committed serious human rights abuses, and Garang was accused of autocratic behavior, centralizing all authority in his own hands. His movement's command council was not called to meet for six years, and anyone challenging him for leadership within the movement or threatening to form a rival party was handed over to Mengistu's internal security apparatus. Garang also branded as warlords any southern commanders who led militias independent of the SPLA command structure.

Why and how did Numayri fall from power?

Jaafar Numayri's reign grew more corrupt, abusive, and incompetent the longer he held power, particularly during the second half of his tenure. In January 1985, he had the liberal reformer Mahmud Muhammad Taha and four of his allies arrested when they advocated the repeal of Sharia law and the restoration of civil liberties. Taha had been a well-known figure in Sudanese politics since independence and founded and led the Republican Brothers, which advocated liberalization and modernization of Islam, woman's rights, democracy, and human rights. He opposed both Marxism and Nasserite socialism and supported peace with Israel; thus he represented everything Hassan al-Turabi opposed. Taha and his associates were convicted of apostasy and hanged, shocking the Sudanese middle class and intelligentsia, for whom Taha was a respected, if controversial, figure.

Earlier in his rule, Numayri had appointed highly skilled technocrats as cabinet ministers, but as time passed he began to make decisions without consulting anyone except a few corrupt cronies and shadowy figures in his inner circle. This led to disastrous investment decisions on some large-scale development projects, including a sugar refinery that lost money.

By 1985, the economy had spun out of control, with rising inflation, static wages, defaults on the government's massive debts, a dramatic decline in exports, and growing social inequality that caused widespread popular disenchantment and unrest. Over his sixteen years in office, Numayri handed out tens of thousands of jobs to loyalists, increasing the burden on the government's finances and the national economy. At the same time the great Sahelian drought had engulfed northern Africa, spreading epidemics and famine. This caused hundreds of thousands of deaths in rural Sudan alone, as well as mass population movements of the starving rural poor to cities. Numayri ignored their suffering and resisted Western aid agencies' relief efforts. In Darfur, the region hardest hit by the famine, the widely respected and popularly elected governor Ahmed Ibrahim Diraige resigned in protest in 1984 because Numayri refused his requests to send food.

Unrest on the streets of Khartoum led Numayri to unleash the military to crush strikes by the labor unions.

Students' groups, labor unions, and professional groups, propelled by the collapsing economy, organized mass demonstrations against the regime. This time, instead of crushing the demonstrations, the SAF intervened, just as it had after independence. On April 6, 1985, while Numayri was visiting the United States, Major General Siwar al-Dhahab, commander-in-chief of the SAF and minister of defense, appeared on national radio and television to announce that the military had taken control of the government, ousted Nymayri, and would hold elections in one year. General al-Dhahab was known for his Islamist sympathies and his admiration for Hassan al-Turabi's movement. He announced the creation of a transitional council that included John Garang—who had publicly dismissed the new government as "Numayrism without Numayri" and refused to participate—and promised to turn power over to an elected government as soon as possible. During the elections held exactly one year after the coup, Khartoum used the SPLA's insurgency as an excuse to exclude half of the South from voting. The two major northern parties, the Umma and DUP, took over 67 percent of the vote, while Turabi's party received 18 percent, and Turabi himself lost his own campaign for the National Assembly in his home district. Negotiations during the transition between the new government and the SPLA led to a joint statement, the Koka Dam Declaration: A Proposed Programme for National Action, which called for a Sudan free of discrimination and a national reform process. The declaration was supported by the Umma Party, opposed by the DUP, and attacked by both the Muslim Brothers and the NIF. It served as the first statement of principles of what a "New Sudan" would look like, even if the new government did nothing to implement its provisions.

The tumultuous sixteen-year reign of Jaafar Numayri was at an end; a new democratically elected coalition government took office, led by Sadiq al-Mahdi and his Umma Party, which had received the largest number of seats in the National Assembly, albeit not a majority.

What was the reaction of Sadiq al-Mahdi to the Second Civil War?

While the Second Civil War was catching the attention of Khartoum as something a little more than peripheral unrest, Sadiq (even before he was elected prime minister) had begun formulating a strategy for addressing southern civil war. In 1986, he published a tract—which for the southern Sudanese has become a legendary and infamous manifesto of northern strategic intent—on why the South would ultimately lose the Second Civil War. In this tract, he argued that the South's tribal rivalries would lead to its ultimate defeat—which could easily be read as a call for the North to foment tribal war in the South. He also argued—much to the anger of southern elites—that Arab-Islamic culture was fundamentally superior to southern African-Christian culture, which would collapse under the pressure of the war and thus ultimately bring Khartoum victory. This again suggested to the southerners a plan to destroy southern culture and society, which in fact unfolded in reality as the war progressed.

When he became prime minister, Sadiq's policy for winning the war became clear. First, he argued the war must be kept at all costs in the South and away from Khartoum, limiting the damage and chaos of the war to the South. Second, the central government would organize, arm, and fund the Arab tribes along the North–South border to form militias as a supplementary force to the national army. Third, using these tribal militias, along with the northern military, the North would raid and burn southern villages, inciting massive population displacements, which would undermine southern culture and society, making people much more susceptible to Sadiq's policy of forced Arabization and Islamization. Later, these displaced southerners would be driven into concentration camps run by the government, where they would hear the Quran read continuously from loudspeakers all day, every day. They were designed to drive southerners to embrace Islam and Arab culture in order to survive. (This strategy ended up doing the opposite.) Fourth, Sadiq proposed that the central government should use its resources—weapons, money, and jobs—to turn one southern tribe against another. Indeed, most of the deaths in the Second Civil War were actually caused by one group of Khartoum-backed southerners attacking southerners aligned with Garang and the SPLA.

Instead of breaking the opposition, the northern campaign against the southern civilian population strengthened popular support for Garang and the SPLA, increasing the flow of new recruits. As more southern tribal militias joined the SPLA, its image as a Bor Dinka army—which had hampered it from the very beginning—began to change, and it began to be perceived as an intertribal alliance. Sadiq's tactics were backfiring, driving more tribes and young men to join the SPLA as more villages were burned, more cattle stolen, more women raped, and more children abducted into slavery. Despite or because of these tactics, the northern army suffered successive defeats against Garang's troops. In late 1989, Khartoum's military high command gave Sadiq an ultimatum: sue for peace with the South, or they would remove him from office. Sadiq shifted his position against a negotiated peace and decided to meet with Garang in Addis Ababa to arrange a settlement. This infuriated Turabi (at this point he was Sadiq's foreign minister) and the NIF cadres, which withdrew from Sadiq's coalition government, suspecting that such a peace would at least require the repeal of Sharia law for non-Muslims and the rewriting of the Islamic constitution, and would reestablish autonomy for the South, all of which were anathema to them.

As if the military and political setbacks were not enough, Sadiq also faced growing economic problems. When he took office, the annual inflation rate was about 40 percent; by the time he left, it had risen to 80 percent. Numayri had left the country with a massive debt that Sadiq did not or could not address. The war itself consumed a majority of the national budget, which in a country as poor as Sudan meant that little development was taking place.

What caused the humanitarian crisis of 1988–1989?

As the second civil war spread, three separate factors combined in late 1988 and early 1989 to create a major humanitarian crisis in the South. The Murahalin militia, an Arab group, was created under Sadiq al-Mahdi in the 1980s as an alternative force to the regular Sudanese armed forces. During the Murahalin raids in the South, these Arab horsemen burned homes, farms, crops, and businesses to the ground and stole livestock, depriving villagers of income and livelihoods. People ran in terror during the raids—children were separated from their parents and husbands and wives from each other, and everyone went without food, water, and their animal herds. These villagers became vulnerable to starvation, disease, and dehydration. Three years of drought and famine had already put farms and cattle herds under severe stress. But what was most destructive was the eight inches of rainfall that covered parts of eastern Sudan in a fourteen-hour period in August 1988, causing the already high waters of the Nile to inundate Khartoum and the cattle-herding areas of the South. The floods led to the spread of cattle diseases and, combined with the Murahalin raids, reduced the Dinka and Nuer herds by at least 2 million head. According to southerners, when cattle herds die, people die, since as much as 70 percent of the Nilotic herders' calories can come from cow's milk. Further complicating the food and nutritional crisis, a locust plague descended on Sudan, devastating whatever crops had survived both the drought and the floods.

With layer on layer of these natural disasters combined with violent assaults by militia, famine was inevitable. The death rates in some areas of the South were four times higher than those of the great Sahelian famine of 1984–1985 in the North.

As people began to die, families turned to traditional methods of survival to protect themselves. Under Dinka custom, when a girl marries a boy, a dowry must be paid by the boy's family to the girl's family, known as the bride price (typically 150 cows). Thus, girls add to a family's wealth— and its chances for survival in a famine—while boys reduce it. When cattle are dying or being raided in massive numbers, parents are forced to make painful decisions about reducing the number of mouths to feed so that the larger family can survive. This traditionally involved shedding their teenage boys, sending them out to fend for themselves.

These shed boys moved toward the Ethiopian border, where it was well known that the SPLA had set up their base camps. The southerners who perished in the famine were disproportionately composed of boys 6–18 years old on the move. This is one reason why the UN refugee camps formed in 1988 and 1989 in Ethiopia consisted of nearly all young males, effectively providing a recruitment and training ground for the SPLA.

As the famine spread and death rates rose, UNICEF, the International Committee of the Red Cross, NGOs, European aid agencies, and USAID offered humanitarian assistance to save lives. Sadiq's government believed it could break the Garang's movement by preventing food deliveries to the South and thus refused the international assistance. In late 1988 and early 1989 in Washington, Julia Taft, director of the Office of Foreign Disaster Assistance at USAID, faced opposition to this aid effort from the State Department's East Africa Office, which did not want to offend Sadiq al-Mahdi's government. Taft, who was well connected to senior officials in the Reagan administration, intervened directly with U.S.

Secretary of State George Schultz, who then overruled the East Africa Office's opposition, and a large U.S. relief effort followed. Taft then visited each of the governments in the region and told them that the United States expected their cooperation in the international effort to get food and medicine into southern Sudan, expectations that, she warned, would have serious diplomatic consequences if they were not met.

Jim Grant, the executive director of UNICEF—which had been designated the lead agency in charge of the UN's aid effort—followed Taft to each of the capitals in Africa and negotiated the terms of the aid agreement. In March 1989, a UN-led international aid conference was held in Khartoum at which Sadiq finally endorsed the effort and pledged his government's cooperation—though not before 250,000 southerners had died and massive civilian displacement taken place. The new aid architecture, called Operation Lifeline Sudan (OLS), was supposed to provide access for humanitarian agencies to provide short-term assistance to address a humanitarian crisis it was thought would end quickly. But OLS would operate for sixteen years—it was phased out in August 2005. Its longevity is evidence of the brutal and seemingly irresolvable nature of the war. Had the aid conference been held six months later—after the Bashir government had deposed Sadiq—OLS would likely have been still-born, as Sadiq's successors were even more stridently opposed to any provision of aid to the South than he was. The Bashir government obstructed humanitarian aid efforts for sixteen long years because it believed that by feeding the southerners whom his government was trying to starve into surrender the international community was prolonging the war, and as a result hundreds of thousands of southerners died.

Thus it was that the Khartoum government's initial stonewalling of the UN and donor government humanitarian relief effort in 1988 and early 1989 led to the mass movement of young men to the Ethiopian refugee camps that Garang had converted into SPLA training camps. Unknowingly, Sadiq had become the chief recruiter for the expanding SPLA.

What were the patterns of fatalities in the Second Civil War?

The great famine of 1988–1989 was the most visible humanitarian crisis of the Second Civil War but not the only one. Another regional famine caused by the war took place between 1998 and 1999, killing between 50,000 and 100,000 people. It was the brutal implementation of the four pillars of Sadiq's strategy described earlier that led to most of these deaths. Sadiq's (and later Bashir's) government used displacement, disease, and starvation as a weapon of war to kill off the southern population and their villages because they were the support base for Garang's army. In the 1990s, as the rebellion spread to the Nuba Mountains in southern Kordofan (which is in the North and 40 percent Muslim), Khartoum's tactics lead to the deaths of between 60,000 and 70,000 people, according to author Julie Flint's estimates.

Many of the tactics used by Sadiq were not new in Sudan. Successive Khartoum governments had used some combination of these strategies, from the Turco-Egyptian colonial period through post-independence governments, but no one had integrated them into a coherent war strategy. In some respects, Sadiq's plan was a strategic redirection of Khartoum's failed military campaign in the war. Sadiq faced a dilemma: strengthening the Sudanese military to prosecute the war meant strengthening his political adversaries, since the military at the time increasingly served as a bastion of Khatmiyya support (his Umma Party's great historical political rivals) and increasingly of Turabi's party, the NIF. Sadiq chose to create instead a paramilitary force, the Murahalin militia from the Misiriyya and Rizaiqat tribes, which had been Umma Party supporters. They committed some of the worst atrocities against southern civilians in the history of a very long war, as noted, burning Dinka villages to the ground, raping or kidnapping their women and children, raiding their livestock, and murdering their men. Forced displacement of people and the deliberate destruction of livelihoods killed the most people. Human rights groups and NGOs reported that Sudanese air force helicopter pilots were ordered to shoot as many cattle as they could to destroy the southern food supply. When a village was attacked by the SAF, the Murahalin, or some other militia, those who survived would flee without food or water and simply die in the countryside. Disease spread rapidly among displaced people, who were malnourished and whose immune systems were compromised, and would usually kill them before they starved to death.

One of the incentives behind these Murahalin raids was cattle rustling, a common practice traditionally done on a small scale among Sudanese tribes, particularly when nomads are in economic distress. With the great Sahelian drought and famine of the mid- to late 1980s and the subsequent damage to the tribes' herds, such desperate conditions spread across Sudan. These raids were much more devastating than formerly because Sadiq's government provided modern weapons and coordinated these attacks with the Sudanese military, which made them much more destructive. Hundreds of thousands of animals were looted. Barbarity was commonplace. One of the first cables I read when I joined USAID in June 1989 came from the U.S. Embassy in Khartoum and reported that an infamous SAF commander (a relative of Sadiq) fighting in the South was crucifying SPLA prisoners.

According to rigorous research done by American demographer J. Millard Burr (whose methodology was peer reviewed by the American Statistical Association) and published by the U.S. Committee on Refugees, 1.3 million southerners died in the Second Civil War between 1983 and 1993, most of them civilians. In addition, more than a million people perished between 1993 and 2003, according to a subsequent study. Much of this chaotic brutality is dramatized in the moving biographical novel *What Is the What*, by David Eggers, which is based on real events surrounding the life of Valentino Deng, a Dinka boy whose village was raided and burned by these Arab militias during this period. The pattern of Murahalin violence against the Dinka was used as a model by the Bashir government to defeat rebellious Darfur tribes in the civil war of 2003–2004, and again in the Nuba Mountains in mid-2011 as the South finally achieved its independence.

While the Numayri, Sadiq, and Bashir governments were directly responsible for hundreds of thousands of deaths in the South during the Second Civil War, it was southerners killing southerners that took the largest number of lives. Successive Khartoum governments knew how to exploit the traditional southern tribal rivalries. Over the course of two decades, the North armed, equipped, and funded as many as seventy southern militias to attack the SPLA, which was seen in many areas as a Dinka-dominated army. The Dinkas had many enemies in the South, particularly the Nuer, the second largest tribe. The Dinka and Nuer killed each other and burned each other's villages using northern weapons and equipment. The worst atrocities of the war took place after the split within the SPLA in the early 1990s. The North also supported, armed, and equipped the Lord's Resistance Army (LRA) in northern Uganda, which was carrying on an insurgency against the Museveni government and maintained a permanent military base in the Kit Valley. Terrible atrocities during the Second Civil War were committed by the LRA in their periodic incursions into southern Sudan—incursions that remained a serious security problem in the South in 2011.

6

THE BASHIR-TURABI COUP OF 1989, THE RISE AND FALL OF HASSAN AL-TURABI, AND U.S. POLICY TOWARD SUDAN

How did Omar al-Bashir and Hassan al-Turabi take power?

On June 30, 1989, just as Sadiq was about to leave for Addis Ababa, a group of midranking army officers led by Brigadier Omar al-Bashir staged a coup in an attempt to stop the peace negotiations and toppled his increasingly unstable coalition government. The country would suffer through fourteen more years of civil war and another million and a half deaths before another peace effort would come this close to success. The third period of democratic rule in modern Sudanese history was now at an end.

More than a hundred senior career military officers and twenty major political figures were immediately arrested and imprisoned, including Sadiq, who was subjected to mock executions by the new regime. Somewhat mysteriously, Turabi was also arrested and imprisoned, though he was treated with more deference than the other prisoners. In prison he told his fellow inmates a new Islamic day was dawning in Sudanese history, foreshadowing his coming revolution. The evidence is compelling that the new military rulers had arrested Turabi to disguise the true nature of the new government and its strategy, in order to avoid causing alarm in Arab capitals—Cairo and Riyadh in particular—where many viewed Turabi as a dangerous radical. This would give the new government enough time to consolidate its power and seize control of the political and economic systems.

Who is Omar al-Bashir?

Omar Hassan Ahmad al-Bashir comes from the village of Hoshe Bannaga in the Nile River Valley north of Khartoum. He was of the Ja'aliyiin tribe—one of the Three Tribes. Bashir joined the army as a soldier in 1960, graduated from the Sudan Military Academy in Khartoum in 1966, and trained as a paratrooper there and later at the Malaysian Military Academy. He rose rapidly through the ranks, and he served in the Egyptian army during the October (Yom Kippur) War against Israel in 1973 and then in the 1980s as the commander of the armored parachute brigade in Khartoum for six years.

Until their falling out in 1999, Bashir was a devoted follower of Turabi. While Bashir converses in Arabic to foreigners through an interpreter, he speaks fluent English, which he will use if he wishes to make his point more

Omar al-Bashir, president of the Islamic Republic of Sudan.

emphatically. Analysts of the Khartoum government report him to have a detached leadership style, leaving the daily minutiae of governing to his subordinates while engaging actively in major disputes or issues of national consequence. When angered or offended, Bashir often becomes truculent and confrontational, making public statements he must sometimes retreat from later. He has two wives, the first of whom is his cousin (marriage of cousins is a common practice in traditional Arab societies), but no children of his own.

Bashir's worldview, values, and temperament have been profoundly influenced by his military training and career. He is a general first, last, and always, but he has developed the skills needed to traverse the factional infighting, Byzantine intrigue, and bureaucratic intricacies of Khartoum politics. He prefers socializing with other military officers rather than civilians in his own government, and he often sleeps in military quarters. He begins most cabinet meetings with some sort of attempt at humor. In all of the meetings I have had with him, he has been well briefed and could argue his point of view clearly. While the National Congress Party (NCP) has a deserved reputation for making agreements they have no intention of honoring, in my dealings with Bashir he has been straightforward and never misled me.

What was the true nature of the new government?

In the months following the coup, Bashir's government was a mystery to everyone outside its inner circle. Bashir claimed in his first public address to the nation that he was removing Sadiq because of his government's human rights abuses, among other charges. Egypt warmly endorsed the coup, as did Libya, because they had had increasingly acrimonious relations with Sadiq and did not support his peace initiative with the South.

The Islamist nature of Bashir's government slowly but irrevocably unfolded over the next six months as it set new

policies into motion. It was not simply another military dictatorship using repression to crush dissent and internal opposition; it was reconstructing Sudanese society—abolishing,
weakening, or completely transforming existing institutions
in a manner that would be difficult to reverse.

Treatment of women provided early evidence of the new
order. Well-educated Sudanese women from elite families
who had been in book clubs with expatriate women in Khartoum were ordered by the new internal security apparatus to
stop reading Western books and to end all contact with
Western women. New dress codes were announced and enforced. Thousands of women in professional jobs in Khartoum were removed from their positions. The diminished
public role for women in Sudanese society was peculiar, for
in his lectures and writings Turabi had argued for a more, not
less, prominent role for women, reflecting the views of his
progressive wife, Wisal al-Mahdi, the sister of Sadiq al-Mahdi.
(Turabi had, thus, married into the first family of modern
Sudan, only to overthrow its titular leader and his own
brother-in-law, Sadiq.)

A network of "ghost houses" was constructed by the new
internal security apparatus where dissidents, opposition
political figures, and senior military officers of suspect loyalty
were taken and tortured. Academics, intellectuals, and
journalists—many from the Three Tribes—who were not of
one mind with Turabi's worldview disappeared into the
prison system.

This all culminated in December 1989 with Turabi's
release from prison. He met with the new government ministers, including Bashir himself, all of whom made a personal
oath of allegiance and loyalty to Turabi, an astonishing act
of fealty on behalf of a sitting government to a man who
held no official position. At this point, Turabi was viewed by
his followers as the preeminent Islamist scholar and theologian in Sudan rather than a common politician. A new
Islamic day had indeed arrived, but of a kind that neither

the Three Tribes nor the non-Arab or non-Muslim populations had ever seen before. After Iran, this was only the
second time in twentieth-century history that an Islamist
government had taken control of a country. Sudan did not
have a history of repression on this scale; even the two
former military governments had acted with comparative
restraint during times of political crisis and were removed
from power with limited loss of life.

Who is Hassan al-Turabi?

Hassan al-Turabi was born in 1932 in the town of Wad al-
Turabi, near Kassala, a city to the southeast of Khartoum close
to the Eritrean border; his father was a prominent Islamic
judge, and his mother's ancestors came from the Muslim
Fulani (African) tribe of West Africa, whose ancestors settled
in Sudan on their way on pilgrimage to Mecca. This meant
that Turabi was not entirely Arab, something he has chosen
not to publicize widely. He attended the University College of
Khartoum (formerly Gordon Memorial College, later called
the University of Khartoum), graduating in 1952; attained his
master's degree in 1961 at the London School of Economics;
and eventually finished his academic career with a Ph.D. in
law from the Sorbonne in 1964.

It was at the University College of Khartoum that he first
came into contact with the Muslim Brotherhood, which had
been founded and organized in Egypt and had established a
branch on his campus the year after he entered. At a meeting
of the Brotherhood in Khartoum in 1954, Turabi spoke and
impressed the movement's older leadership with his bril-
liance and fervor. When he returned to Sudan in 1964 from
Europe, he was named dean of the University of Khartoum
Law School. He was to have transformational influence as an
intellectual, theologian, and organizer on an entire generation
of Islamist activists. In 1964, he organized and was elected
first director general of the Islamic Charter Front (later the

National Islamic Front), an offshoot of the Brotherhood. During the Numayri regime, Turabi was arrested and released seven times for his outspoken criticism of the government, which eventually forced him into exile. In the years he spent in prison, he fulfilled his ambition to memorize the entire Quran. When Numayri announced a reconciliation effort in 1977, Turabi returned from exile and in 1979 became minister of justice, a post he held until 1983. As described earlier, he married the sister of Sadiq al-Mahdi, so he became related to the most famous family in modern northern Sudanese history. His marriage also connected him to the Fur tribe of Darfur, as his wife is the maternal descendant of a Fur princess (who married the Mahdi in the 1880s).

Hassan al-Turabi has been one of the most influential figures in modern Sudanese politics, but in many ways he remains an enigmatic figure. His writing, rhetoric, sermons, and public pronouncements often contradict his actions while in office, as least at first glance. In two long conversations I had with him, in 1991 and then in 2007 as U.S. envoy to Sudan, Turabi made clear his commitment to the rule of law, human rights, democracy, and constitutional government—yet he had organized a coup in 1989 that overthrew a democratically elected government. As we shall soon see, he was the architect of the Popular Defense Force (PDF), which committed widespread, deliberate, and systematic atrocities against hundreds of thousands of southern civilians in the 1990s. He served for ten years as the ideological architect and then senior advisor to a government that, according to extensive reporting by the UN and human rights organizations, had employed widespread arbitrary and extrajudicial arrest, torture, and execution of labor union officials, military officers, journalists, political figures, and civil society leaders. He and his wife—again, one of the leading and most progressive women's rights advocates in Sudan—helped found the International Organization for Muslim Women. Yet through the NIF government, he imposed draconian restrictions on the role of women in Sudanese society.

One explanation for these seemingly contradictory, even hypocritical, positions is that Turabi did not worry himself over the details of implementation: he was the architect, not the engineer, of the policies and therefore did not fully appreciate the real-world implications of what he was doing. Yet such an explanation demeans Turabi's organizational and intellectual gifts. Given his extensive network of informants and NIF loyalists across Sudan, it would be nearly impossible to imagine he did not know what was occurring under his watch.

When Western scholars and writers interview him, they tend to accept him for what he appears to be—urbane, charming, witty, and brilliant. Turabi knows how to speak to Western audiences, using language calibrated to be inoffensive but also misleading. Few Westerners listen to his fiery sermons when he speaks in Arabic. Turabi's use of the word "democracy" refers not to Western constitutional democracy but instead to Islamist democracy—rule by an elite of virtuous Muslim faithful, the *umma*, who impose their interpretation of Allah's will on all subjects, including those who are not "Believers." He has argued that there will be no need for legislation passed through democratically elected bodies because the Quran and Sharia law provide a complete set of guidelines to govern a society.

Two Hassan al-Turabis exist in parallel universes: the moderate and thoughtful Islamic scholar who can be found when he is out of power or when he speaks to Western audiences in English or French, and the religious zealot who emerges when he is in power or speaking in Arabic. It is this Turabi that the Sudanese people and society have had to contend with, for one of the pieces of national legislation he pressed for was that apostasy be punished by the death penalty, a position he has since disavowed. When he talks about women's rights, he is referring exclusively to Muslim women, whose honor and virtue will be protected within the context of Sharia law, even if it restricts their activities in a Western context. Christian or non-Muslim women may be treated as property without rights or protection. As for human rights, Turabi would likely argue that the ends—the reestablishment of the *umma* and Islamic purity—justify the means: the imprisonment, torture, and execution of political opponents and dissidents. Perhaps one of the reasons why he did not take an official position in the NIF government at the outset was that he wished to maintain plausible deniability in the face of allegations over the more egregious abuses of the government that he created.

How did Turabi build an Islamic state in Sudan?

After his return from exile in 1977 and appointment in 1979 by Numayri as minister of justice, Turabi employed his intellect, extraordinary energy, and impressive organizational abilities to lay the groundwork for his Islamist revolution. Between 1977 and the 1989 coup, he slowly rebuilt the cadres of the NIF, which had suffered under Numayri. This structure became the party apparatus of the Bashir government, which, like Numayri's, had no popular base of support apart from the NIF.

To ensure that the Sudanese military would remain loyal to the new government and that Turabi's revolution would extend into its ranks, some officers who were not NIF Islamists were retired, some were arrested, and some were executed. In order to ensure loyalty, NIF operatives were sent as "military advisors" down to battalion level, a practice Turabi likely copied from the Soviet military system. He personally approved all new and up-and-coming officers, so that by 1998, 50 percent of the officer corps consisted of Islamists who were chosen not for their military competence but their ideological purity, suggesting that any future military coup against the Bashir government is likely to be attempted by Islamists even more militant than the government it overthrows.

When some senior officers attempted a coup in 1990, the Revolutionary Command Council (RCC), the ruling body of the Bashir government, crushed the rebels, arresting and shooting twenty-eight of the core organizers within a single day. Shortly thereafter, the commander of the Sudanese air force and 200 enlisted men who were thought to be disloyal were arrested, tried, and hanged. In 1991 a systematic purge of noncommissioned officers (NCOs) took place in which eighteen senior NCOs were executed, all of whom were ethnic Nuba from the Nuba Mountains in southern Kordofan, from which much of the NCO corps had originated.

Turabi also sought to limit the Sudanese military through the creation of a parallel and competing institution to protect him, his followers, and his revolution—the new PDF militia. Its 150,000-strong lines of foot soldiers were drafted into service through a very unpopular forced conscription. Turabi believed that the SAF should necessarily be kept small—given its secularism, sympathy to the Egypt-leaning Khatmiyya sect, and professionalism—while the PDF should serve as what its name implied: a people's army. It may have been "of the people" simply considering its method of recruitment, but it was not a real army. The Sadiq's Murahalin militia was merged into the PDF, and all soldiers underwent political education overseen by Turabi's deputy, Ibrahim al-Sanoussi, who became an Islamist ideological commissar of sorts. The PDF received a couple of weeks of military training, during which recruits were taught how to fire a weapon and not much else. The career Sudanese military personnel detested the new PDF and understood it for what it was—a populist mob that was effective at killing unarmed southern civilians, raping women, and burning villages, all of which did not require, and indeed went against, military training. In the North, the Bashir government used the PDF to suppress labor union unrest and student dissent, duties the career military had been reluctant to undertake, given the levels of brutality needed to keep the streets under control. When the PDF first faced the SPLA in direct combat in Blue Nile province, Garang's forces decimated Turabi's legions; they were expendable fodder for Turabi's revolution.

The Islamist revolution spread beyond the government ministries and the military. Turabi, who had been dean of the Law School at the University of Khartoum, sacked judges with a secular legal philosophy and replaced them with Islamists, many his former students. The Sudanese Bar Association, which was a widely respected institution in northern Sudanese society, known for its juridical expertise and its autonomy from the national government, was simply banned by the Bashir regime. A new law called the Special Courts Act created a parallel system of courts with special jurisdiction that would be managed by seventy-five new magistrates appointed on the basis of their Islamist purity and loyalty to the revolution rather than their legal scholarship. The rule of law was now the rule of Hassan al-Turabi and his interpretation of the Quran and Islamic law.

The Islamist transformation of the PDF and of the SAF was bolstered by Military Intelligence, an internal security apparatus that became one of most feared in the state system. Each branch of security apparatus reported directly to President Bashir and the RCC rather than through each other, so that none by itself would be strong enough to attempt a coup.

The roots of Turabi's revolution began to grow deeply into the private market economy more than a decade before the June 1989 coup. In May 1978 Turabi and his acolytes took advantage of a presidential decree issued by Numayri in his effort to cultivate the Muslim Brotherhood and the NIF, establishing the Faisal Islamic Bank, using Saudi money given on very favorable terms. Though the Muslim Brotherhood were banned in Saudi Arabia, Turabi enjoyed a close relationship with some of the more conservative members of the Saudi royal family, some of whom saw him as a Sudanese expositor of Wahhabist theology. This became the basis of the Sudanese Islamic banking system, which did not charge interest on loans, a practice prohibited by the Quran, and instead used a fee-based structure so that bank profits could be shared with both depositors and borrowers. This system allowed Turabi to provide scholarships to promising Islamist recruits to attend the newly opened Islamic University in Omdurman, as well as other schools, and to extend financing to Islamic NGOs loyal to the revolution.

Five years later, in September 1983, Numayri swept away the remaining traditional Sudanese banking system, as well as its commercial infrastructure, and required all banks to conform to Islamic principles. By doing so, he inadvertently gave license to Turabi's Islamist networks to expand their influence over the business and finance sectors. Any enterprise that needed capital had to be part of Turabi's network to gain access to financial markets. Over time, this has concentrated economic power in the old families from the Three Tribes who were loyal to the new regime and who gradually took over—either through outright expropriation or political pressure—the business interests of the old Lebanese-Christian, Greek, Iraqi-Jewish, and Armenian families who had run the economy under the British. The new business elite simply transformed themselves into Islamists after the Bashir government took power.

During the 1990s, Turabi's revolution drove a generation of Sudanese professionals and young people—perhaps as many as 2 million—out of the country and into the West and the Gulf States. The British public health system, for example, reportedly employs more than 10,000 Sudanese doctors. Turabi's political organization shut off the state patronage to non-Islamists hoping to join the civil service system; rising entrepreneurs trying to secure capital to start new businesses; students aspiring to a university education; and ambitious young men with an interest in politics.

Professional Sudanese women who had no career options were driven out of Sudan.

Even young people from families of the Three Tribes who did not embrace Turabi's ideology were unable to get jobs in the government or were blocked in promotions where they did work, as were southerners, whose race and religion rendered them second-class citizens, if citizens at all. The University of Khartoum, which had used English as the language of instruction for almost a century, was now forced to shift exclusively to Arabic. Southerners, whose lingua franca was English, not Arabic, had few options available inside Sudan. Turabi's revolution created Islamic institutions that served to exacerbate the long-standing inequities of Sudanese society. Many members of the Three Tribes were hostile to his agenda and thus excluded from state patronage and contracts—unless they had transformed themselves into Turabists.

The Islamist state has made it unlikely any future successor non-Islamist government could gain power without a bloody purge, given the sheer number of Islamists who have been recruited, educated, and cultivated over the twenty years (and counting) of Bashir rule. John Garang told me on several occasions that the "de-NIF-izing" of northern Sudan—by which he meant the dismantling of Turabi's Islamist infrastructure—would have been his first and most challenging task if SPLM had ever taken power.

How did Sudanese foreign policy change under Bashir and Turabi?

The Islamist revolution inside Sudan was initially viewed with mild interest by Western analysts, but they grew increasingly concerned once its foreign-policy manifestation became clear. Turabi's aspirations were global, and his theology sought to purge the Arab world of the corrupt secular governments in the Arab world. He dreamed of a new Islamic world order that went far beyond the artificial limitations of the nation-state, which he viewed as a Western invention inconsistent with historic Islam's structure of governance.

Turabi's ultimate objective was the reestablishment of the moral order of the ancient Islamic caliphate—the government of Islam first established by the Prophet's associates after his death—which would recognize Sharia as the legal code and the Quran as the only source of truth. Successive dynasties ruled the caliphate; the last were the Ottoman Turks, before Kemal Ataturk, in 1922, abolished the system in Turkey and established a secular state in its place. Theoretically, with the reinstatement of the caliphate, the world community of faithful Muslims—the *umma*—would be reunited. This could only be accomplished by the replacing of Arab governments with some form of Islamist rule, about which Turabi was never very specific. For two decades before the 1989 coup, he had worked to cultivate a network of Islamists across the Muslim world, from Algeria to the Philippines. And now he had an operational platform—the government of Sudan—from which to execute his grand Islamist strategy.

One of Turabi's earliest diplomatic initiatives was the forging of an alliance between Sudan and Iran—a challenge, given the historic animosity between the Sunni tradition, dominant in Sudan, and the Iranian Shi'a tradition. Bashir himself visited Iran and met Iranian president Rafsanjani in November 1989, only five months after the coup, and the Sudanese and Iranian intelligence services signed a secret agreement of cooperation. By 1992, Iran had become Sudan's closest ally and the principal supplier of arms to the North's security forces engaged in the war against the South. In exchange, Iran could use Sudan as a platform to promote its Islamist revolution in Africa. Even now, whenever Western pressure on the Sudanese government rises, its leaders will play the Iran card, filling the Khartoum news media with new exchange visits, trade agreements, and examples of military cooperation between Iran and Sudan.

A second Turabi initiative was the creation of an international organization that would tie together virtually every radical Islamist group in the world. In 1991 in Khartoum, the General Assembly meeting of the first Popular Arab and Islamic Congress (PAIC) brought together delegates from these organizations, among many others: Jama'at al-Islamiyah (the extremist subsidiary of the Egyptian Muslim Brotherhood, which had assassinated Anwar el-Sadat); Hamas (the Palestinian party founded in 1987 as an offshoot of the Muslim Brotherhood); al-Qaeda (under the leadership of a young Saudi Islamist radical named Osama bin Laden and the Egyptian Ayman al-Zawahiri, former head of Egyptian Islamic Jihad); and Hezbollah (an Iran-backed Lebanese Shi'a organization). The Sudanese government announced that the meeting was "the most significant event since the collapse of the Caliphate." Turabi organized the PAIC in order to challenge the legitimacy of the Arab League and the Organization of the Islamic Conference—more traditional organizations—as the official representative of Arab states and faithful Muslims.

The PAIC emerged soon after the Sudanese government's support for the Iraqi invasion of Kuwait backfired and undermined Turabi's support in Saudi Arabia, where the royal family saw their country as the next target of Saddam Hussein's aggression. At this first PAIC General Assembly meeting, Turabi was elected secretary general. The funding for the conference reportedly came from a $100 million donation from the Iranian government and from Osama bin Laden. The 1995 PAIC General Assembly meeting in Khartoum convened 300 delegates from eighty countries, the largest single meeting of radical Islamist organizations ever sponsored by a sovereign government.

Turabi and the NIF network in the Sudanese government ensured that his Islamist allies from the around the world, now organized formally through PAIC, found in Sudan a safe haven, a place where they could train their operatives without interference, operate their Islamic charitable front organizations, and launch Islamic business enterprises that supported their global political operations. By 1991, Turabi was providing sanctuary and training facilities for the Algerian Islamic Salvation Front as it engaged in a brutal Algerian civil war in which 75,000 people were killed. Audiotapes of Turabi's incendiary sermons were being distributed across North Africa and served as inspiration for Islamic militants across the Arab world. Turabi supported the Tunisian revolutionary Islamist group Al-Nahda, which sought to overthrow the Tunisian government. He even arranged for a Sudanese diplomatic passport for its leader, Rashid al-Ghannushi, an action that eventually led to the breaking off of diplomatic relations between the two countries.

One of the beneficiaries of Turabi's hospitality was Osama bin Laden, who first met Turabi on a trip to Sudan in 1984, when he was searching for business investment opportunities, and had a subsequent meeting with him in London. Bin Laden had sent Mamdouh Salim, a member of al-Qaeda's governing council, to Khartoum to determine whether conditions in the country would facilitate their work. Salim returned with a favorable report. Bin Laden then moved one of his business holding companies to Sudan, six months after the Bashir coup.

After Gorbachev withdrew Soviet troops from Afghanistan in 1991, bin Laden scaled back his activities in support of the Mujahidiin in the Afghan civil war and moved his base of operations to Khartoum, with his now-growing family, business interests, and al-Qaeda leadership. While he was a guest in Sudan, bin Laden reportedly took Turabi's niece as one of his wives (after one of his wives divorced him) and developed a business relationship with Turabi's son Isam, trading Arabian horses. Turabi arranged a series of government contracts to build the highway connecting Khartoum with Port Sudan on the Red Sea, where bin Laden's construction company was located. When the government could not pay the bills for construction work, the regime essentially expropriated almost a half million hectares of farmland that had been under the traditional ownership of some African tribes in Blue Nile State and gave them to bin Laden, igniting an ongoing land dispute. Bin Laden's home in a wealthy suburb of Khartoum remains a "tourist" curiosity today. Thus, these two rising Islamist stars were tied together by their family's business interests, by marriage, and by their political activities.

Bin Laden's welcome in Sudan grew cooler with the solidification of his and Turabi's support for insurgency and terrorist operations in other Muslim countries. Turabi's PAIC supported bin Laden's activities in more than ten countries and acted as a front for al-Qaeda's worldwide operations.

One event demonstrated just how revolutionary the Sudanese government's foreign policy had become. On June 26, 1995, as Hosni Mubarak's armored limousine—which by luck or fate he had brought with him from Cairo—sped through the streets of Addis Ababa to a meeting of the Organization of African Unity, gunmen fired on his motorcade, but failed to kill him. Through interrogations of the gunmen, the Ethiopian intelligence service soon discovered that the plot had been carried out by Jama'at al-Islamiyah. The assassination attempt had the active support of the Sudanese government. The weapons used were transported on the government-owned Sudan Airways from Khartoum; the Sudan's National Intelligence and Security Service (NISS) had provided Yemeni and Sudanese passports to the assassins; and the plot had been planned in Khartoum by senior officials in the Bashir government. The Egyptian government was outraged. The official press in Cairo excoriated Turabi (who, Mubarak believed, was behind the attack) as well as the Sudanese government and Omar al-Bashir, and war fever spread through official circles. The United States and Egypt pushed a resolution through the UN Security Council condemning the assassination attempt and imposing sanctions on Sudan.

While the furor cooled down over time, the incident marked a turning point.

As noted in chapter 2, Egypt's relations with Sudan have historically been intimate, deeply interwoven, and complex. Egypt has been a colonizing power; a source of one of Sudan's major Sunni traditions of Islamic teaching; a self-interested facilitator during the independence movement; and a model for Sudan's political system—both the Jaafar Numayri and Omar al-Bashir took inspiration from Abdel Nasser's revolution. The only times in modern Sudanese history that relations between Sudan and Egypt were fully breached were the revolutionary period in the late nineteenth century under the Mahdi and the period under Omar al-Bashir. There are parallels between the Mahdi and Turabi, but Turabi's activities outside the country were far more revolutionary than anything the leaders of the Mahdist state ever conceived. The attempted assassination of Mubarak—leader of a country with twice as many citizens and an economy eight times larger than Sudan's, and a much larger and stronger military—demonstrated just how out of touch Turabi and his acolytes in the Sudanese government were with the political reality.

On the face of it, Turabi's attempt to use Sudan as a staging ground for a worldwide Islamic revolution at the time was preposterous. Sudan was poor, underdeveloped, and unstable—a failed state if there ever was one. The centrifugal forces that had been pulling the country apart since 1956 did not miraculously disappear after the June 1989 coup; in fact, Turabi's Islamic revolution helped accelerate them. The Second Civil War in the South continued to suck scarce tax revenues out of the national treasury. Another war raged in the late 1980s and early 1990s between the Fur and the Arab Rizaiqat tribe in Darfur (described later). In some respects, Sudan wasn't even a nation-state but was instead an increasingly unstable amalgamation of tribal alliances. Under these circumstances, Turabi's plan to overturn the existing international order using Sudan as a base of operations made very little practical sense. Turabi's insight into the fundamental weaknesses and lack of legitimacy in the public's eyes of secular Arab states has proved correct over time given the Arab revolutions of 2011.

Why did Turabi's ideology drive Sudanese foreign policy for as long as it did?

Turabi's ambitions lasted longer than reality should have allowed because of other unrelated events around the world. The collapse of the Soviet Union and the Eastern Bloc saved Turabi's Sudan, or it at least postponed the country's day of diplomatic reckoning. Before the collapse of the Eastern Bloc, the North suffered defeat after defeat in the Second Civil War; Garang's military grew steadily from the start of the war in 1983 until 1991.

From its start, the Second Civil War had been dependent on the support of Mengistu's Ethiopia for sanctuary, training, and weapons—and to ensure that the SPLA remained united and the only rebel movement in the South. The weapons had come indirectly from the Soviet Union, as Ethiopia was its chief client state in Africa. In 1990, Mikhail Gorbachev decided to drastically reduce arms shipments to the Soviet Union's client states, including Ethiopia. By April 1991, the Ethiopian rebel militias had overrun Mengistu's army and forced him into exile. The new Ethiopian government was formed by Meles Zenawi, the former rebel commander of the Tigrayan People's Liberation Front, who had received assistance from Khartoum to take power in Ethiopia. Zenawi immediately cut off all arms shipments to Garang, shut down the SPLA bases in western Ethiopia, and ended the training and support programs. Zenawi even seriously considered allowing the SAF to use Ethiopia as a base from which to attack the SPLA. The external base of support for Garang's war disappeared in a single moment.

Members of his own central command, who had long resented his autocratic leadership, thought they could remove

Garang with European and American support, which had been withheld from him due to his alliance with Mengistu. Some Western advocacy groups apparently encouraged the internal rebellion (which was not to be the last time meddling by Western advocacy groups had unfortunate outcomes).

On August 28, 1991, three senior commanders, Riak Machar, a Nuer, Lam Akol, a Shilluk, and Gordon Kong, another Nuer—later known as the "Nasir Faction"—broadcast on the SPLA internal radio network that they had removed John Garang as commander and taken control of the liberation movement. In their announcement they criticized his autocratic style, his human rights abuses, and his endorsement of a united Sudan. They had hoped that a sufficient number of other dissatisfied commanders would join them. The support never materialized. Instead, this revolt split the SPLA and weakened the southern position. From the start, the Nasir Faction's leadership did not include any Dinka commanders, which gave their framework a tribal cast that would lead to disastrous results in the ensuing years. In fact, the Nasir Faction attacked Bor County, Garang's home area, massacring or displacing a majority of the civilian population. (The Bor massacre continues to haunt the new Republic of South Sudan and thus Vice President Riak Machar publically apologized in August 2011 for the bloodshed in an attempt to heal the wounds.) What is more, Khartoum later supported the Nasir Faction with funding and weapons—support that was as odd as it was opportunistic, given that the Nasir Faction's coup had been driven by their insistence on complete southern independence. Khartoum's support, however, was *very* consistent with Sadiq al-Mahdi's grand strategy to crush Garang's forces by turning one tribe against another using weapons, patronage, and money. Khartoum was temporarily successful in this regard, despite their larger ideological disagreements with Machar. The split also led to some of the most terrible atrocities of the war, with southerners killing southerners—most of whom were civilians. Effectively, the split among the southerners gave a failing northern military campaign new life.

By 1990, Garang's forces reached the peak of their military successes in the seven-year Second Civil War. By the end of 1991, their prospects had fallen to their lowest point—because of Mengistu's fall, the Nasir Faction's coup, and the subsequent SAF military advance to take advantage of southern split. The SPLA retreated to the Sudd marshes, which the northerners could not easily penetrate. In late 1991, the SAF could have inflicted even more, perhaps fatal damage to Garang's remaining forces but did not, because of the fear (unwarranted, as it turned out) that the U.S. military would repeat in Sudan what it had done to Saddam Hussein in Iraq during the first Gulf War. (Sudan had supported Hussein in that war.) It would take several years for Garang to rebuild his military position. The schism in southern Sudan saved Turabi's revolution.

What was Garang's war strategy?

Garang once described to me in detail a four-pronged military strategy that he gradually developed over time during the 1990s in order either to defeat the North, or at least force Khartoum to negotiate a political settlement:

1. Open a new front in the east near Kassala (which the SPLA briefly captured twice during the war) to threaten the highway lifeline linking Khartoum with Port Sudan. The second front was also designed to threaten the Sennar Dam on the Blue Nile River located 200 miles south of Khartoum, which provided electrical power to the capital and its suburbs, as well as water for the vast Gezira irrigation scheme. This would bring the war indirectly to Khartoum and thus would undermine Sadiq al-Mahdi's strategic principle that the war be kept away from the capital at all costs.

2. Encourage and support other rebellions in other northern states that would cause the central government to

redeploy troops to meet the new threats and weaken their position in the South. This fit particularly well into Garang's exposition of Khartoum's predatory policy of sucking resources from the periphery. Garang did not, as some in Khartoum believed, invent grievances in the northern periphery; all of these regions already harbored deep resentments against Khartoum. They were a powder keg waiting to explode; Garang provided a match.

3. Shut down the oil fields that were due to start producing steep increases in revenue for the central government by 1998. Garang knew that if oil revenues continued to increase, his leadership would eventually suffer, because Khartoum would apply these new resources to the war effort.

4. Either surround or liberate more southern garrison cities, which were the only remaining northern footholds in the South. The cost incurred by Khartoum in provisioning these garrison cities through air lifts and pacifying the local population drained scarce resources from the chronically stressed national treasury. This would bleed the northern government if it could be accomplished before oil revenues began to pour into the national treasury.

Garang's strategy was to use the North's weaknesses against itself. One of the inherent limitations of the Three Tribe system was its extraordinarily modest political base—the three governing tribes made up only 5–6 percent of Sudan's population. The Sudanese military's officer corps was composed of officers from these governing tribes, while the army of NCOs and foot soldiers that they commanded disproportionately came from the periphery: Darfur, the Nuba Mountains, and the South. Garang's strategy struck at the heart of the system's vulnerability. In fact, the military almost forced a political settlement in 1989, before Sadiq al-Mahdi was overthrown by the Bashir coup, ending the potentially promising negotiations.

The Nile River's rich fishing grounds. (Henrik Stabell/NPA)

Why and how did the Bashir government sever its ties with Turabi?

The attempted assassination of Mubarak and the Sudanese government's direct support for Islamic insurgency move ments in more than a dozen countries had isolated Sudan in the world community, particularly from its Arab neighbors. None of the insurgencies it supported were successful at the time; all of the governments it opposed remained in power. (Nonetheless, the prospects for Turabi's Islamist allies across North Africa eventually taking power grew in 2011, as the Arab Revolution spread through Tunisia, Egypt, Yemen, Libya, and Syria, and the Muslim Brotherhood was legiti-mized as a political party with a disciplined and devoted following capable of fielding candidates for office while other parties were only in their infancy.) Osama bin Laden embodied the radical Islamist revolutionary impulse and was a symbol of the Sudanese government's growing international vulnerability. Rumors circulated in Khartoum that al-Qaeda had developed a plan to assassinate Sadiq al-Mahdi, which enraged Mahdi's Ansar Army and supporters, a development the RCC could ill afford, given its already weak popular support base. The RCC decided to deport Osama bin Laden and contacted the Saudi Arabian government. Bashir insisted in a meeting with King Abullah that he would only turn bin Laden over if the king would agree not to harm or imprison him. The king refused, fearing internal destabilization in his country if he accepted bin Laden under any circumstances.

An in-depth investigation by the *Washington Post* confirmed that as an alternative, Bashir offered to turn bin Laden over to the United States and dispatched General Al-Fathi 'Urwah, later named Sudanese ambassador to the UN, to meet with senior officials at the CIA in Rosslyn, Virginia, in February 1996, to whom he extended the same offer. The Clinton administration refused. The United States was virtually at war with the Sudanese government and deeply suspicious of Khartoum due to its appalling humanitarian record and its support for international terrorist groups.

Realizing that bin Laden's presence was undermining his own reputation and political power in Sudan, Turabi searched for a new home for bin Laden in Afghanistan. He made the deal through Atiya Badawi, the Sudanese ambassador in Kabul—an Afghan-Arab—who had good relations with some of the Taliban commanders. Yunis Khalis, a Mujahidiin commander during the Afghan war with the Russians whose forces were located in Jalalabad, agreed to provide safe haven to bin Laden and al-Qaeda. On May 16, 1996, bin Laden and his family with their al-Qaeda bodyguards boarded a chartered plane for Afghanistan. As he left Sudan, bin Laden grumbled that he had lost $160 million of the fortune he had inherited from his father in ill-advised investments in Sudan and that the Sudanese government was nothing more than a criminal syndicate dressed in religious garb.

Disposing of bin Laden was only the first step in shifting Sudan's foreign relations agenda. Bashir then proceeded to disband the PAIC and expel the radical Islamist groups which he had given unregulated and unlimited safe haven for in Sudan. He has remained in power longer than any Sudanese leader since independence partially because he has left the details of government administration—and of its inevitable divisive controversies—to his subordinates and established policy-making priorities through the consensus of the RCC. His positions on major issues were guided by the dominating factional interests within the ruling elite, and he would only intervene strategically and episodically. Yet by 1998, Bashir's detachment was threatening the survival of his government because he had left too many major policy decisions in the hands of Turabi's acolytes within the RCC—particularly to Nafie Ali Nafie, director of the NISS and later senior advisor to Bashir, and Ali Osman Taha, who served as social affairs minister, foreign minister, and eventually vice president of Sudan (Nafi and Taha were later bitter rivals to succeed Bashir). As a military officer, Bashir was not a revolutionary by nature, though he was sympathetic to the conservative Islamist agenda. Just after he took over as president in 1989, he publicly criticized the use of limb amputations as a punishment for violation of Sharia; it was, he said, inconsistent with the merciful spirit of Islam. He did not act on his views until 1995, when the police and courts finally banned the punishment. Bashir engaged in the mechanics of government just before it was nearly hijacked by Turabi.

In March 1996, in an effort to restore his position in Sudanese politics, Turabi decided to run as a candidate in the National Assembly elections, the first held since the NIF coup of 1989. He was elected unopposed for the seat he had lost during the 1986 election, after the mysterious withdrawal of two highly credentialed Islamist candidates from the same district. Bashir received 75 percent of the vote for president, in an election that was carefully managed by the regime to ensure its own victory. Turabi then ran for speaker of the National Assembly and won. This was the first time he would hold a formal government position since Bashir's assumption of power in 1989.

Turabi changed the name of the NIF to the National Congress Party (NCP) and reorganized its structure. He sought to reduce Bashir's power and proposed legislation for the direct popular election of governors (they had been previously appointed by the president), a constitutional amendment allowing the National Assembly to depose of a president by a two-thirds vote, and the dissolution of the ban on other political parties. All of this, he said, was designed to introduce democratic institutions and practice to Sudan.

Bashir saw the Turabi "reforms" as a power grab. Turabi once told me that Bashir and his allies were simply military dictators and had "no understanding of or respect for constitutions or the rule of law." Yet Turabi did not seem bothered by the first seven years of the Bashir government as long as the government carried out his policies. Only when Bashir put the brakes on his Islamist revolution did Turabi "discover" the constitution; the legal system he had already fatally compromised, he had Islamized the economy, and he had dispensed with democratic political principles.

Bashir and Turabi elevated their quarrel over the powers of the presidency into an increasingly acrimonious public debate. As the quarrel grew and Turabi was increasingly perceived by his followers as engaged in a pedestrian power struggle, his image as an Islamist theologian and intellectual who operated above petty political intrigue gradually became tarnished. He was now no more than a common politician. In December 1999, two days before the National Assembly was to vote on legislation proposed by Turabi to curb presidential power, Bashir declared a state of emergency. His troops surrounded the National Assembly, which he then dissolved, and he called for new elections, which were held in 2000. After winning 86 percent of the vote, Bashir launched a government-wide purge of Turabi loyalists, though it was difficult for the purge to distinguish them from the Islamists who supported Bashir (since both shared the same base support).

Turabi's institutional base of operations disappeared in a single day, though he remained a role model and iconic figure for the more militant, idealistic, and younger Sudanese Islamists. Since the 1999 breach, Sudanese internal security has arrested, released, and rearrested Turabi numerous times, usually after he has made public pronouncements that they find objectionable, yet the harassment has had little effect on his willingness to attack the regime publicly. In its private conversations and public statements, the Bashir government to this day remains paranoid about Hassan al-Turabi, probably because their small base of mostly Islamist support in Sudan may be more loyal to him than to them. Southern Sudanese leaders remain convinced that the breach between Bashir and Turabi is a contrived public relations gambit to disguise their true common radical Islamist agenda and reduce hostile reactions from more moderate Arab states in Africa as well as the West. (In June 2011, leaders of the Muslim Brotherhood in Egypt announced they were sending a senior delegation to try to mend the breach between Turabi's and Bashir's wings of the Islamist movement.) If the southerners are correct, the tactic has only moderately succeeded, as hostility to the regime is greater now than when Turabi was directing government policy. It may be that the breach in the ruling party was real but the internal dispute concerned timing and not ultimate intentions. Bashir's faction may simply be postponing its Islamist jihad in Africa until they strengthen the Sudanese state, while Turabi continues to believe that Sudan should unleash his Islamist revolution now.

In any case, by the end of the 1990s, Turabi's vision for an Islamist revolution had faltered. His Islamist cadres had been absorbed into the power structure of a Bashir government that was now more intent on survival—they enjoyed the perks of power and the massive increases in oil revenues a bit too much to be revolutionaries—than in transforming the world. While Khartoum remained hard-line Islamist inside Sudan, its aspirations outside the country's borders had been tamed by the realities of the world. No Arab or African government fell to their revolution. Turabi had become a liability to his own allies and was more expendable than he had perhaps understood. His vision was never very clear or specific regarding what Sudan (or for that matter the Arab and African worlds) would look like after the revolution had been fully realized. Like his friend and fellow Islamist, Osama bin Laden, Turabi had no plan to improve governance or implement reforms to relieve the crushing poverty, the unending famines, or the continuous state of civil war that plagued his country. In fact, he exacerbated all of these problems. Hassan al-Turabi did leave one enduring legacy: the Islamist apparatus of state authority, which the Bashir government has maintained.

The debate over presidential power ended in a victory for Bashir for one simple reason: he remained commander-in-chief of a military that appeared to be loyal to him personally, particularly at the senior staff level, despite Turabi's earlier efforts to Islamize it. Bashir's cultivation of the military command structure over the course of his presidency has been less a conscious strategy than the natural inclination of a man who was, at heart, a military officer. Whenever a senior officer died, he would visit the grieving family with a truckload of tea, sugar, flour, rice, and herbs financed through a large offline account in the budget he uses to reward friends and loyalists, particularly among the military. During the peak of international pressure on the government in the first half of 2007, when the NCP believed the United States was preparing for military action against Sudan over the Darfur crisis, Bashir's closest friends among Sudanese generals, who disliked the NCP, urged him to orchestrate his own coup in order to take complete control of the government himself. They had hoped that he would abolish the NCP and RCC power structures, arrest the civilian leadership in the government, and rule entirely through the military, which perhaps tells us more about the way the SAF views the civilians in the government than anything else. We do not know how seriously Bashir considered the advice.

The 1999 breach between Bashir and Turabi forced two of Turabi's most prominent acolytes within the RCC—Nafie Ali Nafie and Ali Osman Taha—to make a choice between him and Bashir. It was not really a choice. Debates within the RCC had exposed the recklessness of both Turabi's foreign policy and his domestic intrigues. And events suggested that Bashir would survive.

Neighboring Arab countries, particularly Egypt, celebrated Turabi's purge from the government. With Mubarak welcoming Bashir to Cairo after his victory, the Egyptian-Sudanese rift was over, and good relations restored.

After more than two decades in office, the Bashir government has shown a penchant for pulling back from the precipice. In 1998, as Bashir and the RCC stood at a cliff's edge staring into the abyss, there were two circumstances that extended the life of this increasingly weak and isolated government: the purge of Turabi and growing oil revenues. Bashir's breach with Turabi had also eroded the government's already weak base of popular support, so he needed new political allies, and he may have believed he could find it in the South, just as Numayri had thought in 1972. The war was not going well in any case. Events outside Sudan likely also contributed to the decision to shift policy and chart a new course.

How did oil change Sudanese politics?

While oil was discovered in the 1970s, the infrastructure needed to pump the oil out of Sudan and on to global markets

was not constructed until the 1990s. By 1998, rising oil revenues were breathing new life into the Bashir government.
A year after the coup of 1989, Chevron had ended its Sudan
operations under pressure from Western churches outraged
by Khartoum's atrocities. Chevron had spent $1 billion on
exploration, with little to show to investors except high levels
of risk and public embarrassment. But Canadian and
Swedish—followed by Chinese, Indian, and Malaysian—oil
companies bought the oil concessions. Later in the 1990s,
heavy pressure and criticism from church groups and human
rights organizations led to the withdrawal of all Western oil
companies. This withdrawal was accelerated after these
groups made public the oil companies' complicity in Khartoum's scorched-earth policy in the oil fields. The Sudanese
government, its Murahalin militia, and Major General Pau-
lino Matip (a southerner, a Bul Nuer who had been initially
allied with Garang but later incorporated his militia into the
Sudanese army, effectively becoming no more than a hired
gun) burned Dinka and Nuer villages to the ground, stole
their cattle herds, raped and kidnapped their women, and
killed any young men who might join the SPLA. The whole
point of it all was to make way for oil exploration.

In May 1999, Bashir inaugurated a tanker terminal near
Port Sudan that was connected to the new pipeline running
toward the Heglig and Unity oil fields. This event symbolized
a seismic shift in Sudan's future economic prospects, as oil
revenues began to pour into the Sudanese government's
national treasury, creating the first trade surplus in a decade.

The economic situation in 1994—before oil—had reached
a state of crisis as Sudan came to be crippled by an annualized
inflation rate of 80–100 percent. The government was forced
to devalue its currency and sustained enormous budget deficits, experiencing very little or even negative economic
growth. The IMF imposed draconian economic reforms in
1993 after the Sudanese defaulted on their external debt of $23
billion; the IMF plan was supported and implemented by the

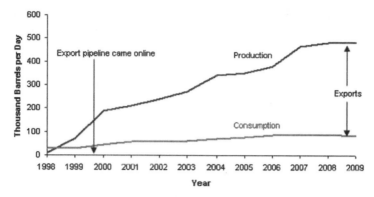

Sudan's oil production and consumption. (U.S. Energy Information Administration)

finance minister Adel Rahim Hamdi, who was a free market advocate and fiscal disciplinarian. These reforms, coupled with the infusion of rising oil revenue, arrested the Bashir government's slide into economic oblivion. By 2001, the economic outlook of the country, at least in the Arab Triangle, looked bright. Greater Khartoum had a rising middle class, a construction boom, new businesses opening across the city, and a semblance of public services. When I traveled to Khartoum in the late 1980s and early 1990s, the city was a poor backwater in suspended economic animation; by 2006 it looked increasingly like the booming Gulf States, with dozens of construction cranes towering over the skyline against the backdrop of the Nile River.

Yet the periphery of the country saw little of the oil boom revenue in their regions. Many looked no different than they had a century earlier (except for the roads, air strips, and oil installations constructed to extract mineral and energy wealth). In many ways, the periphery was much worse off than when the British had governed: at least they had kept order, strengthened functioning traditional institutions, and developed an elemental justice system.

Oil revenues not only saved an anemic economy but also increased the resources available to the central government to expand government apparatus. Since independence, Sudan has been a patrimonial state, held together through the regime's patronage networks, which dispense jobs, state contracts, access to natural resources, and monopoly control over various sectors of the economy to its supporters. Rising oil revenues allowed the Bashir government to dramatically expand those networks. Alex de Waal, one of the leading Western scholars on Sudan, reports that government expenditures were less than 10 percent of the country's GNP in the 1990s but "rose quickly after 2003 to reach 23 percent in 2006, at a time when the GNP was growing 6 percent to 10 percent per year." This allowed the government to add tens of thousands of Islamists to the payroll of the national and provincial governments, consolidating Bashir's control over Sudan's economic and political order.

Oil revenues also affected the combat preparedness of the Sudanese military, which was in desperate condition by 1998 after having sustained repeated defeats by the SPLA in 1996 and 1997 (it had partially recovered from the Dinka-Nuer split). As much as half of the rising oil revenue was directed toward the modernization of the military, principally in new weapons systems such as artillery, tanks, and aircraft purchased in Russia, Bulgaria, Poland, the Ukraine, and China. But some funds were also diverted to an expanded recruitment effort. A new draft, consisting mainly of students taken from the Greater Khartoum area, had been extremely unpopular with the public and violated the regime's traditional policy of keeping the war away from the Arab center of the country. Now, defeats were felt by the new Khartoum middle classes when their sons did not return from distant southern battlefields. It was a measure of its desperation that the Bashir government would institute such an unpopular draft, given their already weak base of public support.

Another sign of this increased desperation was the NIF-dominated army's narrowing recruitment of only the most committed Islamists from the Shaiqiyya tribe, one of the Three Tribes, to serve as officers in the army. This tribe had traditionally dominated the officer corps in the past, and it was a recipe for a weak and ineffective military when a single tribe that represented 2 percent of the population was providing the majority of the officer corps. While the weapon modernization program did marginally improve the battle readiness of the SAF—leading to stalemates rather than southern victories in battles with the SPLA in the Nuba Mountains and for Wau, the capital of western Equatoria— these purchases could not correct the structural weaknesses of the armed forces.

The expansion of oil exploration and extraction across the South had a very different effect than it had in Khartoum. It fanned the flames of the civil war (now entering its sixteenth year) and profoundly changed the political and economic calculations. Now, there was now something tangible worth fighting over that would change the lives of whoever controlled it. I had not visited southern Sudan between 1996 and 2001, and on my return as USAID administrator in July 2001, I discovered that virtually everyone I met—from tribal chiefs to SPLM officials, to people in civil society, to Christian pastors and priests—seemed to be focused on the North's "theft" of the South's oil riches. This angered southerners, as the oil field development was being implemented through an ethnic cleansing campaign of murder, rape, and pillage by government militias loyal to Khartoum that were recruited from among southern tribes and funded by the oil companies. Oil was subtly contributing to the growing sense of shared grievance and nationhood among southerners. Where before tribal identity had been the only identity that mattered, now tribal loyalty competed with a sense of being a southern Sudanese.

The oil also changed Khartoum's perception of the Second Civil War, support for which in the North had been steadily eroding over time. The war had contributed to the economic sinkhole into which the country was sliding. As noted, casualty rates among northern young men were rising. Mass protests against the war in Omdurman by the troops' mothers had surprised the security apparatus. And on several occasions, Garang's army temporarily cut Khartoum off from Port Sudan and briefly took control of Kassala, located on the southerly edge of the Arab Triangle, threatening the Gizera Dam. For a time, fear—though unwarranted—spread in Khartoum that the SPLA could not be stopped. And now a new rebellion in Red Sea State among the Beja tribe had commenced in 1996, with the support of the neighboring Eritrean government, only ending in 2002.

At the start of the Second Civil War, the SAF had ridiculed Garang's army as illiterate cattle herders. This clearly was no longer the case: the SAF had been defeated so many times in frontline combat at the hands of the SPLA that they were now demoralized and in retreat. (A UN security official whom I met in 2001, who was a retired European army commando, had witnessed the annihilation of an entire SAF battalion by the SPLA, which he described to me in some detail.)

From the time of the Bashir coup, the principal justification for the war came from Turabi, who insisted that the defeat of the SPLA was essential for the spread and consolidation of Islam in Sudan and the broader Salafist Islamization of Africa. With the demise of Turabi and Bashir's new-found realism, this become moot. Had Turabi's jihad continued to serve as justification, the peace process that produced the CPA would likely have never taken place. Oil replaced religious expansionism as the reason for war, and since the war was inhibiting oil exploration, peace became a logical policy. Garang controlled most of the South, where both existing and prospective oil fields were located, and SPLA attacks had shut down some of the existing fields and disrupted the construction of new ones.

How did U.S. policy change toward Sudan during the 1990s?

On August 7, 1998, suicide truck bombers blew up the American embassies in Dar es Salaam, Tanzania, and Nairobi, Kenya, killing 224 people, of whom twelve were Americans, and wounding 4,000 others. (A third attack planned on the U.S. embassy in Kampala, Uganda, failed because of operational problems.) Osama bin Laden's al-Qaeda orchestrated the attacks, though he had been expelled from Sudan two years earlier and was then operating out of Afghanistan. Some of the operatives who had planned the bombings had Sudanese passports, and others had regularly passed in and out of Sudan. Thus Turabi's policies, if not his overt operational involvement, had put Sudan not only in a direct collision course with Egypt—with the assassination attempt against President Mubarak—but also with the United States. Under international law, embassies are sovereign territory of the states to which they are posted. Sudan had just cooperated on a direct attack against U.S. sovereignty.

In response, the United States decided on retaliatory strikes in Sudan and Afghanistan. President Clinton himself made the targeting decisions. Intelligence agencies suspected that al-Shifa, a pharmaceutical plant in Khartoum, was manufacturing VX, a nerve gas, for use in the South (the owner of the plant had rented a home to Osama bin Laden in Khartoum), and so the U.S. military bombed the plant on August 20, 1998, in what they named Operation Infinite Reach. This facility turned out to be the largest pharmaceutical factory in the city, with more than 300 employees, who produced malaria and veterinary medication. One employee was killed and eleven wounded. Although never confirmed, Garang had told me in 1994 that he had evidence of poison gas use by the Sudanese military against the SPLA and southern villages, but he suspected that the gas itself was coming from Iraq; the SPLA had captured an Iraqi army major during one of their operations. The Clinton administration later came under severe criticism for the bombing raid because officials could not produce any evidence that nerve gas was being produced at the plant. It appeared that the decision to bomb may have been based on faulty intelligence. In addition, President Clinton was facing a pending impeachment motion before Congress just as he ordered the bombing raids, leading critics to argue that his decision was an attempt to divert public attention. This was the one and only military action taken by any U.S. administration against the Bashir government.

On October 12, 2000, two al-Qaeda operatives drove a small boat loaded with 400–700 pounds of explosives into the USS *Cole*, a U.S. naval guided missile destroyer, while it was anchored in Aden Harbor, Yemen, killing seventeen people (including themselves) and injuring thirty-nine. Three days later, related operatives attempted to assassinate the British ambassador to Yemen. Seven years later, in March 2007, a U.S. judge ruled that the Sudan government had been involved in the attack on the *Cole*, making it liable in a lawsuit by victims' relatives.

The Clinton administration's Sudan policy could be summarized in one word: confrontation. Given the Kenya and Tanzania embassy and USS *Cole* bombings, the U.S. administration maintained a steady barrage of rhetorical criticism, aggressive diplomatic demarches, and condemnatory UN Security Council resolutions. It also imposed new economic sanctions, downgraded diplomatic relations, withdrew most U.S. embassy personnel from Khartoum, and, finally, endorsed military action. The administration even encouraged and supported a hapless Sudan regime change plan organized by Tanzania, Uganda, Eritrea, and Ethiopia, which failed.

This aggressive diplomatic policy frightened the Sudanese government and affirmed their view that the Clinton administration's ultimate objective was regime change in Khartoum. Yet none of the U.S. actions actually threatened the Bashir government in any tangible way, nor did they weaken the government's hold on power. The U.S. policy was one of regime change without actually changing the regime. The violence against the southerners, the contrived famine of 1998 in which 50,000–100,000 southerners starved, the killing of 60,000–70,000 people from the Nuba Mountain, the atrocities committed against the Masalit tribe during the Masalit-Arab war in Darfur of 1995–1999, and the ethnic cleansing of the oil fields all took place during this period. If the policy of confrontation acted as some sort of constraint on Sudanese government behavior, there is no evidence of it. It may have contributed, though, to Bashir's decision to end Turabi's foreign Islamist ambitions, since they threatened the vital national interests of other countries and many allies of the United States, and did little to promote Sudan's.

Like previous and successive U.S. policy stances on Sudan, the Clinton policy was based on misunderstanding of the Bashir calculation. The central imperative of the NCP and the Bashir government once it dispensed with its Islamist jihad was survival at all and any cost; losing power would have subjected the leadership to the revenge of a population brutalized by atrocity after atrocity. (Later in 2011 this fear must have grown more palpable as Khartoum witnessed the Arab Revolution in which long time dictators Zine El Abidine Ben Ali, Hosni Mubarak, and Muammar Gaddafi fell from power.) To survive, the Khartoum government believed that it had to do two things. First, it had to increase oil revenues to fund weapons acquisition, the expansion of the security services, and additional payments and jobs used to control the country's tribal and social networks. It therefore had to protect the oil fields and apply military pressure to the SPLA. Second, Khartoum believed it had to suppress any other rebellions in the periphery of the country through brutal force, regardless of the cost in terms of internal or international opposition. So the only way to stop the Khartoum government's abuses would have been to remove the Bashir government from power. No American president was prepared to undertake the sustained military campaign necessary to do so, thus there was a perpetual gap between public rhetoric and diplomatic and military reality.

The U.S. policy of confrontation was in marked contrast to that of the Europeans, who took a much more accommodating, and equally ineffective, approach, consisting of quiet diplomacy and subtle pressure. In fact, the French government had amiable relations with Khartoum under the Mitterrand and Chirac governments—as did the British—even making a deal with the Sudanese to turn over the infamous international terrorist Carlos the Jackal to French intelligence. Thus U.S. policy put it at odds with its allies, a circumstance the Sudanese exploited by playing the Europeans against the Americans. This diplomatic tact is one of Khartoum's most effective survival mechanisms.

7

THE THREE REBELLIONS
OF DARFUR

What caused the rebellions in Darfur?

The three successive Darfur rebellions beginning in 1987 had deep roots in the Sudanese past. The British colonial rulers broke the military power of the Fur sultanate in one last great battle in 1916, in which Ali Dinar, the last reigning Fur sultan, and his two sons were killed. From that battle until independence in 1956, neither successive Fur sultans nor the Fur nobility challenged British power, nor did they challenge Khartoum's authority after independence, at least not until seismic shifts in the politics and economy of the Sahel changed their calculations. Darfur was gradually and peacefully absorbed into Sudan under the British-Egyptian Condominium. British power affirmed the existing Fur hierarchical order, and, equally important, the Pax Britannica brought order, which facilitated agricultural activity and commerce in the province, though the British invested very little in infrastructure or public services. The second half of the nineteenth century had been a period of political instability, famine, epidemics, and war, with brief, temporary periods of peace; the British colonial period brought a welcome respite.

Darfur's participation in the national life of Sudan after independence was manifested in three ways. First, the traditional base of support of the largest and most popular national political party—the Umma Party—was in the province. Darfur had a connection to national political life through elections (even if elections were sporadic, given the history of military coups). Second, Umma Party activists, the Ansar Army of military and religious warriors, recruited many of the party's adherents in Darfur. This provided an opportunity for thousands of ambitious Darfuris to rise through the ranks of what amounted to a religious militia. Third, Darfur, as we've seen, was also the traditional recruitment grounds for foot soldiers and NCOs in the Sudanese military. This tied Darfuri society into national life, even if few of these soldiers could ever rise into the officer corps. Thus, the Darfuri tribes found organized institutional outlets for their martial spirit and values, allowing for some stability in the province.

Unfortunately, forces were at work in Darfur over which the people and their leaders would have little control. The Sahara Desert has periodically moved south into Darfur and then receded back to the north, causing migration from northern to southern Darfur. By 2002, the population of southern Darfur was twice the size of that in northern Darfur. Darfur has also suffered from periodic droughts, some of which have lasted several years and led to devastating famines. In the mid-1960s, the 1970s, and again in the mid-1980s, drought-induced famines caused political unrest that eventually reached Khartoum. Historically, when famines strike anywhere in the world, they sometimes bring with them ethnic conflict, violent crime, and population movements of starving poor seeking food, often leading to political upheaval. All of these struck Darfur. Numayri's failure to respond to the human suffering during the great Sahelian famine of the mid-1980s was one of several reasons for his overthrow in 1985.

The Darfuri people were afflicted with more than famine. The population increased from 1 million in 1950 to 6.5 million in 2000, heightening tensions among those who

LIBYA

Northern

S A H A R A   D E S E R T

SUDAN

CHAD

Overview Map

N
W — E
S

Mallit

North
Darfur

North
Kordofan

Kutum

Kutum
Rural ▲

Kulbus
▲Sirba

Kabkabiya
Kebkbaiya
Town ▲

Abu
▲Shouk

Al Fasher

Arddamata
Camp
▲

Al
Geneina

Zallingi
▲Morni ▲Nertiti
Zalingei

Gulu▲

Jebel
Marra

Dar El
▲Salam

Um
Kadada

Habillah

▲Garsila

Kass ▲
Kass

Kalma
▲

Shearia

West
Darfur

Edd Al
Fursan

Nyala

Adayla

Mukjar

Ed Daein

▲Sharef

Tulus

Relied
Al Birdi

South Darfur

South
Kordofan

Al Deain

Buram

CENTRAL
AFRICAN
REPUBLIC

Kotto R.

SOUTH SUDAN

0		100 miles
0	100 km	

depended on the land for their livelihood. Since land is a temporal resource, a sixfold increase in the population of farmers and herders on the same amount of land will eventually drive them into conflict, particularly when the desert is moving south, reducing the arable land and animal pasturage. This 650 percent population increase led to a corresponding increase in the number of domesticated animals in the state: camels, sheep, goats, and cows in southern Darfur alone. This placed a severe amount of stress on the fragile pastureland of Darfur but also across North Africa, driving tens of thousands of Arab pastoralists, seeking water and pastureland for their stressed herds, from Mali, Niger, and Chad, to Darfur.

In 2007, the Sudanese government began encouraging this migration of Sahelian Arabs to Darfur—promising pastureland, citizenship, and financial support—in order to expand the Arab base for Janjawiid troops and to increase the size of the Arab constituency in preparation for the 2010 national elections. The national census announced in May 2009, as required under the CPA (the North–South Peace Agreement described in chapter 9), showed more than a 40 percent increase in the Arab population of Darfur, while the African tribes increased by less than 5 percent. The Darfuri population had been estimated by demographers at 7 million; the census showed 8.5 million. While Khartoum could have easily invented the higher number through census fraud, evidence suggests that the elevated census figures reflect the sustained migration of these Arab tribes to Darfur as part of Khartoum's strategy.

The campaign represented Khartoum's single most irresponsible action in Darfur since the atrocities of 2003 and 2004. It resulted in the addition of as many as a million and a half Arab nomads onto a pastureland that was already heavily stressed, and could be setting the stage for a possible fourth Darfur rebellion in the future. Had the farmers and herders of Darfur been of the same race, tribe, and language, conflict would still have been inevitable, but it would have perhaps been less severe and brutal. But these tribes spoke a variety of African languages or Arabic; they identified themselves and each other as Arabs or Africans (as we've seen, Sudanese Arabs call the Africans "blacks" though they themselves are black) even when they intermarried and traded with each other. In Darfur everyone professed themselves Muslims, but Arabs regarded themselves as the true heirs and guardians of the Prophet's teachings and considered African tribes' devotion to Islam somehow inferior.

Racial, tribal, and linguistic identity in Darfur has historically been much more fluid than in other societies. The Zaghawa tribespeople in Darfur identify themselves as Africans, while in southern Libya the same tribe is recognized as Arab. When a smaller tribe transitions from herdsmen to farmers, they will sometimes change their identification from Arab to African, or vice versa. This all changed with the polarization of race, tribe, and ethnicity during the three Darfur rebellions, as political figures in the region pitted groups against each other to achieve their short-term political objectives.

During the 2004 conflict, I was in one of largest refugee camps outside El Fasher, the capital of North Darfur. The USAID staff took me to the former headquarters of the Turkish Red Crescent Society's humanitarian aid program, which had been distributing U.S. government food aid until a mob of African IDPs burned down the Red Crescent compound during one of the many upheavals in the camp. When asked why they had done this, the IDPs replied that it was because it was an Islamic NGO (the Red Crescent Society symbol uses the Islamic crescent, just as the Swiss cross is used to represent the Red Cross Societies, but neither has any religious significance). The IDPs were all Muslims. They were burning down the NGO offices perceived to represent their own religion because they saw them as a front for the Arabs. This would have been inconceivable in any of the earlier Darfur rebellions.

Why and how did Libya influence the Darfur rebellions?

Libya and Chad have had more influence over the conflicts of Darfur and its recent history than the central government in Khartoum. To understand this peculiar circumstance, we must review the Libyan state's connection to the history of the region.

In September 1969, King Idris I of Libya was overthrown in a bloodless coup by a group of young officers led by a 27-year-old captain from a desert Bedouin Arab tribe named Muammar Gaddafi. The officers abolished the monarchy and established Libya as an Arab socialist republic, modeled in part on the pan-Arab nationalist movement of Abdel Nasser of Egypt, whose ideology Gaddafi has sought to emulate during his decades of rule in Libya.

Gaddafi's ambitions extended beyond Libya's borders. He sought to become a new Che Guevara—a revolutionary leader who would overturn the international order. He did this by subsidizing radicals around the world and, early in his rule, by supporting groups that used violence to depose or attack governments he opposed. In 1974, he publicly called for the assassination of President Numayri and armed and financed at least two coups against him, including one mounted by Sadiq al-Mahdi himself. Several assassination attempts against Hissen Habre, president of Chad from 1982 to 1990, originated from Libya as well—likely on Gaddafi's orders. In July 1977 the Libyan government carried out an unsuccessful assassination attempt against President Sadat of Egypt through some local accomplices, which led the Egyptian army to briefly invade Libyan territory in what was called the "Sand War."

To increase Libyan influence in the Organization of African Unity (now the AU), Gaddafi used Libya's oil wealth to pay the dues in arrears of poorer African countries, and thus Libya had a disproportionate influence in the AU. Gaddafi saw himself as pan-Africanist—and called himself the Father of Africa, a title many African leaders found preposterous.

Despite his penchant for provocative outbursts and grand and bizarre pronouncements, as well as his constantly changing tactical maneuvers, Gaddafi's foreign policy showed a remarkable degree of consistency over his forty-two years in power and had a profound influence on the course of events in Darfur. He sought to expand the influence of the Arab race and culture first, his own interpretation of Islam second, and third, the Libyan state across Africa. He effectively collapsed the Sirte Peace Conference (which his government had helped organize) on Darfur in 2007, arguing that the Sudanese government ought to be able to address its internal problems in Darfur without outside interference, particularly from the UN, which he regarded as a front for Western powers. The Darfuri rebel groups (and Western diplomats—I was one of them) listening to his opening speech were shocked by his views, and considered leaving the conference in protest.

Part of Gaddafi's vision was the creation of a Libyan empire—essentially a sphere of influence in North Africa that encompassed Chad and Darfur (as an afterthought). His plan for a greater Libyan sphere of economic influence was not as outlandish as it might seem at first. For four centuries, Darfur has had closer economic ties to Libya than to the Nile River Valley. The open-air markets of Darfur today feature more goods from Tripoli and the Libyan coastal plain than from Khartoum and Port Sudan. These modern trade routes are not a contemporary contrivance; they were forged by camel caravans a thousand years ago, when Saharan desert salt was bartered for African slaves and ivory across four principal trade routes. For centuries, these routes have tied Chad, Libya, Darfur, and the Sahelian countries of northern Africa together along the southern border of the vast Sahara Desert. Gaddafi used oil revenues to build or modernize roads through the desert in order to project Libyan influence southward. While Khartoum was ignoring Darfur, Gaddafi was bringing it into his expanding sphere of influence. That is why Gaddafi had far more influence over the course of events in Darfur than successive Sudanese governments, let alone the UN or the AU. Gaddafi had seventy security agents in Darfur during the course of the third rebellion using money, weapons, and equipment to support rebels against the Khartoum government and its allies.

Three Gaddafi foreign-policy initiatives directly affected the course of events in Darfur. First, he intervened repeatedly in Chad, attempting to overthrow President Nhartha Tombalbaye (1960–1975), who came from the Christian and animist Chadian South and was a member of the African Sara tribe. Under Tombalbaye, Chad received foreign and military assistance from Israel and had an intimate, if contentious, relationship with the country's former colonial masters, the French, who controlled most of the Chadian economy after independence in 1960. On all these counts, Tombalbaye was on a collision course with Gaddafi's worldview: he was a Christian ruling what Gaddafi believed should be a Muslim country; he was an African ruling Arabs (who lived in the northern and central regions of the country); he allied Chad with Israel (which Gaddafi despised); and (though Tombalbaye deeply resented them), he allowed French military, diplomatic, and economic influence to continue.

The attempt on Tombalbaye's life was not the only time Gaddafi would attempt to unseat or manipulate the Chadian government. Battles continued between Chadian and Libyan forces until a peace agreement finally ended the war in 1988. Idriss Deby seized control of Chad two years later in 1990, with Gaddafi's active military and financial assistance. Unlike previous Chadian leaders, Deby was a Muslim and a member of the Kobe Zaghawa tribe, which Gaddafi regarded as Arab. The Kobe Zaghawa's homeland covers parts of Chad, Libya, and Darfur, and it has been at the forefront of the Darfur rebellions since 2001 (in Darfur the Zaghawa are regarded as Africans).

The second Gaddafi initiative that was to have a profound influence on the Darfur rebellions was his support for two Arab supremacist groups—the Islamic Legion and Arab Gathering—to further his expansionist ambitions. The Arab Gathering was a loose alliance of Arab groups whose common objective was to roll back the rising presence of African farmers and herders along the northern part of the Sahel, in order to make room for Arab nomads who had been pressed southward by the advance of the Sahara Desert and the Great Sahelian drought and famine of the mid-1980s, which had killed as many as a quarter million people. Gaddafi formed the Islamic Legion—composed of Sahelian Arab tribespeople, Pakistanis, and other foreign Muslims who immigrated to Libya for work—to act as ground troops for his war in Chad.

To write their history of the Darfur rebellions, *A New History of a Long War,* Alex de Waal and Julie Flint obtained internal documents from both the Arab Gathering and the Islamic Legion that confirm their racist and Arab supremacist outlook and objectives, as well as their willingness to use violence to achieve them. While the two movements were loosely tied to each other and had a good many followers in common, the Islamic Legion was formed, trained, and armed by Gaddafi in the 1980s and 1990s. Officially disbanded in the 1990s, they didn't simply disappear but instead turned into a ticking time bomb, waiting to explode in Darfur.

For generations, Darfuri tribes were assigned their own specific land, or *dar,* for their farmers and herders. *Darfur* itself means "the land of the Fur." Some of the smaller Arab tribes, particularly in the North, where profound environmental changes occurred, were never assigned their own dar and thus were landless and impoverished. They and their sheikhs believed that their nomadic way of life and their very existence as tribes were at risk of extinction. They did, in fact, face a growing crisis as the population increased geometrically and animal herds expanded proportionately, despite the temporal limit on arable land to which they had no firm claim. This, however, does not excuse the violence or racist ideology embraced by these tribes as a solution, but it does suggest that their grievances were real and fears well founded.

The leaders of the Arab Gathering and Islamic Legion later organized and led the Janjawiid militia in the Darfur rebellions of the 2000s, committing some of these conflicts' worst atrocities. Perhaps the most notorious leader of the Arab Gathering and the Islamic Legion in the Fur War was Sheikh Moussa Hillal, a Darfuri Arab and leader of the Um Jalal clan of the Abbala (camel-herding) northern Rizaiqat tribe. The Rizaiqat are the largest Arab tribe in Darfur, but the Um Jalal clan is without its own dar.

Gaddafi's third contribution to the Darfur rebellions was the introduction of automatic weapons to both Chad and Darfur, with predictable consequences, massively expanding the number of people killed in tribal conflicts, which were becoming more and more frequent. (The collapse of the Gaddafi government and Gaddafi's own lynching by rebel forces in Sirte in October 2011 will likely profoundly change the course of events in Sudan described in the final chapter.)

When and why did the first Darfur rebellion take place?

The rebellion that took place in Darfur during the first decade of the twenty-first century, so well known to the outside world because of its savagery and destructiveness, was not the first rebellion since independence; it was the third. The first Darfur rebellion took place between 1987 and 1989, pitting the Darfur Arab tribes against the Fur. In 1987 Chadian rebels, seeking to overthrow President Habre and Libya's Islamic Legion, moved their forces into Darfur—with arms, training, and financial support provided by Gaddafi and tacit approval provided by Sadiq al-Mahdi, then prime minister of Sudan—to set up base camps for an invasion of Chad. These troops' movements, combined with the drought and famine of the mid-1980s, caused growing tensions between the Arab Baqqara Tribe and the Fur.

The Libyans regarded the Fur tribe and its nobility with contempt, and the Fur reciprocated by denigrating Gaddafi's acquisitive ambitions south of Libya's borders. Darfur was their homeland, the 400-year-old Fur sultanate was their proud inheritance, and their rich agricultural system in the Jebel Marra provided the livelihood for its people. In 1988, surrounded by enemies and with their land invaded and plundered by Libyan and Chadian forces, the Fur nobility formed the Federal Army of Darfur, a militia of 6,000 fighters whom they armed and trained to defend Fur villages from these attacks. They were proud Muslims, but they had no intention of ceding their dominant position in Darfur to Arab tribes.

As the Fur armed themselves, the Arab nobility of Darfur demanded weapons from Khartoum and Libya. They received weapons far more powerful than anything the Fur could muster. The arms disparity resulted in the death of thousands of Fur, the burning of hundreds of their villages, the looting of tens of thousands of livestock, an assault on their mountain fortress in Jebel Marra, and the plundering of crops—all done by Darfuri Arabs, Chadian rebels, and Libyan forces. The Arabs, unsurprisingly, reported far lower casualties. Two years later, and only eight days after the Bashir coup in July 1989, a tenuous peace settlement between the Arabs and the Fur was finally signed, with a subsequent agreement being signed in December 1989. The two agreements called for the disarmament of both the Janjawiid and Fur militias, the deportation of Chadians, the return of displaced people, pasturage, and water rights for Fur and Arabs, and the reestablishment of local government and police authority. As with many peace agreements in Sudanese history, Khartoum never implemented it, which only served to exacerbate local bitterness toward the central government.

Some of the Fur displaced during this period had yet to return to their traditional villages as many as twenty years later. This was because Khartoum pursued a strategy of weakening the Fur hold on Darfur, limiting their claims to their own dar, and constraining their political power. Khartoum arbitrarily appointed a competing Fur *magdum* (a supporter of the regime who would do what he was told) to undermine the authority of the legitimate magdum, Ahmed Adam Rijal (whom I alluded to earlier), a vocal opponent of Turabi's NIF government. In 1994, Khartoum split the single Darfur Province into three new states, a move that was deliberately designed to weaken Fur influence further and would only add to the list of Fur grievances.

The chronic neglect of Darfur's economic development, the ongoing discrimination against non-Arabs within the political appointment process in Khartoum, and the brutality of the Arab-Fur rebellion led young Darfuri men to organize. Initially, these young activists looked with hope to the Islamist Muslim Brothers and its offspring, Turabi's NIF, which they saw as a new reform movement, to rid Sudanese politics of its racial and geographic prejudices. Now they saw both for what they were: a front for the Three Tribes and their Arab allies in Darfur.

How were the three Darfur rebellions related to the Second Civil War?

Daud Yahya Bolad embodied the rising Darfuri political awareness and activism, ultimately leading to the alliance between the Fur, John Garang, and his southern movement. In 1973 Bolad, then a young Fur activist with Islamist sympathies, while attending the University of Khartoum, ran for president of the student association and won, marking the first time in the school's history that the winner was not an Arab. Bolad and his supporters had high hopes that Sudan was changing. He soon discovered that his election did not signal any shift in the Three Tribes' control or their underlying prejudices. In early 1991 he returned to Darfur angry and disillusioned, abandoning the Islamist movement that had proven itself nothing more than a traditional Riverine Arab-only club, and joined John Garang's SPLM movement. Garang did not require much persuasion to support Bolad; the Darfur rebellions fit well into his own narrative of what ailed Sudan: chronic neglect and abuse of the periphery of the country by Khartoum.

By December 1991 Garang had armed and trained Bolad, who was now one of Garang's SPLA commanders, and his second-in-command, Abdul Azziz al Hilu, whose father was a Darfuri Masalit and a Muslim. Hilu's subsequent career included leading the SPLA forces in the Nuba Mountains of South Kordofan, where he was born. He rose in the ranks, becoming deputy director general of the SPLM in 2009 and deputy governor in southern Kordofan in 2010. Bolad and Hilu launched a military campaign against the Khartoum government presence in Darfur. The campaign was a disaster, as the Sudanese military and the Arab Fursan tribal militia—which Khartoum had recruited and armed— defeated Bolad's forces, capturing him and seizing a notebook he carried with him into battle that contained the names of individuals in his clandestine organizational network. He was tortured and disappeared into the Sudanese gulag, where he was likely executed. The Sudanese internal security methodically arrested and disposed of Bolad's entire underground network of activists, destroying Garang's Darfur organization and postponing the third rebellion for another decade. Bolad remains a martyred hero to the current generation of Darfuri rebels. Though it failed utterly, his rebellion was the first major alliance between the southern and Darfuri uprisings.

What caused the second Darfur rebellion?

In 1995 the second rebellion began, this time between the Darfuri Arabs and the Masalit tribe, whose dar was situated in western Darfur. The Masalit, like the Fur, were African Muslims who saw themselves as the dominant power in their dar and jealously protected their territory and prerogatives. During the famine of the mid-1980s, the Masalit tribes blocked humanitarian aid to the Arab tribes, many of whom had migrated from Chad to western Darfur decades earlier, because they saw them as newcomers and interlopers. The Masalit sultan exercised traditional authority in western Darfur and was thus either a critical ally of or a competitor to successive Khartoum governments. Unlike the Fur, who were suspicious of Sadiq al-Mahdi (despite his great-grandmother's Fur pedigree), the Masalit had embraced his Umma Party in the 1985 elections and were rewarded with all of the region's seats in the National Assembly. The sultan's cousin was also named to the new five-man collective presidency, the Council of State. The Masalit were the backbone of Umma power in western Darfur, along with the Rizaiqat Arabs in the North and South, who, as we've seen, provided the foot soldiers of Sadiq's Ansar Army.

When the Bashir coup deposed Sadiq in July 1989, the new government was determined to break the Umma's power in Darfur, and one of its first targets was the Masalit. This was a chance for the marginalized Arabs to seize power from the dominant Masalit, who had exercised authority over them for so long—just as Darfuri Arabs had attempted to break Fur power in the first Darfur rebellion. Bashir appointed new local authorities in the Masalit region—all but one of whom were Arabs—who were then given the title Amir ("prince"), implying equality with the sultan. Thus the central government was replacing the Masalit sultan by installing these new powerbrokers in the region. Then, in a subsequent "reform," Khartoum announced that henceforth the sultan would be appointed by a council of these amirs. The very idea that the western Darfur sultan would likely be an Arab in the future enraged the Masalit.

By 1995 the central government's heavy-handed tactics, combined with the polarized relations between the Masalit and Arab tribes of western Darfur, had thrown the region into conflict. It is unclear from historical accounts which group fired the first shot in the second Darfur rebellion: each side blames the other. What is clear is that the Bashir government decided that the only groups it could rely on in the province were the Arab tribes—the Masalit were now deemed adversaries, just as the Fur had been a few years earlier in the first Darfur rebellion. In this second rebellion, Khartoum armed the Arab tribes of western Darfur: Marhariya, the Um Jalul of the Rizaiqat, Beni Halba, and the Misiriyya. Prominent Masalit intellectuals and civil society members were arrested and tortured by NISS.

Alex de Waal and Julie Flint provide persuasive evidence that the Janjawiid attacks on Darfuri villages began during this second rebellion. A strategy took shape: the Sudanese military visited Masalit villages, disarming everyone, and a day or two later the Janjawiid militias would arrive and loot and burn the villages. Dar Masalit lay in ruins, with thousands of casualties. Deep and festering Masalit grievances and bitter memories emerged from the destruction.

The second rebellion did not end until 1999, when Khartoum finally tried to restore some form of representational balance in the local government councils by appointing an equal number of Arabs and Masalit. Yet the only reason that this became necessary was because Khartoum's Arab-only policy had incited the Masalit rebellion in the first place. By arming the local Arab militias against the Masalit, the central government had provoked and then exacerbated the animosity between the tribes.

What was The Black Book *and how did it affect the third Darfur rebellion?*

A book published in May 2000 had an explosive affect in Darfur and other regions of Sudan already riven with simmering resentments and expanding grievances. In late 1996 the Justice and Equality Movement (JEM)—a Darfur rebel group with roots in Turabi's NIF—began conducting painstaking research on the ethnic and geographic origin of the Sudanese elite who have ruled Sudan since independence. The JEM was almost entirely run by Darfuri and Kobe Zaghawa, an African tribe that was later allied with the Fur and Masalit during the third rebellion. Their research, later published in two hardcover volumes titled *The Black Book: Imbalance of Power and Wealth in Sudan,* confirmed what John Garang had been arguing for so many years: that Sudan was run by the Three Tribes of the northern Nile River Valley—the Shaiqiyya, Ja'aliyiin, and Danagla. These tribes made up only 5.4 percent of the Sudanese population yet had completely dominated the institutions of Sudanese society since independence, holding 70 percent or more of its senior positions and concentrating development resources and the wealth of the country nearly entirely within the Arab Triangle. Banks, universities, the military officer corps, the government's civil service, the police and internal security apparatus, the judiciary, corporations, and the news media were composed of and controlled by men from the Three Tribes. While Garang had argued that the South had been excluded from the centers of power, resource, and influence since independence, *The Black Book* revealed that most of the country outside the Arab Triangle had been marginalized, not just the South.

In May 2000, one Friday after prayers, JEM arranged to have copies distributed as the faithful left their mosques in Khartoum and other cities in Sudan. Reportedly, government ministers, including President Bashir himself, returned from

Friday prayers to find a copy of the book on their desks. The NISS immediately bought all available copies and unsuccessfully tried to confiscate the remainder for destruction. This clumsy attempt at censorship only increased the demand for the book. Newspapers allied with the NCP attacked *The Black Book* and claimed that it had been written by "tribalists," a term that only served to legitimate it, given that most Sudanese identify themselves with some tribe.

Like Sudan watchers, I was fascinated by the book when it was first published, because it explained so much about the many crises facing Sudan. A northern Sudanese friend who had served as a minister in Numayri's cabinet told me many years ago that four ministers serving in the same cabinet had all come from his own home village in the Nile River Valley north of Khartoum. This had seemed odd to him, given that the village had fewer than a few thousand inhabitants.

Sudan has of course been dominated by the Three Tribes since the Egyptian invasion of 1821. It is a problem that has existed for nearly two centuries under many different political regimes and thus will not be easy for any future reformers to correct.

What was the relationship between the Darfur rebellions and Hassan al-Turabi?

The Darfuri Zaghawas who wrote *The Black Book* were men who had joined Turabi's movement in their youth because they believed his Islamist vision offered the best hope for correcting the injustices of Sudanese society. They had been disappointed, more perhaps by the Bashir government than by Turabi himself. *The Black Book*, which was to become the rallying cry for the third Darfur rebellion, was published six months after Turabi had been deposed as speaker of the National Assembly by Bashir in the internal military coup described in chapter 6. The NCP, as we've seen, had thereafter moved rapidly toward a more realist foreign policy and away from Turabi's Islamist adventurism. Domestically, the NCP's policy was focused on two objectives—regime survival and collection of oil revenues—rather than on Islamic revolution. Their cynicism disgusted young idealistic Islamists. By May 2000, when *The Black Book* was released publicly by JEM, Turabi had become one of the leading and most outspoken critics of the Bashir government. Did Turabi orchestrate the publication of *The Black Book* as a retaliatory intellectual strike against Bashir? Following the 9/11 attacks on the Twin Towers in New York City, Khalil Ibrahim, the founder and leader of JEM, began to distance himself from Turabi, given the latter's relationship with Osama bin Laden. Ibrahim referred to Turabi as his political godfather until 2001 and reportedly continues to take advice from him. In 2000, Ibrahim joined Turabi's new opposition party—the Popular Congress Party (PCP)—which Turabi had formed after his expulsion from Bashir's party and from his position as speaker of the National Assembly. Both the timing of *The Black Book*'s publication and Ibrahim's embrace of Turabi's new party suggest that Turabi was behind JEM. The fact that Ibrahim joined Turabi's party after the latter's break with Bashir suggests that Ibrahim was already alienated from Khartoum and still remained loyal to Turabi even when it was politically dangerous for him to do so.

While I was U.S. envoy to Sudan, Bashir and his senior leadership repeatedly told me that they believed Turabi was the architect of the third Darfur rebellion. They may have done this to justify their brutal repression of the rebellion. I wondered why Turabi should care about what happened in Darfur. It may have been Turabi's plan to use Darfur as a base of operations to depose the NCP from power in Khartoum as revenge for his ouster by Bashir in 1999. As noted, Turabi's wife was a descendant of the Fur Sultan through her paternal great-grandmother, so Turabi continued to have a familial connection to the non-Arab tribes of Darfur, which may explain, along with Turabi's Islamist ideology, Ibrahim's continuing loyalty to him.

How did the third Darfur rebellion start?

The first two Darfur rebellions—the Arab-Fur and Arab-Masalit conflicts—took place against a backdrop of growing tribal polarization, the widespread distribution of automatic weapons into the hands of the Arab militias, chronic under-development, an encroaching northern desert, population growth, and the use of Darfur by Libya and Chad as a staging ground for their own military campaigns. *The Black Book* inflamed the simmering grievances of the non-Arab Darfuri tribes even more. All these were factors in the third rebellion, which was set off by the publication of *The Black Book*. The third rebellion was the most destructive civil conflict in Darfur in more than a century. The three largest and most powerful Darfuri African tribes—the Fur, Masalit, and Zaghawa—united into a broad military alliance driven by four historic issues: the marginalization of the periphery; poverty and underdevelopment; human rights abuses by Arab supremacist groups; and the absence of democratic institutions through which to seek redress from their grievances. While most observers mark February 2003 as the beginning of the third rebellion, on paper it actually began on July 21, 2001, when Fur and Zaghawa leaders signed a pledge—on the Quran—to resist the Arab supremacist movement that was spreading across Darfur.

The three Darfuri rebellions really represent one long war interspersed by temporary phases of tenuous peace. All three share the same poisonous racial component; were led by many of the same men; and were met with the same reaction by Khartoum: to arm Arab militias, such as the Janjawiid, and use them to wipe out the rebel base of operational support. The results were the same: displacement of the civilian population; looting of their animal herds (which represent rural farmers' savings accounts and insurance policies against economic hardship); killing of young men likely to join the rebellion; and slaughter of tribal elites. This third conflict brought this long war to its horrific climax.

In July 2001, two months after taking over as Administrator of USAID, I traveled to Sudan to assess the humanitarian situation. We attempted but failed to travel to the Nuba Mountains (Sudanese military intelligence stopped our trip), where there was an ongoing ethnic cleansing campaign against tribes allied with John Garang's SPLM. From there I traveled to Darfur, where I visited rural drought-affected areas and was treated to a sumptuous meal by the new governor of North Darfur (he had been appointed in April 2001), General Ibrahim Suleiman, at his official residence in El Fasher. His wife, a grammar school principal in Khartoum, had come from the capital to supervise the feast. The week before, we had been treated to a cool reception in Khartoum, and my delegation took this gracious and conciliatory response from the governor and his wife to be a sign that the Sudanese government wished to improve relations with the United States. In Nairobi a few weeks later, Secretary of State Colin Powell and I announced a new emergency aid program focused on food security and the livelihoods of Darfuri residents. The State Department hoped the program would also send a signal to Khartoum that it wanted to move U.S.-Sudanese relations in a more constructive direction. This also included a reversal of the Clinton administration's ban on humanitarian aid to anyone in the North (except displaced southerners outside Khartoum). My visit there nearly coincided with the secret pledge made by Fur and Zaghawa leaders to resist, but the signs of rebellion were hidden beneath the surface.

Suleiman, who had been Bashir's minister of defense and the army's chief of staff (very unusual, given that he was not from one of the Three Tribes), was appointed governor by Khartoum to calm the tribes, end the emerging conflict, and negotiate a peace. Suleiman was a good choice for the job. He had been born in Darfur, belonged to the Berti tribe (an African Darfuri tribe), and understood the legitimate grievances of the rebels and their tribes, grievances he believed were negotiable.

By the end of 2001, the rebel leaders sent Zaghawa fighters, who had a long warrior tradition of desert warfare, to train the much larger Fur tribe, who had been more pacific in their recent history. The first joint campaign took place on February 25, 2002, when the two tribes attacked an SAF garrison, defeated the government troops, burned the garrison, and looted its arms. The Zaghawa-Fur alliance in and of itself would have alarmed the central government, but the subsequent addition of the Masalit panicked the security services in Khartoum. Their reaction was predictable: they mobilized Janjawiid units recruited from the Arab Gathering and Islamic Legion. With the support of the SAF, Janjawiid militia units entered each village in Dar Masalit of western Darfur, dragged the village sheikhs and local leaders out of the dwellings, and summarily executed them to intimidate and disorient their followers. In all, nearly 2,000 members of the local Masalit nobility were assassinated by the Bashir government and its Janjawiid allies.

Janjawiid attacks against Fur villages intensified, and in May 2002, alarmed Fur members of the National Assembly met with President Bashir to air their grievances about the destruction of hundreds of Fur villages, the rape of their women, and the murder of their young men. Khartoum responded by approving Governor Suleiman's plan to arrest Arab and Fur militants, who were seen as fomenting the violence. This included the future commander of the Janjawiid, Sheikh Moussa Hillal, whom General Suleiman had arrested and sent to prison in early 2003 in Port Sudan for murdering African tribespeople. Vice President Ali Osman Taha countermanded Suleiman's wise decision in April 2003 and ordered Hillal's release. While Hillal came from a noble family—his father was also a well-known sheikh—his temperament, ethics, and personality had devolved over time and turned him into a brutal militia leader and killer. Although Khartoum initially denied any connection to Mousa Hillal, he told Western researchers that he was provided with weapons and his orders by commanders in the SAF. (Later, in 2007, he was made a major general in the SAF to ensure his continuing loyalty to the regime that began wavering because he feared Khartoum intended to turn him over to the ICC for prosecution for the atrocities in Darfur to save themselves.)

In August and September 2002, two conferences were convened with Khartoum's support—one in Nyertete and the other in Kaa, both in South Darfur. The first produced a statement that diplomatically assigned blame to both sides and proposed some practical measures to bring peace. The second conference, in Kaas, focused blame for the entire conflict on the Fur; the new governor of South Darfur—Major General Salah Ali al Ghali, an active supporter of the Arab Gathering—had orchestrated the event and ensured its outcome.

What is not clear is why Khartoum appointed such contradictory figures to deal with the crisis: Suleiman, a moderate and conciliatory figure (in the context of Darfur) as governor in North Darfur, and Ghali, an Arab supremacist, as the new governor in the South. The latter appointment decision could have been partially a result of internal politics within the NCP and motivated by tribal factionalism, or it may have been because the political stock of Khartoum's hard-line security services was on the rise. In any case, the effect was immediate. In late 2002, the government sent the SAF and Janjawiid forces to surround and attack Jebel Marra, the center of Fur culture, killing hundreds of Fur villagers.

Why did the Bashir government move from negotiation to an ethnic cleansing campaign?

In February 2003, the Darfur rebels formally announced their intention to rebel. The military campaign started off badly for the government when, in April 2003, the rebels, now joined by the Masalit, attacked El Fasher Airport and the Sudanese air force base there, destroying two Antonov aircraft. During the battle, they captured Major General Ibrahim Bushra, commander of the Sudanese air force, as well as so much weaponry that they could not take it all with them. This marked the public beginning of the third Darfur rebellion, though, as mentioned earlier, fighting had occurred earlier. The nine months between February and October 2003 brought the worst military disasters to the SAF in Darfur since Sudan's independence: of thirty-eight pitched battles, the SAF won only four, while the rebels won thirty-four.

Peace negotiations between the SPLM and NCP in 2003 were showing signs of progress. However, Khartoum did not anticipate the consequences among the rebellious regions in the northern periphery that were not included in the talks. The more progress in the North–South negotiations, the more unrest brewed in the northern periphery, including Darfur, for which there was no prospect for a resolution of grievances. Khartoum feared that a peace deal with the South might create momentum for reform in the North, or even the over-throw of the Bashir regime. The events in Darfur from February through October 2003 panicked Khartoum into a brutal counterinsurgency campaign against the Fur, Masalit, and Zaghawa alliance because the government feared it was losing control of the country. The North believed it faced the prospect of the dissolution of the entire Sudanese state, and the only way they thought they could deal with it was with repression and more violence—which accelerated rather than slowed the dissolution.

The security apparatus in Khartoum panicked. The defeats aided the rise of a hard-line faction in the NCP and led to the forced retirement of General Sulieman as governor later in June 2003. (Later, President Bashir took Suleiman with him on Hajj; this was widely interpreted as a form of apology for not heeding Suleiman's wise advice on the conflict in Darfur.)

The ascendancy of the hard-line faction had also led to Moussa Hillal's appointment as the commander of the Janjawiid: President Bashir offered Hillal a dar for his Um

Jalal clan—in exchange for which his clan would be expected to recruit Janjawiid troops. Hillal readily accepted. Any dar offered to the Um Jalal, however, could only be given at the expense of some other tribe, likely one of the three in rebellion, many of whose members were crowded into displacement camps. All of the other arable land was already taken. Thus, in order for Bashir and his advisors to crush the rebellion, they had to virtually guarantee a new one. Khartoum's new hard-line tactics did not contain the rebellion; young Fur and Zaghawa men flocked to the cause, outraged by the Janjawiid and SAF attacks on their farms and villages.

The rebels' hit-and-run tactics proved very effective against the SAF's fixed defenses, as well as against such targets as police stations, air bases, and government buildings. When the SAF troops would rush to respond to the attack, the rebels would fade into the vast countryside on small pickup trucks mounted with machine guns. Often, SAF forces would follow them and attack their villages.

As the SAF combat position further deteriorated and the hard-liners grew more powerful, Khartoum's military high command changed tactics. Instead of retaliating directly against the rebels, they focused on their villages, which were relatively defenseless. Leaders of the NCP were sent to Darfur to encourage—with offers of weapons and money—the Darfur Arab tribes to contribute troops to the Janjawiid militia, which the government was equipping and training to lead the counterattack. Their appeals filled the Darfur newspapers and Sudanese media. Many Darfur Arabs refused, remembering that similar calls from Sadiq and al-Bashir in the 1980s and 1990s against the South had brought retaliation from Garang's forces.

Bashir summoned Saeed Mahmoud Ibrahim Musa Madibu—nazir of the Baqqara Rizaiqat and the most revered and powerful Arab leader in South Darfur—to Khartoum in 2003 to appeal for his support. He firmly and absolutely refused, reportedly stating that Bashir would not be president forever, while "the Rizaiqat are here forever and revenge will continue forever." I met with the tribal aristocracy of the Baqqara Rizaiqat who represented Madibu in 2007, and, repeating Madibu's own arguments of 2003, I encouraged them to remain neutral in the conflicts. They replied that Madibu remained committed to neutrality but that central government agents were still trying to recruit young Rizaiqat men to form a new Janjawiid unit. The nazir was unyielding in his opposition to the rebellion. The government, he said, was destroying Darfur. When the Janjawiid attacks intensified, he ordered those under his authority to protect the animals of Masalit and Fur farmers and herders, returning them only when it was safe. In other words, this was not a war of all Arabs against all Africans; the situation was far more complex, varying by region. Attempts in the West to demonize all Arabs in Darfur have led to a serious mischaracterization of the complex politics of the region, one that ignores the principled position of men like Nazir Madibu. A number of the Arab tribesmen refused to acquiesce to Bashir's hard-line strategy.

So, too, did some elements of the SAF, a large proportion of whose NCOs and foot soldiers were from Darfur, often recruited from the tribes leading the rebellion. When they confronted rebels in combat, some would drop their weapons and refuse to fight. Many SAF units were told by their commanding officers that they were being sent to Darfur to protect the civilian population from rebel attacks, only to find when they arrived that the local people were hostile toward Khartoum and supportive of the rebels. This only served to demoralize the SAF troops. Four Sudanese air force pilots who were ordered to bomb rebel villages refused to carry out their orders in late 2003 because they were from Darfur. They were arrested and disappeared into the Sudanese prison system. It was one thing for the SAF army and air force to kill southerners during the two civil wars; it was quite another to destroy their own home villages in Darfur.

By 2004, the Sudanese high command realized that soldiers recruited from Darfur were unreliable and decided to force tens of thousands into early retirement, replacing them with Janjawiid irregulars. Another of the reasons the Janjawiid were recruited and placed on the regular military payroll was so the SAF could exercise greater control over them. At times the Janjawiid would invade cities in Darfur controlled by Khartoum to steal food in the markets, and when they were challenged by government police they would open fire. The only way Khartoum could restore order in these circumstances was for NISS agents to bribe the Janjawiid commanders with cash to withdraw from the cities. These new Janjawiid recruits, however, proved poor soldiers: shabby, undisciplined, difficult to train, and nearly all illiterate, they quarreled with regular troops and panicked when they faced fire. Many of these new soldiers moved their families to Darfuri cities, sold off or gave away their animal herds, and abandoned their old nomadic way of life.

The third Darfur rebellion brought other profound changes to Darfuri society: rural Fur, Zaghawa, and Masalit were driven from their farms into IDP camps, many of which were becoming permanent communities outside large cities, heavily dependent for their viability and livelihood on food aid from donor governments. The Janjawiid, whose attacks depopulated the dar of the rebellious tribes, now were abandoning these same rural areas—at least those recruited onto the regular military payroll. Some had been transferred from Darfur into SAF units in other regions. Even that did not end the conflict. In 2010, Janjawiid units quarreled with regular units and engaged in firefights during training exercises on a military base north of Khartoum.

In 2010, another trend appeared, one that demonstrated Khartoum's waning influence on the ground. Realizing that the central government was never going to reclaim control of Darfur, some rural Janjawiid who were not recruited into the military or urbanized were making informal agreements with

Fur farmers to protect their villages, animal herds, and crops in exchange for food. Some say these deals are no more than disguised protection schemes; others argue that they show the Janjawiid hedging their bets, once they began to realize the central government was untrustworthy, and that in the future they were going to have to cohabit with tribes they had preyed on. In September 2010, more than 2,000 Janjawiid irregulars switched sides and joined the rebels. This had happened in earlier years for short periods of time—until they were bribed back into the Khartoum's fold. This time was different: the Janjawiid were hedging their bets in a more permanent fashion.

8

THE THIRD DARFUR
REBELLION CONTINUED

How did the Darfuri rebels arm themselves?

To understand the complexity of the third Darfur rebellion
we must now review the four sources of weapons that supported rebel combat operations. First, the rebels captured
weapons, vehicles, and military equipment during their victories over the SAF in 2003. So, in a very real sense, Bashir's
government unintentionally acted as quartermaster for the
rebellion.

The earliest outside support for the rebels, and the second
source, came from the Eritrean government, which had been
virtually at war with the Bashir government from its
independence in April 1993 until a peace agreement was
signed with Sudan in June 2006. The Eritrean government
had intelligence agents on the ground in Darfur to assist the
rebels, deliver weapons, and provide cash. Turabi and the Sudanese government had supported Eritrean Islamists, seeking
to overthrow the newly established secular Eritrean
government in 1993. In retaliation, Eritrea supported a rebellion among the Beja and Rashaida tribes between 1999 through
2006 along the border it shared with Sudan in the Red Sea
region. Eritrean support for the rebels ended in 2006—as did
Eritrea's covert Darfur operations—after they were promised
discounted oil prices by the Sudanese government as well as

no further interference in their internal affairs. After 2006, the Eritreans switched sides and supported Khartoum's efforts for a political settlement in Darfur.

The SPLA was the third source, sending weapon shipments into Darfur in early 2003 and training the rebels in guerilla warfare. John Garang's strategy included an effort to unite the periphery against the center to form a chain of alliances that would keep Khartoum busy fighting wars around the country, not just in the South, and eventually force it to engage in broad reform of the Sudanese social structure, giving the periphery a chance to seize control of the country's power and resources. In late 2010, the southern government in Juba formed a new alliance with JEM and other secular rebel groups from Darfur to exert military and political pressure on the Bashir government, so that it would have to make concessions in negotiations between the North and the South on postindependence planning.

Finally, in volume and regularity the weapons from Chad and Libya were perhaps the most significant of all of the sources of rebel support. Much of this weaponry was sent across the Chadian border into Darfur, but its original source was Libya. As described earlier, Gaddafi saw the third Darfur rebellion as an opportunity to support the Darfur Zaghawas, whom he categorized as Arabs, and to extend Libyan influence into Darfur. President Deby of Chad, a Kobe Zaghawa, had alienated his father, brothers, and other tribal leaders by remaining neutral in the Darfur conflict, while his Zaghawa kinsmen were being murdered and their villages laid waste by the Janjawiid and the SAF. Deby's neutrality was a careful diplomatic calculation. He realized that supporting his own tribe in Darfur would lead Khartoum to retaliate against him.

But his position created opposition against him within his own tribe. Deby reversed his stance, agreeing to supply arms to the Zaghawa rebels in Darfur and allowing them to use Chad as a base of operations. This infuriated Khartoum. In early 2008, Sudanese internal security organized and armed a large body of Chadian rebels that managed to cross the desert to the capital, N'djamena, and engage Deby's forces in bloody street battles. Hundreds of bodies littered the streets for days, while Deby summarily executed anyone he deemed loyal to Khartoum and its Chadian allies.

Having crushed the coup attempt, Deby realized that he had gone too far in Darfur and again pledged neutrality. Yet he was in an untenable position: no matter what position he took in Darfur—neutrality or support for the rebellion—he put himself and his government at risk.

All this illustrated just how complicated the political situation in Darfur had become, and how difficult it would be to piece the region back together again, given the competing strategic interests of Sudan's neighbors. It also demonstrated that Khartoum could not even control its own borders. Its neighbors, particularly Libya, exercised more control over the country's periphery than it did. This was a direct result of the central government's chronic neglect of the regions outside the Arab Triangle. This neglect might have been easier to understand when Sudan had limited resources to develop the rural areas, but with oil revenues now pouring into the national treasury, the NCP's myopic policy accelerated the centrifugal forces pulling the country apart.

What limited the rebel movement's effectiveness in the third rebellion?

As news of the rebel successes spread, new recruits poured into their ranks. By 2004, there were 11,000 irregulars under arms, organized into thirteen battalion-sized units. Ironically, their combat victories became their undoing. The early cohesion among the rebel leadership and the disciplined coordination of their initial military campaign soon deteriorated with the burgeoning of their forces and expansion of their combat operations.

Tensions among the three Darfuri rebel tribes (and sometimes within the same tribes between clans) as well as
personal rivalries among leaders hindered decision-making.
A few of the older rebel commanders had been trained in
military tactics as SAF soldiers, but they were often pushed
aside by more aggressive younger men, many still in their
early twenties, lacking combat experience and leadership
skills. During my tenure as USAID administrator in late
2004, I traveled to North Darfur to urge rebel commanders
to halt the rising incidence of attacks on and looting of
humanitarian aid convoys that brought food aid and other
assistance to the displaced camps (USAID was providing 60
percent of the humanitarian aid through UN agencies and
NGOs at the time). The rebels had been using the looted aid
for combat operations, which was one of many reasons
Khartoum stonewalled aid efforts, which they saw as merely
provisioning the rebellion (either by feeding the IDPs in
camps or through rebel groups looting food aid and the
trucks transporting it). The meeting's organizer was Suleiman Jamous, a man then in his sixties and the only rebel
leader at this meeting of this age group; the rest were between twenty and thirty years old. While Khartoum claimed
that the rebels were thieves and criminals, most recruits
were initially farmers and herders trying to defend their
families and villages against government attacks. Similarly,
Khartoum accused the rebel leadership of seeking support
for the rebellion from abroad. To some degree this was again
from necessity. For example, Abdul Wahid Nur, a Fur lawyer,
had organized his tribe for rebellion in 2001 and signed an
oath pledging to stop the Arab Gathering. After he and his
forces were surrounded by the SAF, Garang dispatched a
plane to rescue him. Had Abdul Wahid been captured, he
would likely have suffered the same fate Daud Yahya Bolad
had in 1991 and been tortured to death.

   After a number of such close calls, Abdul Wahid and his
forces went into exile, moving between Eritrea and Kenya.

After the Abuja conference in April and May 2006, he moved to Paris, where he refused to leave or participate in any peace process. I met him several times in Paris while I was U.S. envoy and found him vehemently opposed to any diplomatic efforts to end the conflict in Darfur unless all of his nonnegotiable demands were acceded to before the negotiations began, while also insisting that only he could lead the negotiations. Fur military commanders in the field who were part of his movement grew impatient with his inept and chaotic leadership and tried to split away and form their own movements. Abdul Wahid dispatched his remaining operatives to assassinate dissenting commanders. The same divide between so-called hotel rebels, such as Abdul Wahid, and their field commanders, who were under fire, lacked food, and lived off what they could loot from aid agencies, was also growing among other rebel factions.

Was Khartoum's counterinsurgency campaign in Darfur ethnic cleansing?

Khartoum's campaign of terror followed a repetitive pattern. Sudanese air force helicopter gunships—often flown by foreign mercenaries, because the SAF did not trust its own pilots to conduct raids—would carpet-bomb a village, bringing destruction and sowing panic, followed shortly thereafter by the arrival of Janjawiid troops on horseback or on trucks with mounted weapons. The Janjawiid would kill any likely recruits for the rebel army and bury them in mass graves, or dump their bodies into the village wells, rendering them unusable. They would rape village women to humiliate their fathers and husbands, who would be forced to watch helplessly at gunpoint. And they would loot anything of value, particularly animal herds, and burn crops on their way out of the village.

Khartoum's strategy indeed amounted to an ethnic cleansing campaign, purging the countryside of the Fur,

Masalit, and Zaghawa populations who were providing the troops and support for the insurrection. When the rebellion spread, Khartoum targeted an additional five smaller African tribes, also because of their sympathy and support for the rebellion: the Dajo, Tunjur, Meidob, Jebel, and Berti. This displaced 1.8 million people, who were driven into sixty-five IDP camps in Darfur, and another 240,000 people into twelve refugee camps in Chad (although some of these individuals were displaced by conflict within Chad itself not directly related to the Darfur rebellions). From 2006 to 2010, the UN regularly reported the number of IDPs in Darfur at 2.7 million. In 2010, after a careful review of the census figures in the camps, the UN revised the figure downward to 1.8 million, having admitted that the figures had been inflated by IDP leaders and that some of the rebel commanders were diverting humanitarian food aid in the camps.

Khartoum's explanation of the IDP camps' size reflects its general response to the entire Darfur catastrophe: either completely denying what happened or claiming that its enemies had invented reports of the atrocities to put it on the defensive. Khartoum claimed most of the people in the camps were not displaced at all, but were simply there to take advantage of free services provided by the UN humanitarian agencies, the Red Cross, and NGOs—free clean water, health care, food aid, and schools for their children, which they could not easily obtain in their own cities. Finally, Khartoum reported that far fewer had died in this third rebellion and that higher Western estimates were grossly exaggerated.

Here we must examine Khartoum's claims. There are three sources of information about the atrocities. First is the Arab television network Al Jazeera, which Khartoum promptly threw out of Sudan after closing its offices. Second are reports from humanitarian aid workers on the scene, though most arrived after the peak of the violence. Khartoum threatened to assassinate UN human rights reporter Gaspar Biro, a Hungarian human rights lawyer and law professor, after his report came out documenting the ethnic cleansing. Finally, there is a report containing more than 1,136 interviews with Darfuri refugees in Chad, conducted by the International Coalition for Justice, a human rights organization associated with the American Bar Association. The interviewers were not NGO or human rights field officers but judges, police detectives, and prosecutors from the U.S. criminal justice system. The report was commissioned by U.S. Secretary of State Colin Powell before he made his genocide finding, and was funded by the State Department and USAID. All of these reports consistently described the same pattern of atrocities against the three rebellious tribes (Fur, Zaghawa, and Masalit): the bombing of the villages; the murder of young men; the widespread and systematic use of rape as a weapon; the looting of livestock; and the burning of the crops.

It is probable that as many as 10–15 percent of the 1.8 million people in the Darfuri displacement camps were not displaced at all, but that is far less than the 90 percent figure posited by Khartoum. Humanitarian organizations made repeated efforts to target only those who were truly displaced, but their efforts caused demonstrations and riots. Aid workers' lives were threatened by those who would lose their benefits in the camps, so the organizations suspended the reduction efforts. Refugee and IDP camps around the world often attract a portion of the local population who are drawn to the free public services, so these developments in Darfur are not unusual. However, it is a small percentage of the population in the camps, not the majority claimed by Khartoum.

So it was ethnic cleansing. Was it also genocide?

The mortality figures remain the most provocative issue surrounding the third rebellion and the subject of ongoing debate. The lowest estimates of deaths come from, unsurprisingly, Khartoum, which claims that 20,000 civilians perished.

The highest estimates of deaths in Darfur come from American advocacy groups—notably the Enough Campaign, the Save Darfur Coalition, and Eric Reeves, an English literature professor from Smith College and advocate. Reeves in his most recent estimates claimed that 544,000 people died—304,000 from violence and 240,000 from the disease, dehydration, and hunger caused by forced displacement in Darfur in what advocates called an "ongoing genocide." He calculated this extraordinarily high figure by extrapolating from the number of original family members reported by Darfuri refugees in Chad, a method not accepted by international public health experts or demographers who are the technical experts in the discipline of mortality rates.

We know from detailed UN reporting (although there are likely some incidents that go unreported, the UN's investigations are thorough) that the deaths peaked from September 2003 and May 2004, subsiding substantially afterward principally because Khartoum's counterinsurgency strategy had been successful in destroying the base of rebel operations in the villages; the humanitarian aid agencies had arrived to provide services to those displaced; and Khartoum may have felt more pressure from the international community as a result of its murderous tactics.

Aid agencies in 2004 indicated that the mortality rates in some displaced camps were between six and nearly ten times higher than normal, thus indicating a "major humanitarian crisis" (which occurs if more than one person per 10,000 people dies per day). These deaths were caused by acute malnutrition and starvation, dehydration, and disease spread among displaced people in ad hoc camps, or camps whose aid delivery system was not yet fully functioning.

To set up this structure, aid organizations sent 1,000 expatriate workers to Darfur, providing food and housing for them, and then hired 12,000 local Sudanese staff to assist them in setting up this structure, a process that would take months. The sharp decline in death rates by late 2004 and early 2005

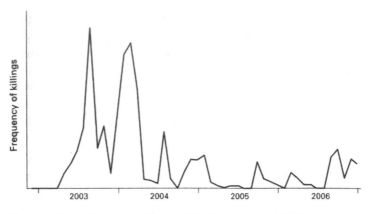

The correlation between time and the frequency of killings in Darfur. (Adapted from Julie Flint and Alex de Waal, *Darfur: A New History of a Long War* [London: Zed Books, 2008])

was largely a result of the aid agencies' success in setting up this infrastructure.

In a lecture he gave at Yale Law School in 2009, Luis Moreno-Ocampo, the chief prosecutor of the International Criminal Court (ICC), claimed that 5,000 people were being killed in Darfur every month, but he produced no evidence to support this statement. The UN security office in Darfur investigates each reported incidence of violence by site visits, and its data do not come even remotely close to 5,000 killings per year, let alone per month. No other international humanitarian casualty reporting system exists, and Moreno-Ocampo has no staff on the ground in Darfur. By 2005, the mortality rates in the IDP camps were lower than those in other peaceful and stable areas of Darfur because of the humanitarian aid being produced the IDPs.

While I served as U.S. envoy to Sudan in 2006 and 2007, I combed through evidence on atrocities and violence against civilians collected by the UN special rapporteur (the title given to the Hungarian human rights lawyer appointed by the UN to investigate reports of atrocities by Khartoum in Darfur), reports by the UN Security Office, a panel of experts appointed by the UN to investigate conditions in Darfur, aid agency and human rights reports, and the U.S. State Department analysis. Toward the end of 2006, civilians began to report (three independent sources with staff on the ground in Darfur reported this) that the Janjawiid told them during attacks that they could loot and burn their villages but were no longer permitted to kill them (probably because Khartoum was bowing to international pressure or had already achieved its political objectives of destroying the base of the rebellion). Alex de Waal and Julie Flint report in their book that by early 2005 Khartoum had adopted a more restrained strategy in dealing with the third rebellion.

The most rigorous and comprehensive retrospective study of Darfur mortality rates (and the closest we will likely ever get to the truth of what happened) was published in January 2010 in the *Lancet*, the most respected British journal of public health, by the Center for Research on the Epidemiology of Disasters at the Université Catholique de Louvain La Neuve, Belgium. The study reported a mid-range average of 298,000 deaths from all causes in Darfur during the entire conflict (2003–2010), with steadily declining death rates from early 2004 to 2008. According to the Louvain study, approximately 80 percent of deaths were caused by disease and malnutrition due to the forced displacement of the population, meaning that 20 percent of the deaths were attributable to violence, mostly committed in early 2004. This would have meant that about 60,000 people were actually killed in the conflict (Arabs and Africans).

The declining death rates noted in the *Lancet* study had been earlier confirmed by the UN. On April 27, 2009, Rodolphe Adada, the joint AU-UN representative for Darfur, stated at a UN meeting in New York that "Darfur today is a conflict of all against all." He reported that from January 1, 2008, until March 31, 2009, there had been some 2,000 fatalities from violence. Approximately one-third of them were civilian. During intertribal fighting, 573 combatants had died and another 569 people had been killed. This amounted to roughly 133 deaths per month for the period covered. These figures were obviously far lower than those made by advocacy groups, which themselves had been under heavy criticism by scholars for exaggerating death rates. In early 2009 John Prendergast, the founder of the Enough Campaign and one of the sources of these original claims, debated Mahmoud Mandani, Africa scholar and critic of such estimates, at Columbia University. Prendergast admitted in the debate that "most of these figures are wild estimates. They are simply crazily wild estimates."

But was it "genocide"? The somewhat promiscuous use of the word by advocacy groups to describe the third rebellion after 2004 misled many observers with regard to the details, causes, and timing of the conflict. Genocide may be defined as the "intentional murder of part or all of a particular ethnic, religious, or national group," but required evidence of intent.

In the 1980s before the Bashir coup, a few members of the Arab Gathering publicly advocated the "extermination" of the African tribes across North Africa in newspaper advertisements, but this does not prove genocidal intent by Khartoum twenty years later. Some sympathizers with the Arab Gathering do hold positions in the NCP hierarchy, but we do not have evidence that the extermination of the African tribes was either official government policy or their actual intention.

More accurately, Khartoum's strategy in Darfur amounted to the ethnic cleansing of the three rebellious tribes from their villages, as part of an unlimited and unconstrained counterinsurgency campaign whose purpose was to deprive the rebels of a base of supply and operations. Ethnic cleansing "can be understood as the explusion of a population from a given territory." Alex de Waal has called the strategy a "counterinsurgency campaign on the cheap." Even Prendergast, in the same 2009 Columbia University debate with Mahmoud Mandani, backpedaled on his characterization of the Darfur conflict as "genocide" when he stated that he wouldn't "fall on my sword" over the use of the term. President Obama, in a public statement on Darfur in 2009, used the term "geno-cide" to describe the event but referred to it in the past tense.

I myself used the term sparingly in my congressional testi-mony and public statements, though it was then a finding of the Bush administration, and as a representative of the president, it was my job to reflect administration policy. Had I presented the foregoing analysis at that time, it would have created a firestorm from the advocacy groups. At one U.S. Senate hearing in early 2007, Senator Robert Menendez (D-New Jersey) and I had a tense exchange over Darfur in which he demanded six times that I corroborate his assertion that genocide was ongoing when, in fact, it wasn't.

The atrocities committed by the Sudanese government and their allies, the Janjawiid militia, against the poor villagers of rural Darfur were real and horrific. Advocacy groups could have made their arguments and calls to action without distorting what was already bad enough. They chose instead to mischarac-terize the situation in order to keep their followers motivated, a strategy that strengthened Khartoum's case that the West did not understand what was happening in Darfur and made it much more difficult to find a diplomatic solution to the crisis because it became politically impossible to offer diplomatic carrots to the Sudanese government to end the tragedy and encouraged rebel intransigence in the diplomatic negotiations.

Could anything have been done to stop the atrocities during the third rebellion?

In 2006 and 2007, advocacy groups used full-page newspaper ads in the United States and Europe, mass emails, blogs, and public statements to accuse the international community and the Bush administration of standing by while the Sudanese government exterminated the Darfuri tribes in rebellion. Newspaper columnists such as Nicholas Kristof attacked the Bush administration, saying that no one appeared to care in the U.S. government about the Darfuri victims.

The international response to Darfur took three separate routes—humanitarian, diplomatic, and military peacekeeping operations—that were only tangentially connected to each other yet affected each other in profound ways. The humanitarian track mobilized first because it is the least dependent on support from the combatants, of the three responses enjoyed the greatest level of support in the UN Security Council, and was the least threatening to Khartoum.

Roger Winter, former director of the U.S. Committee for Refugees and then assistant administrator of USAID in charge of the humanitarian bureau, took early action to respond to the humanitarian crisis. In August 2003, USAID allocated $40 million to care for IDPs in Darfur through UNICEF, which dispatched its emergency aid workers to Darfur, to be followed later by the World Food Program. Numerous NGOs deployed staff at this time as well. As the attacks and displacement spread, Winter and I held a meeting with career staff in my USAID office in early March 2004 and arrived at three decisions—first to contract with a commercial satellite company to photograph villages in Darfur before and after Janjawiid attacks to show the devastation. When the photos did not appear to have sufficient resolution to convince skeptical officials at the UN Secretariat and members of the Security Council (I presented the photographs to them myself in June 2004), President Bush approved the use of National Geospatial-Agency Intelligence satellites to photograph the villages. We released the photographs at a UN Darfur-aid-pledging conference in Geneva in July 2004 and also provided them to the UN Security Council Permanent Five members (United States, United Kingdom, France, China, and Russia). Second, we decided to ramp up the size and scale of the USAID aid program on the ground and dispatch a Disaster Assistance Response Team with technical staff to manage the U.S. government's effort. Third, we decided to commission a report to be produced by the USAID career public health and agricultural and food security staff on anticipated death rates in Darfur, should the

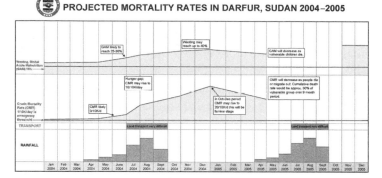

PROJECTED MORTALITY RATES IN DARFUR, SUDAN 2004–2005

USAID study of projected mortality rates in Darfur. (USAID/OFDA)

humanitarian aid effort fail or be delayed (which was released at the same UN Darfur aid conference).

Roger Winter took a field trip to Darfur in March 2004 to gather information on what was happening, and when he returned testified before Congress on March 11, providing powerful evidence of the atrocities being committed by the Sudanese government. In the same month, a National Security Council meeting was held in the White House at which the U.S. State Department and President Bush's staff decided to propose a UN Security Council resolution condemning the atrocities and calling for a no-fly zone to constrain the Sudanese air force bombing attacks on Darfuri villages (which several Security Council members insisted be deleted from the resolution). Secretary of State Colin Powell commissioned the field report described earlier to document the atrocities, and then with White House support testified before Congress on September 9, 2004, and later to the United Nations, that genocide was occurring in Darfur.

President Bush—who had called President Bashir on a total of eleven occasions to press him to support the North–South peace negotiations—again called Bashir in March 2004 to insist that he stop the attacks against civilians in Darfur, which he told him were completely unacceptable. Bush told me that although Bashir had listened to his arguments on the North–South negotiations and on the compromises needed to finalize the CPA, he stonewalled him on Darfur. Some U.S. diplomats feared that if the United States took too aggressive a set of actions against Khartoum to get it to stop the atrocities in Darfur, it would compromise the North–South peace process. Even more serious was that any U.S. military action would endanger the entire humanitarian aid effort, which Alex de Waal has argued ultimately saved hundreds of thousands of lives. The U.S. NGOs themselves feared military action, and in early 2007 in a letter to the Save Darfur coalition. Sam Worthington, president of the U.S. NGO consortium InterAction, threatened publicly to criticize Darfur advocacy groups if they did not stop demanding military action. Save Darfur toned down its full-page ads demanding action, giving the NGO community virtual veto power on their content.

Some of us even tried to confront the leader of the Janjawiid. In late 2006, I asked the U.S. embassy in Khartoum to arrange for me to meet Sheikh Moussa Hillal privately (it would have created a firestorm among the advocacy groups and the news media had it become public) at an AU military base in Darfur. We talked for two hours, and at the end I told him the purpose of our meeting was to warn him against any further killing of innocent civilians. He replied that had he known I would threaten him he would not have come to the meeting. As he left, an AU military commander told me that two truckloads of heavily armed Janjawiid were stationed outside our building, as Hillal was afraid the real purpose of the meeting was to arrest him for war crimes.

It was not just the United States and other Western governments that acted on the tragedy in Darfur. Both the AU, led by Alpha Konare, former president of Mali, and the UN, led until the end of 2007 by Secretary General Kofi Annan and afterward by his successor Ban Ki-moon, took action to address the crisis. The AU supported the U.S. government's

effort to negotiate the April 2004 N'Djamena (Chad) Humanitarian Ceasefire Agreement, which created a structure for
providing humanitarian assistance, a ceasefire, and AU peacekeeping troops. The ceasefire broke down quickly: rebel
groups used the break in violence to initiate new combat
operations, and Khartoum responded by resuming its
bombing campaigns. The Darfur humanitarian protocols
remain in place to this day, though often violated by
combatants.

The AU and later AU/UN (in their first joint operation)
peacekeeping operations did provide an international military
presence in Darfur, though they were unable to protect noncom-
batants or aid workers from attacks by rebel groups looting
food aid and stealing trucks. The UN Undersecretary General
for Peacekeeping Operations, Jean-Marie Guehenno, argued
that sending in a peacekeeping force to Darfur was unwise
given there was no peace agreement to enforce, and thus would
be ineffective. Much of the international diplomacy in 2007 (and
much of my own efforts as President Bush's Envoy to Sudan)
focused on forcing Khartoum to accept the UN/AU peacekeeping forces: in late 2006, Bashir had declared publicly: "Blue
Helmets (UN PKO troops) will never step foot in Darfur." That
they eventually did was due to the persistent diplomacy of Ban
Ki-moon, the AU, and the Western democracies. President Bush
asked President Hu Jintao of China to press Bashir to accept the
UN peacekeeping troops, and he did so (and I believe this may
have been the decisive factor in changing Bashir's mind).

The *Lancet* mortality study quoted earlier, juxtaposed
against the broad history of humanitarian crises, does suggest
that international intervention has been more successful in
saving lives—though not in bringing peace—than has been
appreciated outside Sudan. As the intervention scaled up on
all fronts—diplomatic, peacekeeping, and humanitarian—
death rates declined. This should not be surprising since,
according to the *Lancet* study, 80 percent of the deaths in
Darfur were caused by disease and malnutrition; most deaths

from violence had occurred in 2004, before the AU and UN peacekeeping operations had been implemented.

The real failure was in how long it took for outside help to arrive in Darfur. The delays were a function of three factors: the complexity of the international system in which many countries that had to be consulted and convinced to undertake the effort; the logistical difficulty of moving aid workers and troops to one of the most remote places in the history of humanitarian intervention; and Khartoum's resistance of the entire project every step of the way, using every bureaucratic impediment at its disposal.

Why was Omar al-Bashir indicted by the ICC, and what was the consequence of the indictment?

In July 2008, the aforementioned Luis Moreno-Ocampo, as chief prosecutor of the ICC, issued an order for the arrest of Bashir for crimes against humanity. On March 3, 2009, the ICC affirmed the order, and in July 2010, ICC jurists added an indictment for genocide.

Within days of the announcement, Bashir ordered the expulsion of thirteen U.S., British, and French NGOs on the grounds that they had been providing information to the ICC. Unlike most war crime indictments, which are usually served against former heads of state or public officials, this ICC warrant was issued against a sitting head of state who controlled an army and a ruthless security force and had a growing number of internal and external allies. Bashir had the means of reprisal at his disposal, and he was swift to use them.

The arrest warrant virtually eliminated the chances for free and fair multiparty elections required under the CPA; Bashir decided to orchestrate his own reelection in order to ensure that he would never be arrested. (Bashir had privately told other Arab leaders before the ICC action in 2006 that he was considering not running for reelection to the presidency.) Advocates of the ICC decision believed that it would pressure

Bashir and his government to improve their behavior, but there is no evidence that it did.

The ICC warrant also gave Darfuri rebels no incentive to pursue peace negotiations, and have encouraged them to avoid serious negotiation. The louder the demands for war crimes trials made by international advocacy groups, the media, and foreign politicians, the longer the list of nonnegotiable demands made by the rebels, and thus the more remote the possibility of any political agreement, which carried the only real hope that refugees and displaced people could return to their homes and villages. The traditional form of reparation for murder in Darfur has been blood money, paid by the perpetrator to the victim's family. Before the ICC's intervention, some Darfuri rebel leaders argued that blood money should be the basis for a peace agreement. Khartoum had told UN envoy Jan Eliasson privately that it would be willing to spend $300 to $400 million in "reconstruction" money in Darfur as part of any peace agreement, though the Sudanese government insisted that it not be called either "reparations" or "blood money" (this would have been an admission of guilt).

After the ICC indictments, rebel demands escalated to levels that Khartoum—no matter who was in power—would never accept. Abdul Wahid Nur demanded $10,000 be paid to every displaced Darfuri. Khalil Ibrahim, not to be outdone, insisted on double what Abdul Wahid had demanded: 15,000 euros (slightly more than $20,000 at the time) for every IDP, and, in addition, 20 billion euros to rebuild Darfuri villages.

The ICC arrest warrant actually undermined the ICC itself. The Arab League and AU both condemned the indictment and refused to cooperate in its implementation. Twenty African countries—original ICC signatories—announced later in 2008 that they were considering a withdrawal from the ICC treaty over the Bashir indictment. Prior to the indictments, Bashir and his government had been isolated among Arab and African governments; afterward, they embraced him and rallied to protect the Sudanese government.

It was unclear from my conversations with exiled political leaders in Darfur after indictments against lower-level Sudanese officials issued in late 2007 just who would comply with these demands. Sudan's leaders were not going to arrest themselves, and the international community had neither the political leverage nor the combat troops to do the job. The internally displaced people and their leaders said they welcomed the ICC's decision against Sudan's leaders. But for justice to be served, they insisted to me, the tens of thousands of Janjawiid who had committed the atrocities must also be arrested and prosecuted, which was completely impractical.

Advocacy groups such as the Enough Campaign argued that the ICC indictment of Bashir could be used as a diplomatic chit to get Khartoum to negotiate peace in Darfur and implement the CPA. However, the ICC protocol is based on the Napoleonic Legal Code, which does not allow for the kind of plea bargaining proposed by these advocacy groups. Under Article 16 of the protocol, a UN Security Council vote (which would be difficult to obtain under any circumstances, let alone each year) can postpone prosecution for one year, continuously, but it cannot erase an indictment. The ICC action holds out little promise of bringing either peace or justice to Sudan.

9

THE COMPREHENSIVE PEACE AGREEMENT

Why did Khartoum negotiate an end to the Second Civil War?

The third Darfur rebellion devolved into a disastrous conflagration while the most sustained effort to resolve the North–South war since Sadiq al-Mahdi's overthrow was under way. As we've seen, these wars were interrelated: the rebel movements expressed the same grievances, demanded similar reforms, and suffered the same atrocities from Khartoum and its allies as did the SPLM. Later in the peace process, the Darfuri rebels had pressed to be allowed to join the negotiations. John Garang welcomed the Darfuri rebels into the process, as long as they would agree to unite with the SPLM and be part of a single negotiating team. While the leaders of the rebellion in the Nuba Mountains and Blue Nile had formally joined Garang's movement early in the war as commanders of the SPLA, the rebels refused and wished to keep their independence. The Darfuri rebels refused Garang's offer and insisted on taking an independent negotiating position. From his past experience, Garang knew that lasting peace could not be achieved without a united front, because the North would manipulate one rebel faction against another.

Khartoum had agreed to begin serious peace negotiations with Garang as early as 2002. Beginning in 1998, its military position had been deteriorating across the South, and prospects grew even dimmer after 2001, when Garang and Riak Machar resolved their differences—thus reuniting the two largest southern warrior tribes in the SPLA—in response to heavy pressure from the Bush administration. The quarrel between Garang and Machar, which started in 1991, had renewed the North's hopes for a military solution to the war. The war was costing the North half of its oil revenues (and even more, given the revenue forfeited as a result of the inaccessibility of new oil fields due to Garang's attacks). Khartoum realized that an end to the war would bring economic relief to the North.

The theme stressed repeatedly by NCP leaders in public and private after the signing of the CPA was that of "making unity attractive"—a phrase they insisted be integrated into the text of the peace agreement itself. Northern and southern leaders believed the other was responsible for making unity attractive and thus not a fundamental part of their own responsibility. This perception meant neither side took ownership of the task. Bashir constantly repeated to me it was the western donors' responsibility to make unity attractive, not his duty. Additionally the North believed that with Garang's leadership the southerners could be convinced to end the war and remain part of Sudan with some negotiable degree of independence. As the 2011 secession vote came closer and closer and southern opinion unified behind independence, this miscalculation became undeniable. Bashir and his party did not understand how to make unity attractive, nor did they accept this as their responsibility. Nor could they bring themselves to undertake the necessary reform of their political and economic system. Khartoum did fund some development projects in the South to make unity attractive but did not realize that was not what the southerners wanted the most. They wished to be treated with respect, as equals, and to fully participate in the political life of the country. Instead, Khartoum saw the southerners as another group to be manipulated and bought off. Juba's leaders suspected that the North viewed southern autonomy in much the same condescending way President Numayri had—as superficial and easily superseded. Khartoum never understood—and this was to be its greatest miscalculation—how reviled the Northern Nile River Arab elites and their Islamic agenda were by the southern people.

The NCP willingness to negotiate peace may have also been related to its quarrel with Turabi, a quarrel that had split the northern Islamist movement into two factions. Just as Numayri had turned to the South for allies after he had alienated northern political parties, perhaps Bashir thought he could turn to the South for an alliance following his break from Turabi. (Indeed, in January 2011 with southern independence looming, Bashir started reaching out to the South after the northern Islamists seemed to have abandoned him because of southern secession.)

Many have argued that the NCP initially negotiated with the South in 2002 as a delaying tactic—it was waiting until the increased oil revenue gave it the means to supply the weakened SAF with more modern weapons. Garang understood that the oil revenues flowing to the North would strengthen the NCP. He had his own reasons to negotiate a political settlement at this particular moment.

Khartoum most feared U.S. military action, a fear that surfaced repeatedly in conversations I had with NCP leadership, during which the bombing of the pharmaceutical plant in Khartoum by the Clinton administration arose over and over again. The U.S. military campaigns in Afghanistan from 2001 and Iraq from 2003 frightened Khartoum—it feared that Sudan might be next—into considering making a serious effort toward peace negotiations. Yet the Sudan peace process began well before Iraq, and some of the warming of relations occurred even before 9/11. The NCP knew that the U.S. domestic alliance supporting the South had broadened beyond its core supporters in the U.S. Congress, and that this could cause serious trouble for Khartoum. Relations between the United States and Sudan would never improve without an end to the Second Civil War as well as an end to the North's support for violent Islamist groups. The expulsion of bin Laden from Sudan in 1996 and then of Turabi from the ruling party in 1999 addressed this second issue, and would later facilitate cooperation between the United States and Khartoum on counter-terrorism issues, yet the Second Civil War remained a major roadblock.

Why did the Bush administration decide to focus on ending the Second Civil War in Sudan?

As George W. Bush began his campaign for the presidency in 1999, he assembled a team of senior foreign policy experts that included Condoleezza Rice, then provost of Stanford University. After his election, she urged him to make Africa a foreign-policy priority, increasing foreign aid and using American influence to end the six ongoing civil wars on the continent, the most deadly of which was Sudan. When Colin Powell became secretary of state, he also urged the new president to focus on Africa, and made it his first foreign trip. In their first meeting, Walter Kansteiner—the new Bush administration assistant secretary of state for Africa—and Colin Powell agreed that a less confrontational approach was needed to address Sudan's problems and help resolve the North–South conflict. Thus, from the beginning of his administration, Bush, Rice, and Powell—the latter two of whom are African Americans with a deep personal commitment to Africa—all believed that a new approach to Sudan was needed. Just after President Bush took office in January 2001, he met in the Oval Office with Franklin Graham, president of the evangelical NGO Samaritan's Purse with programs in Southern Sudan, and son of Billy Graham. Graham urged Bush to initiate a peace process in Sudan. The support of conservative evangelical Christians, the Catholic Church, black American churches, and mainline Protestant churches—

particularly Presbyterian and Episcopal—would also later play a role, but was not the only factor in the decision by President Bush to act.

In June 2001, Colin Powell and I announced at a press conference in Nairobi that the U.S. government had rescinded an earlier policy that prohibited emergency humanitarian assistance to the North (with the exception of southern Sudanese IDPs around Khartoum). Henceforth, provision of emergency assistance would be based on need alone. The following month, I reached an agreement with the Sudanese foreign minister, Mustafa Osman Ismail, to send a shipment of humanitarian assistance across conflict lines in the Nuba Mountains, where an SPLA-led insurgency commanded by Abdul Azziz al Hilu was under way, caused by Arab land grabs and a Khartoum-led ethnic cleansing campaign against the Nuba tribes.

After this initial aid delivery proved successful, USAID and the State Department drafted a proposal for a humanitarian ceasefire in the Nuba Mountains. It was to have been delivered to the Sudanese embassy in Washington on September 11, 2001, by Roger Winter of USAID. Circumstances required that it be made by telephone instead.

Five days before September 11, President Bush announced the appointment of former U.S. Senator Jack Danforth (R-Missouri) as envoy to Sudan. Danforth's stature (he had been a finalist for the vice president nomination at the 2000 Republican Convention) suggested that the Bush administration was taking the peace process in Sudan seriously. In October, Danforth's staff, the State Department, and USAID developed four tests to determine whether or not Khartoum was serious about peace: would Khartoum (1) allow humanitarian access to the Nuba Mountains; (2) agree to a temporary suspension of fighting through what were called zones and days of tranquility; (3) end the practice of selling prisoners of war into slavery; and (4) stop the bombing of civilians. These criteria represented a minimum set of requirements. Were Khartoum not serious about these basic issues, it was unlikely to address more complex political and diplomatic issues.

But Danforth needed Western allies to cooperate with him on Sudan. The White House and State Department decided to pursue (as the Clinton administration had in its last year in office) a diplomatic partnership to bring peace to Sudan with Norway and Great Britain (later called the Troika), both of which had a longer history of diplomatic and humanitarian work in Sudan than any other European government (and of course colonial presence, in the case of the UK). For more than a decade, the Intergovernmental Authority on Drought and Development (IGAD)—the East African regional organization composed of Djibouti, Somalia, Ethiopia, Eritrea, Kenya, Sudan, and Uganda—had been unsuccessful in getting a peace agreement, but it had produced a "Statement of Principles" in 1994. The statement, which called for self-determination in the South, democracy, and a secular state in Sudan, was endorsed by the two major rebel movements in southern Sudan—led by Garang and Machar—but not, unsurprisingly, by Khartoum. The Statement of Principles became the philosophical position of the IGAD states and IGAD's organizational structure, as well as the basis for North–South peace negotiations in 2002. The chief mediator in the negotiations was Lazarus Sambeyo, a retired Kenyan general, who was close to President Daniel arap Moi, and whose considerable diplomatic skills proved critical in mediating the negotiations.

Over the course of the next three years (2002–2004), a long and involved peace process would unfold, led by Ali Osman Taha for the North and Garang for the South. The process was supported bilaterally by the Western Troika and the IGAD member states. On July 20, 2002, the two sides announced the Machakos Protocol, which described the broad principles of the peace agreement and was a turning point in the negotiations. It was a seminal moment in the peace process.

At a critical point during the talks, Colin Powell promised Khartoum that if it implemented the Comprehensive Peace

Agreement, as it was now being called, the U.S. government would reciprocate by taking Sudan off the list of countries accused of sponsoring terrorist groups (dating from when Osama bin Laden and others ran their operations there), establishing full diplomatic recognition (rather than the lower level of official presence, which had signaled Washington's disapproval), and removing economic sanctions on U.S. businesses working there (imposed by both Clinton and Bush). This was to be the first of three such offers the U.S. government extended to Khartoum (the U.S. government also made the same offer to Khartoum if it signed the Darfur Peace Agreement negotiated at the Abuja peace talks in 2006 and in late 2010 if Khartoum allowed the referendum on southern independence to take place without incident). However, because of the atrocities committed by Khartoum in Darfur and later in 2011 in the Nuba Mountains in South Kordofan, U.S. policy makers found it politically untenable to begin any improvement of relations with Khartoum or the rescinding of any sanctions.

As I reported earlier, President Bush made twelve telephone calls to Bashir during the negotiations to press him when they became deadlocked. The week before Bashir was to leave for Nairobi to sign the CPA in January 2005, President Bush called Bashir three times to press him to leave for Nairobi when it appeared that hard-line pressure in Khartoum was turning Bashir against the agreement. Each time Bush called Bashir, he also called John Garang on the same day to review progress in the negotiations so as to ensure equal treatment of both sides.

Who is Ali Osman Taha?

Born in 1944, Ali Osman Mohammed Taha came from the Shaiqiyya Tribe—one of the Three Tribes—and from a humble background; his father was a zookeeper. He received a law degree, taught law at the University of Khartoum Law School, set up a private practice, and eventually served as a judge in the Sudanese court system. Following his entrance into politics in the 1980s, he was elected as a member of the Sudanese Parliament as an acolyte of Turabi and joined the Bashir government right after the 1989 coup against Sadiq. As a skilled organizer, Taha rose rapidly in the ranks because of his intellect and organizational abilities and cultivated a large and devoted following within the ruling ranks of Turabi's NIF and later of the NCP. Taha's first cabinet position was as minister of social planning/welfare and social development, a position he held from January 1993 to September 1995; he then served as minister of foreign affairs until February 1998. From 1998 until 2005, he was vice president of Sudan, and he served as the top official in charge of handling the Darfur crisis from 2003 to 2005. In August 2005, he was appointed the second vice president of the new interim Government of National Unity (GNU; Garang served as first), as required under the CPA. As second vice president, Taha handled the organization of the secession referendum in southern Sudan. Still serving in 2011 as second vice president, Taha heads the Sudanese side of the important Sudanese-Egyptian High Committee, which has negotiated several critically important agreements on employment, immigration, and citizenship between the two countries.

The international community has long seen Taha as the leader of the less "radical" wing of the NCP. With John Garang he negotiated the CPA, perhaps the most transformational document in modern Sudanese history. Western diplomats and UN officials have found him easier to deal with than other members of the Khartoum government, which shows how this former Turabi acolyte has shrewdly transformed himself into a mainstream politician.

The seemingly genuine and warm relationship he developed with Garang apparently changed Taha's hard-line Turabist worldview. He has often said that he believes in constructive engagement between the Sudan and the West, while his principal adversary within the NCP, Nafie ali Nafie, believes the West is interested only in forcing Khartoum into making destabilizing and self-destructive concessions. Taha is the sole northern Arab politician who has (marginally) favorable ratings in surveys done among southerners. Taha is an ambitious politician who has tried to position himself to succeed Omar al-Bashir and has been involved in several power struggles with him, all of which he lost to Bashir; these quarrels have reduced Taha's political influence within the government.

What were the major provisions of the CPA?

The CPA provided for the establishment of the autonomous GOSS in Juba and the interim GNU in Khartoum, both of which would have ministerial posts reserved for appointees from each side's ruling parties, the NCP and SPLM. National multiparty elections were required by 2009 (they were actually held in April 2010), and by January 2011 the South would vote in a referendum as to whether to secede. Under the CPA, Sharia law applied only to Muslims. English, rather than Arabic, was to be the official language of the South and used in its school system. Half of all oil revenues from the southern oil fields—which made up more than 75 percent of the known oil reserves of the entire country—would be distributed to the GOSS treasury each month. (Between 2005 and 2010, $7 billion was transferred to the southern treasury by the North.)

All SAF troops would withdraw from the South and all SPLA troops from the North. Joint SAF/SPLA units called Joint Integrated Units (JIUs) would be stationed across the South, Abyei, the Blue Nile region, and the Nuba Mountains. The South would be allowed to maintain the SPLA as an independent army, and the GOSS would be allowed to receive international assistance to transform it from a rebel militia into a conventional force.

The CPA provided for special arrangements for three disputed areas located along the border between the North and the South: Abyei, Blue Nile State, and the Nuba Mountains in southern Kordofan State, all located (though the status of Abyei could change) in the North yet controlled mainly by the SPLA. Because of competing claims by powerful tribes, Abyei is the powder keg of Sudan—the Kashmir of the North–South conflict. The Ngok Dinka claim Abyei as their ancestral home and seat for centuries of their paramount chiefs. The Dinka were driven from Abyei in the 1980s by Misiriyya Arabs who were recruited by Sadiq al-Mahdi and claimed the land as their traditional cattle-grazing region. Tens of thousands of Dinka civilians were killed during these militia attacks. To further complicate the status of Abyei, the region is floating on a sea of oil that offers some of the largest reserves and best quality deposits in Sudan (though oil engineers now believe these oil fields will be exhausted by 2019).

The Ngok Dinka demanded the return of their homeland to the South, and the Misiriyya Arabs threatened war if that happened. More than any other issue between the North and South, the dispute over Abyei represented the greatest threat to the peace negotiations. The U.S. government intervened through special envoy Jack Danforth with a proposal that provided for the eventual creation of a commission (the Abyei Border Commission [ABC]) that would find the exact border in the region based on historical records from the Condominium period); it also called for a referendum—on the same ballot as the vote on southern secession—that would determine whether Abyei would become a permanent part of the North or the South. (The ABC, which included the preeminent scholar Douglas Johnson, conducted research and found that Abyei traditionally was considered part of the South, a finding that was rejected by Bashir as beyond the scope of its authority.)

In the Nuba Mountains and Blue Nile State, "popular consultations" were also to be held at a later date on the future governance of the states (although, as of June 2011, Khartoum abandoned Nuba Mountain and Blue Nile political processes and chose to use force, sending in the SAF to disarm the SPLA armies in the North and impose central control combined with a massive bombing campaign targeted against civilians). Many Sudan analysts fear that if a North–South war does resume in Sudan, it will be ignited in Blue Nile State, the Nuba Mountains, or Abyei—the three areas with ambiguous status and populations that are aggressively hostile to Khartoum.

Garang insisted on several nonnegotiable provisions before he would sign the CPA. First was the SPLA's continued existence as an independent fighting force and the provision of international assistance for its modernization. Second was the eventual referendum on southern independence. And third was the sharing of oil revenues. These three provisions, he believed, would determine whether the South would have sufficient political strength and resources to protect itself from northern pressure and to force the implementation of the CPA.

How did John Garang die, and was his death an accident?

On July 30, 2005, six months after the CPA was signed in Nairobi and three weeks after Garang was sworn in as the new first vice president of the GNU, a helicopter taking him from Uganda to southern Sudan crashed, killing everyone on board. Ugandan president Yoweri Museveni had been meeting with Garang and had provided his presidential helicopter to transport him back to Juba; it got caught in a storm at night and crashed into the side of a mountain. Museveni was Garang's closest friend and ally among sub-Sahara African heads of state. The Ugandan government had provided weapons and funding to the SPLA during the war, and 11,000 of Uganda's soldiers had fought alongside the SPLA in Equatoria Province against the North in the early 1990s, so Museveni's loyalty to Garang and to the southern Sudanese cause could not be questioned.

When the announcement of Garang's death was made public, southern Sudanese—convinced that the Bashir government had assassinated their leader and passed it off as an accident—rioted in both Juba and Khartoum. In all, 130 people were killed in the riots, which continued unchecked for three days. Sudanese intelligence had tried to assassinate Garang several times during the twenty-two-year civil war, so the suspicion was not unwarranted. Rebecca Garang, widow of the dead leader, broadcast a statement that her husband's death was an accident. Only then did the violence stop. For his part, President Museveni suggested that outside influence may have been responsible for the crash, which fueled more conspiracy theories. Other rumors spread of a conspiracy among Garang's enemies in the South to kill him. Many southerners believe to this day that Khartoum's security services orchestrated the crash.

A team of international investigators—including one from the U.S. government—spent months investigating the incident. They found no evidence of an attack on the helicopter or any tampering with its guidance system, concluding that the accident was caused by pilot error. As U.S. special envoy, I requested a detailed briefing from the Federal Aviation Commission inspector who had been assigned to the team of experts, a man with twenty-eight years of experience investigating aircraft crashes. He told me that there was no evidence of foul play and that the evidence produced by the investigation demonstrated pilot error.

As head of the U.S. delegation, I attended Garang's funeral in Juba in early August 2005. Rebecca Garang told the assembly (including President Bashir; Amr Moussa, the secretary-general of the Arab League; and heads of state from Ethiopia, South Africa, Kenya, and Tanzania among others) in attendance that she would not mourn her husband's death because he lived on in the CPA. Were the provisions of the agreement violated in the future, however, his legacy would die, and she would then mourn his death. The Anglican archbishop of Juba called Garang "our Moses," who led his people to the promised land of peace. Bashir promised to carry out the provisions of the CPA just as Garang had negotiated them.

What is Garang's legacy?

More than any other individual, Garang created a new South. He began and led the southern movement in the Second Civil War for twenty-two years, created a political movement that gave purpose to the war and the terrible suffering it caused, and created a sense of identity. He navigated the South's course through a peace process that ended with a political settlement that achieved virtually all of his ambitions, except that of a unified, secular, and inclusive Sudanese state. It is too soon to know whether the new northern state will evolve into an open society or fall into chaos. No single Sudanese leader since independence has had a more profound influence on Sudan than Garang, who rose from Dinka rebel commander to national leader. His legacy has its downside: he was autocratic, concentrated power his own hands, ruthlessly eliminated his southern rivals for power, and, with his Nuer rival, Riak Machar, was responsible for some of the most terrible bloodshed. More recently, some have argued in retrospect that without his autocratic leadership the South would have lost the Second Civil War, and no peace agreement would have been negotiated.

Garang's death dramatically altered the landscape of Sudanese politics. He was the strongest advocates of a united Sudan in part because he believed he was destined for the presidency, where he could have transformed all of Sudanese society.

After Garang's death, the SPLM leadership council met and quickly chose Lieutenant General Salva Kiir Mayardit, deputy commander of the SPLA during the war, as his successor. Kiir, however, did not share Garang's ambition for a united Sudan; like the overwhelming majority of his compatriots in the South, he wanted to be rid of Islamists and the northern state. Garang's greatest legacies are a transformed South, however incomplete, with oil revenues pouring into its treasury; a peace agreement that led to independence; and a large army capable of acting as a deterrent to northern aggression.

Ironically, Garang's death removed the one major impediment to the South's independence. Had Khartoum's security services orchestrated the accident, they would have also have been ensuring the secession of the South. The only faction of the SPLM left supporting unity consisted of northerners, particularly in the Nuba Mountains and Blue Nile State, which remained part of the North, who feared they would be isolated and attacked by Khartoum if the South seceded (which indeed they later were).

How did Garang's successor, Salva Kiir, change the direction of southern Sudan?

Salva Kiir Mayardit comes from a Dinka family in Bahr Ghazal State, where he was born in 1951. He joined the Sudanese army after completing high school and rose to the rank of major, fought in the First Civil War, and was among the first wave of southerners to join Garang's forces in 1983, rising to operational commander of the SPLA under Garang. By temperament and style, Kiir was unlike Garang. He never had a formal college education (though he did well in officer training school). A devout Catholic, he urges his cabinet ministers to attend church (of whatever denomination) and often preaches in his home church.

Kiir is famous for his prodigious memory. I once met with him in Khartoum in 2006 and asked him to comment on a list of ten items I had read out to him. With no briefing papers or taking notes, he methodically went through and commented on each item from memory in the exact order in which I had

Salva Kiir, first President of the Republic of South Sudan.

mentioned them to him. Garang once challenged Kiir to a contest during a commander's conference as to which of them could remember the full names (everyone from the southern part of the country has three names) of the sixty individual commanders as they shook hands with them. Kiir was able to remember each one flawlessly, while Garang could not and conceded the contest to Kiir. On his return to Juba from the UN Security Council meeting in New York in October 2010 he gave on the spot a speech in Arabic that was written in English.

On Garang's death, Kiir was immediately cast into the role of the new president and at the beginning was uncomfortable with being in the spotlight. Kiir had the personal loyalty of the SPLA commanders. Over time, Kiir gradually asserted himself through appointments and policy decisions. He may not have the charisma of Garang, but he is a conciliatory and unifying leader, has a gift for reading people, solid political judgment, and an ability to balance competing interests and tribal loyalties. Yet Kiir has also tolerated a high level of official corruption, which has undermined public and international support for the new government and damaged its ability to provide public services.

How smooth was the CPA's implementation?

From the start, the CPA faced steep challenges. The two men—Garang and Taha—who negotiated its terms did not end up overseeing its implementation. Seven months after he signed the agreement at a ceremony in Nairobi, Kenya, Garang was dead. Vice President Taha, after he concluded the negotiations, quarreled with Khartoum's ruling NCP and left for exile in Istanbul. Hard-liners in the NCP, particularly leaders of the security services, believed that Taha had compromised the North's vital interests. Only Bashir's support saved the CPA. Opposition was not limited to Khartoum; Kiir himself had led a revolt of SPLA commanders in 2004 to try to remove Garang as commander of the SPLM, believing that he had left them out of the negotiating process (as indeed he had). Once Kiir and other commanders saw what was in the CPA, however, they rallied to support it and Garang.

The 125-page document that is the CPA includes a large set of detailed provisions that would have been a challenge for a well-run and well-organized government to implement. Unfortunately, the governments in Khartoum and Juba were neither. The only truly competent Khartoum bureaucracy was the security services (competent in their brutality), which opposed the CPA; the South had no insti-tutions yet in place to support its implementation. The southerners and international supporters of the CPA often attributed the North's failure to implement key provisions of the agreement—on what was admittedly a very challeng-ing time schedule—on bad faith. While some of these sus-picions were indeed well founded—the NCP felt threatened by the transformational provisions of the CPA and refused to implement them—some of the failures were merely the result of poor management and incompetence. Salva Kiir once told me that Khartoum implemented all of the CPA's easy provisions while constantly reopening negotiations on those it feared would alienate hard-line Islamist and Arab ultranationalist constituencies.

The agreement's implementation required good faith, which simply did not exist. The only reason that the CPA existed at all was that Garang and Taha had developed a bond of trust that allowed serious negotiation and compromise. Over time, Bashir and Kiir forged a working relationship that allowed for the resolution of smaller disputes; the larger ones remained.

Perhaps the greatest impediment to implementation was the fact that the two parties running the Khartoum govern-ment—the NCP and the SPLM—knew they would become opponents in the elections scheduled under the agreement for 2009 (they were actually held in 2010). Asking two political parties that would be vying for power in upcoming elections to cooperate and compromise on implementation may have been too high an expectation.

Another was that the Three Tribes and the peoples of the periphery saw the CPA in profoundly different ways. South-erners held the CPA in reverential awe—much as black Amer-icans view Lincoln's Emancipation Proclamation. Rebecca Garang, John Garang's widow, spoke for many other south-erners when she proclaimed that the CPA was sent by God to save the South from northern oppression.

The NCP, of course, held the CPA in no particular reverence: it was a political agreement that ended an increasingly unpopular war, as casualty rates rose and oil revenues were diverted to fight the war instead of developing the North, and little more. Most Nile River Arabs had only a vague understanding of the CPA's provisions, for Khartoum made virtually no effort to publicize them, fearing that to do so would further weaken its already anemic level of popular support.

In contrast, Garang had organized a major campaign in which he spent months educating the southern people on the provisions of the agreement. He spoke to mass audiences, shifting from English to Dinka, and to Juba Arabic (the local dialect of Arabic spoken by many southerners). For him, the CPA would be the salvation of the South after five decades of bloodshed and political intrigue, and the crowning achievement of his career. This raised the expectations that paradise would soon arrive. It also meant that each time the North botched the implementation of even the smallest provision, tried to reinterpret any part of the agreement, or missed a deadline by even the slightest of margins, southerners reacted with controlled fury.

Northern NCP loyalists claimed that the South was doing exactly the same thing. For example, while the CPA called for joint integrated SAF/SPLA units to patrol the South, few of these units were actually stood up. The truth is that the NCP had been ruling Sudan for sixteen years without having to concede anything to the southerners. The Arab supremacists and ultra Arab nationalists in Khartoum, though not a majority of the Three Tribes, saw the two civil wars as slave rebellions that should have been crushed, not legitimized with peace agreements. The notion of having to compromise with the southerners, or having their actions being scrutinized by the Assessment and Evaluation Commission (created under the CPA and led by a Western diplomat to ensure outside oversight of its implementation), or being forced to listen to the UN, international news media, Western diplomats, and advocacy groups (who, in the NCP's eyes, could never be satisfied) berate them for their failures and abuses was too much to take.

The South began employing its own hardball tactics to end northern delays. Pagan Amum and Yasir Arman, director and deputy director general of the SPLM, respectively, opened a party headquarters in Khartoum and recruited several Nile River Arab sheikhs fed up with the Bashir government to join them. (I spoke at the opening ceremony and called for a full, multiparty democracy in the North that respected human rights—which became the headlines in the Khartoum newspapers the next day.) In protest of procedural violations by the NCP leadership, SPLM delegates walked out of National Assembly meetings. The SPLA announced that it had recruited to its ranks a 3,000-man-strong Arab Misiriyya and Rizaiqat militia that had been earlier a part of Sadiq's old organization the PDF, which had engaged in atrocities against southern civilians. This enraged the NCP leadership (one senior leader told me he would personally see to it that the Misiriyya and Rizaiqat militia paid for their treachery if the Second Civil War resumed).

All this came to a climax in early 2007, just as the international advocacy campaign against atrocities in Darfur reached its most aggressive stage. In a speech at the Holocaust Museum on April 18, President Bush had intended to announce a new set of measures against Khartoum, including economic sanctions. The night before the speech, UN secretary general Ban Ki-moon called the president, informing him that he believed that sanctions would undermine his diplomatic efforts to gain Bashir's acceptance of the joint UN/AU peacekeeping force in Darfur. After the speech, Bush made no more calls to Bashir. Bush announced the measures he was considering but postponed their implementation for six weeks in deference to Ban.

The southerners were fed up with NCP stonewalling and put Khartoum on notice that the peace was at risk. On October 11, 2007, the SPLM withdrew from the GNU; its ministers in Khartoum were temporarily recalled to Juba, and all negotiations were suspended. The South was now doing what the North had done for so long—playing hardball.

In a meeting with Bashir in Khartoum in March 2007, a month before the president's speech, I forewarned him. I urged him not to overreact and to cooperate on UN troop deployments. He showed no emotion, offering little insight as to what he was about to do next. In fact, he would end up retaliating against the South. Following my meeting with Bashir, Khartoum canceled the monthly oil revenue deposit to the GOSS treasury, forcing the Juba government operations to grind to a halt. Bashir ordered SAF commanders, who the CPA required to withdraw across the border to the North by July 2007, to stay in place. In an incendiary speech in June 2007 to commemorate the anniversary of its founding, Bashir called for the remobilization of the PDF, which had earlier committed such terrible atrocities against southerners. The southerners viewed his speech as an act of war. Khartoum's message was clear: we are not without our own resources to respond to U.S. and UN pressure, we will hold hostage your allies and friends in Sudan, over which we have more control than you do, and we will not be pressured into taking actions that we regard as dangerous to our vital national interests and our own survival. One southern official told the U.S. embassy that "blood would flow in the streets."

The South decided to take military action. The SPLM brought the quarreling Darfur rebel groups to Juba to organized them into a military alliance with the NCP's various domestic enemies. They even brought Sheikh Moussa Hillal, the infamous commander of the Janjawiid, to Juba, knowing that he was afraid that the NCP might turn him over to the ICC as a scapegoat. When Khartoum heard that Hillal was in

Juba, it panicked and offered him a senior government post—which he accepted.

The South put in place its military plan: the SPLA would advance on Khartoum from the south; the united Darfuri rebels would move their troops from the west; and the Beja Congress's militia from Red Sea State would advance from the east, all in a triple pincer movement aimed at deposing the NCP. The idea was to bring the war to Khartoum, something the North had sought to avoid from the beginning. Now the prospect of a southern-led invasion of the Arab Triangle by rebel movements from the periphery was becoming a very real possibility. Garang had twice before tried to bring the war to Khartoum, but the SPLA had been repelled by the SAF in both cases. By October 2007, southern troops had massed on the North–South border, south of Khartoum. But now the South had much more advanced weapons with a much larger force than it had during the second civil war. Panic spread in the capital. Sadiq al-Mahdi sent a personal emissary to see me in Washington. Sadiq worried the invaders would be unable to distinguish between the Arabs who were hostile to the NCP and wished for a return to democracy and those who supported Bashir.

The NCP's reaction to the challenge was predictable. Should the SPLA, Darfuri rebels, and Beja militia attack Khartoum, the North's tank battalions would advance on Juba. Security services began purchasing a large number of pistols on the international arms markets, for distribution to the Arab population of Khartoum. Then they mapped out—neighborhood by neighborhood—where the 2.5 million displaced southern Sudanese lived in Khartoum, so that they could massacre them in the event of an SPLA-led invasion.

Events were spinning out of control. I put together a four-point plan to pull both sides back from the brink of war. It called for SAF and SPLA forces to withdraw fifty kilometers north or south, respectively, from the informal border, the deployment of UN peacekeeping troops already in the South under the CPA between the two forces, an accelerated integration of the SAF and SPLA into the JIUs required by the CPA, and the creation of an international commission (which included the United States, United Kingdom, China, and Saudi Arabia) to mediate the ongoing Abyei dispute, which was the source of much of the immediate tension. A month later, SAF generals submitted a set of proposals for immediate action to the Ceasefire Joint Military Committee (which had been set up under the CPA) that were a virtual duplicate of what I had proposed. This astonished UN officials (and me), who had thought neither side would approve the ideas. The SAF proposals revealed more about the state of mind in the North—deep concern, if not panic, at the prospect of a renewal of the North–South war and a southern invasion of the city—than the acceptability of the ideas.

The White House watched the crisis with growing anxiety, and President Bush decided to intervene. In November 2007 he called Kiir and senior GOSS officials to a meeting in the Oval Office, which I attended. He told the southern delegation that the only solution to the crisis was diplomatic, not military. Kiir asked him what the South was to do if it were attacked by the North. The president replied that of course the South would have to defend itself, but that "the South should not provoke a northern attack and make it look like the North was starting the fight." Kiir responded that he had always believed in a political and diplomatic solution and that a return to war would be terrible for the common people.

The diplomatic efforts succeeded. Northern and southern troops were instructed to pull back from the border areas and from a state of alert. Kiir and Bashir worked out a compromise set of agreements on CPA implementation as temporary expedients, and the SPLM rejoined the GNU. Collapse of the CPA and a return to war was temporarily avoided, but just barely.

*How effective was the CPA in the period leading up to the vote
on southern independence?*

Despite the many shortcomings of the CPA's implementation,
it succeeded where other agreements had failed. It ended the
state of war between the North and South, as well as the violence against the civilian population. This allowed 2 million
southerners to return to their homes from IDP camps within
Sudan, particularly around Khartoum, and from refugee
camps in neighboring countries. The SAF withdrew most of
its forces from the South, and the SPLA did the same with
most of its forces in the North (except for SPLA troops who
came from Blue Nile State and the Nuba Mountains in
southern Kordofan—which were in the North—and were
northern citizens). The GNU in Khartoum and the GOSS in
Juba were created, with northerners serving in the GOSS and
southerners in the GNU. A plan was designed and implemented to transform the SPLA into a conventional military
force with U.S., British, Kenyan, and South African technical
assistance (specifically permitted by the CPA) in order to
serve as a deterrent. The Ugandan and South African governments trained southern Sudanese pilots for a small air force
that the GOSS created. The southern tribal militias that had
been on the North's payroll were largely absorbed into the
SPLA, with a few choosing to join the SAF and twenty other
smaller militias returning to the bush (leading to insecurity in
some areas). Between 2005 and 2010, Khartoum transferred to
the GOSS $7 billion in oil revenue, an astonishing amount of
money for a region with 8.5 million people that had never
seen such wealth or development spending. More important
than perhaps anything else, the southerners voted overwhelmingly in a free, fair, and peaceful referendum in early
January 2011 for independence, which formally took effect on
July 9, 2011—an event that critics and skeptics had insisted
would never happen.

10

THE DARFUR PEACE PROCESS

Given the success of the CPA, why hasn't a similar agreement been negotiated for Darfur?

As we've seen, the situation in Sudan is complicated because the second civil war—North versus South—occurred while rebellions were taking place in other regions of the country—in the Nuba Mountains, among the Beja tribe in the Red Sea region, Blue Nile State, and, of course, Darfur. These were all interrelated, and so, too, were their resolutions.

The CPA was signed in Nairobi in January 2005 at a stadium filled with 2,000 southerners and a number of African leaders. Colin Powell represented the United States and acted as a witness, as did a number of foreign ministers from other Western governments. The ceremony took place just at the moment that Khartoum decided to ratchet down the intensity of northern combat operations in Darfur.

From early 2005 through April 2006, African, American, and European diplomats helped facilitate the first of three efforts to fashion a peace process for Darfur, working with rebel groups and Khartoum. All three efforts failed, though the first one came closest to success. Only a political settlement could end the Darfur rebellion. A military victory by one side or the other was highly unlikely: the rebels were too divided, and the SAF lacked the training necessary to fight an insurgency.

The first peace negotiation took place in Abuja, Nigeria, in April 2006 and produced the Darfur Peace Agreement (DPA). Robert Zoellick, then deputy secretary of state under Bush (later president of the World Bank), played a key U.S. role in fashioning the DPA, as did President Olusegun Obasanjo of Nigeria. One of the three rebel leaders at the time, Minni Minawi, signed the document; the two others, Abdul Wahid Nur and JEM leader Khalil Ibrahim, refused to sign. Abdul Wahid, then living in Paris and self-declared leader of the Fur tribe, was particularly erratic. He had initially announced he would sign the document and then refused the next day. One Western advocacy group at the conference urged him not to sign because they argued the peace agreement was flawed, as did hard-line Fur advisers (who lived safely in Canada). In retrospect, the DPA was the only peace effort that could have succeeded, for matters soon became more complicated. Not a few but dozens of rebel factions would eventually form; there was a growing split between rebel commanders and civilian rebel leaders; and Sahelian Arab tribes arrived in 2008 and 2009, settling on the lands originally inhabited by people who had been driven into the camps.

Abdul Wahid attacked the agreement with demagogic rhetoric, misled IDPs in the camps regarding the provisions of the DPA, organized IDP camp demonstrations against the agreement from his Paris office, and thus contributed to its demise. For its part, Khartoum never took the agreement seriously and avoided the implementation of many of its key provisions—which only embittered the rebel groups that did support it—probably because they knew it could not bring an end to the war even if it were fully implemented without full rebel support (which it did not have).

Khartoum decided to try to weaken the remaining rebel groups that refused to sign the DPA by offering them money, jobs, and supplies to break away from the major rebel militias. Thus, the anarchy in Darfur in 2007 and 2008 was partially a function of these divide-and-rule tactics. A year after the DPA conference, there were twenty-eight rebel groups, most lacking a political agenda but awash in captured weapons and equipment. Many consisted of farmers and herders who, to survive, had become little more than brigands who wrapped themselves in a rebel banner and then looted humanitarian aid trucks and the food aid they carried. A lucrative trade developed from such trucks in Chad. While Khartoum had facilitated the breakup of the rebel force, much of the breakdown in rebel cohesion had more to do with the passage of time and the absence of any rebel leader strong enough to enforce a unified political agenda and organizational discipline. Darfur had no John Garang, someone who could unify the civilian and military wings and was capable of implementing a comprehensive military strategy and conducting peace negotiations.

The second effort started in Addis Ababa at an international conference held in November 2006, led by UN secretary general Kofi Annan and Salim Salim (former foreign minister of Tanzania), representing the AU. Annan presented a comprehensive plan, calling for a joint AU/UN peacekeeping force to be dispatched to Darfur, protections to be established for the ongoing humanitarian relief program in the region, and the political process that would lead to the diplomatic talks to end the war in Darfur. Annan did a masterful job building support for the plan among Arab and African countries; in the end, the only country that refused to approve it was Sudan, led by its foreign minister, Lam Akol, who claimed that it violated Sudanese sovereignty (later when the Sudanese government was completely isolated internationally in opposing the agreement the NCP announced it had always supported it). This conference produced a plan for resolving the Darfur crisis, culminating in a peace conference in Sirte, Libya, in October 2007.

In January 2007, I could see how complicated the situation was. I organized a meeting with rebel leaders—military commanders and political leaders as well as their senior staffs—in Abeche, Chad, to determine whether unity was possible.

Khartoum opposed the meeting because they believed that any such unity would ultimately evolve into a military alliance that would be more effective against them in combat operations. They threatened to raid Abeche during the meeting. I had hoped the convening power of the U.S. government would move the rebels to unite to achieve some common negotiating positions. Rebel commanders and IDP representatives held the United States in high regard; President Bush was particularly popular, because he was perceived as the Darfuri people's strongest international advocate and protector. In some IDP camps parents were naming their newborn sons George Bush. With the exception of Abdul Wahid, virtually all armed rebel leaders attended, but they were unable to reach a consensus.

The diplomatic talks finally took place in October 2007 in Sirte, Libya, jointly sponsored by the UN and AU, with bilateral support from Western governments. I led the U.S. delegation to these talks as well as the prenegotiations to them.

The UN and AU sponsors of the Sirte conference made a concerted effort to include the burgeoning number of rebel movements, all the elements of Darfuri civil society, and the Libyan and Eritrean governments in the process. As we've seen, the two neighboring governments had more influence on the ground in Darfur than the international community; they had undermined the DPA because they felt left out of the process. Nonetheless, this second attempt also failed. Several rebel leaders, most notably the still erratic Abdul Wahid Nur, refused to attend the Sirte conference, and it thus did not produce an enforceable settlement.

The third effort began in 2008 in Doha, Qatar, organized by that country's minister for foreign affairs, Sheikh Ahmed bin Abdalla al Mahmoud, with backing by the UN Secretariat, the AU, the Security Council Permanent Five, and the Arab League. The United States played a critical role through my successor as U.S. Envoy, Ambassador Rich Williamson, in getting these talks started. This third attempt produced an agreement, signed in 2009 between the GOS and JEM. Nonetheless, this agreement fell apart, because neither side truly supported it or followed its provisions. As of this writing, negotiations continue in Doha, with a new agreement signed in late 2011 between Khartoum and a new Darfur political leader with no troops in Darfur and no history in the war; U.S. diplomats hoped to get the major rebel leaders' approval later to an agreement they had no hand in negotiating.

What are the prospects for peace in Darfur?

An unpublished survey of the Darfur IDP camps shows that 70 percent of the IDPs were Fur, while the remaining IDPs came from the Zaghawa, Masalit, and a smattering of smaller African tribes. Most of the effective military commands and rebel units are Zaghawa, and divided into a half dozen competing and autonomous militias. No agreement in Darfur can be reached without support from the mass of the Fur population, as well as the Zaghawa military commanders.

The most visible Fur leader remains Abdul Wahid Nur, who simply will not participate in any negotiations and has even tried to assassinate Fur commanders who have broken with him and supported peace negotiations. The highly disciplined Fur historically have followed one leader, but this tradition began to unravel by 2009, as Nur's position has become untenable. In mid-2010, fighting broke out in some IDP camps between pro- and anti-Nur factions—fueled by Khartoum, which had long wanted to close down the IDP camps. Although most members of the Fur elite believed Abdul Wahid had to be replaced, they did not have an alternative and had no means of effectively removing him. Perhaps the only Fur leader capable of uniting the tribal and negotiating an agreement is Ahmed Diraige, elected governor of the province in the 1980s.

Peace in Darfur remains elusive. UN officials, European diplomats, and mediation NGOs have also all attempted to facilitate unification talks through different venues, without success. Scott Gration, the U.S. envoy under President Obama, led an aggressive effort in 2009 and 2010 to unite the Darfur rebels and incorporate Abdul Wahid into the peace process. Nur once again stubbornly refused to cooperate, thus dooming the negotiations. All efforts—Abuja, Addis Ababa, Serte, and Doha—failed because there are so many competing actors with so many conflicting agendas. The rebel groups tried to outdo each other with their demands to incorporate unachievable and wildly unrealistic promises to their supporters in the agreement. As noted, Abdul Wahid, for example, publicly promised each of the 1.8 million IDPs $10,000 in war reparations or blood money from Khartoum, which would have amounted to $1.8 billion. No successful peace process in recent history has included so many competing players or such exaggerated demands.

Equally problematic have been Khartoum's motivations throughout these negotiations. I've argued that it effectively achieved its objectives in Darfur by the end of 2004, when it broke the back of the rebellion and decimated the homes and villages of its supporters. It therefore has no real motivation to compromise on any significant issues. Moreover, it achieved this victory with a devil's deal: it gave away the rebel tribes' land to the Janjawiid tribes and new Arab migrants that Khartoum had invited to settle in Darfur from other countries to buy their loyalty. So Khartoum cannot send people in the IDP camps home to these lands without igniting a new war.

These conditions do not lend themselves to a lasting peace agreement, and there is little that outsiders can do to change this, despite constant pressure from advocacy groups. With a divided rebel movement, weak and ineffective leadership, and an unmotivated government—either local or national—none of this is likely to change any time soon. Khartoum wants a return to normalcy and a political settlement, but on its terms; displaced people are tired of living in the IDP camps, but many of their local leaders have become radicalized and are making demands that are unachievable and unrealistic; and donors are tired of paying a hundreds of millions of dollars a year to feed people and maintain the camps. The more complex the negotiations and the more extravagant the rebel demands, the less likely any workable settlement will be. Many of the refugees would like to settle permanently in the camps if they could be converted into urbanized neighborhoods. Given that the countryside is increasingly incapable of supporting farming and herding, this solution is not so far-fetched. In late 2010, Bashir announced plans to close forcibly the camps located near cities in Darfur for security reasons (and because some of the camps had become weapons arsenals and sites of the major rebel groups' offices). The question is whether the IDPs can find livelihoods to support themselves in an urbanized environment without a permanent dependency on international aid. It remains to be seen whether the international community can restrain Khartoum from carrying out its plan, which would likely involve widespread violence.

The revolution that began in Libya in February 2011 to overthrow the Gaddafi government and led to his lynching in Sirte in October 2011 could have momentous consequences to any peace in Darfur. As we have seen, Gaddafi armed and supported the rebel movements in Darfur over many years, but particularly in the third rebellion in 2003. When he came under attack from within Libya, the three major (and previously quarreling) Dafuri rebel leaders—Khalil Ibrahim, Mini Minawi, and Abdul Wahid Nur—rushed to support him. This was the only time all three men had been united since the first years of the rebellion in 2003 and 2004, because they realized that if Gaddafi was removed from power and a new Libyan government became an ally instead of opponent of the Bashir government, their rebellion in Darfur might collapse. In March 2011, the NATO alliance supporting the anti-Gaddafi rebels became strange military bedfellows with an unlikely and unwanted ally: Omar al-Bashir. Khartoum had correctly seen Gaddafi as a major funder and weapons supplier of the third Darfur rebellion and believed that if he could be removed, it could crush the rebel movement. The Sudanese government decided to send military assistance to the anti-Gaddafi forces (after Gaddafi was killed Bashir claimed Sudan's assistance had taken him down). When the Libyan capital was taken by these forces in August 2011, they also captured Khalil Ibrahim, the most effective Darfur rebel military commander, who had led an attack on Khartoum in April 2008 (described in the next chapter). With his capture and the collapse of the Gaddafi's support for the Darfur rebellion, Khartoum for the first time in ten years might have had some prospect for achieving a military victory in Darfur. However, in September 2011 Ibrahim's troops rescued him from Tripoli, and he returned to Darfur with a new arsenal of weapons Gaddafi apparently had given him before his death. This included surface-to-air, anti-air craft missiles (and a large amount of cash) that could prove decisive, as it was the Sudanese Air Force that protected Khartoum more than any other element of the Sudanese armed forces. President Bashir rushed his army after Gaddafi's death to seal the border between Darfur and Libya and Chad in an effort to prevent these weapons from entering Sudan. If the Darfuri rebels were able to shoot down the Sudanese Air Force, it would leave Khartoum vulnerable to attack by an anti-Bashir, anti-NCP coalition from the periphery of the country. In fact this coalition announced its formal alliance in mid-2011 composed of Darfuri rebels, Abdul Azziz al Hilu's SPLM North army in the Nuba Mountains of South Kordofan, and Malik Agar's forces in Blue Nile State (all areas located in Northern Sudan).

11

THE FUTURE OF NORTH AND SOUTH SUDAN

How has the NCP remained in power for two decades?

Since 1998, the NCP has used rising oil revenues to ensure its survival. Khartoum has built a domestic munitions industry, producing tanks, Kalashnikov machine guns, ammunitions, and small arms to provision the SAF, should international arms suppliers stop selling it weapons. Although Iranian and Chinese arms manufacturers provided the technical support necessary to build the plants, it is unlikely that Sudan currently produces weapons in any considerable quantity or quality, given that none are exported. The 2003 and 2004 battlefield defeats by Darfuri rebels against the SAF as well as its depleted ranks due to repeated purges—because of feared disloyalty—have led Khartoum to seek more advanced weapons from the Chinese and Russians as a substitute for an effective army. This has included fighter and bomber aircraft, helicopter gunships, and night vision goggles. The Sudanese air force contains a large contingent of foreign mercenary pilots many from Russia, Iran, and Egypt; it fears that its own pilots could be disloyal in a coup or refuse to carry out orders to bomb their own tribes and regions. Despite this growing superiority in advanced weaponry, the armed forces have been demoralized from repeated purges and defeats, politicized by the NCP (officers are chosen for loyalty rather than competence), and weakened by the shrinking population base from which to recruit personnel.

The NCP has increased public spending, using oil revenues to fund public sector jobs instead of much-needed infrastructure. Distributing patronage jobs has allowed the Bashir government to expand its base of loyalists and to cement ties to various tribes and factions. As reported earlier government expenditures accounted for less than 10 percent of the GNP in the 1990s but rose after 2003 to 23 percent. While Khartoum has successfully used oil revenues for political purposes, state expenditure of this size is not only unsustainable, it is dangerous. At a World Bank conference held in 2010, experts reported that Sudanese oil revenues would plateau before 2020 and may begin to decline, requiring layoffs and reduced economic growth. Southern independence substantially reduced northern oil revenues after July 2011 and precipitated an economic crisis in Khartoum. The International Monetary Fund estimates that the Northern economy will contract with minus economic growth in 2012 and 2013 because of the loss of oil revenues. At the same time food prices were rising rapidly in the North causing growing popular unrest. Thus, the very patronage strategy that has kept peace in the North will become destabilizing as public employees are laid off because of the loss of oil revenues. Rising food prices, negative economic growth, and then these layoffs may eventually destabilize the Bashir government at the moment it is most politically vulnerable following the loss of 80 percent of its natural resources in the south.

The North's national debt remains at 92 percent of GNP, and while the fiscal imbalances that plagued earlier governments have been reduced, they have certainly not been eliminated. In early 2007 and 2009, a number of civil servants did not receive their wages for a period of several months; the government had been directing funds to other activities, perhaps within the security services and military, while simultaneously experiencing a large drop in revenues due to falling

oil prices. Rumors circulate in the Khartoum business
community that the NCP is also using government revenue
to purchase real estate in the Gulf States, Iran, and Malaysia
under the party's (and not the Sudanese government's)
name—an insurance policy should a popular uprising or
coup depose them. In late 2010, Bashir was accused of diverting $9 billion in revenues into his own or NCP coffers.

The increase of oil revenues since 1998, U.S. and UN sanctions (imposed by the Clinton and Bush administrations), and
Western advocacy group pressure have pushed the Bashir
government to seek Arab and Asian investors (who largely
ignore Western sanctions). Western businesses have largely
abandoned the country. Khartoum has simply shifted its hunt
for investment to the Middle East and Asia, where Western
media, parliaments, and advocacy groups have little influence.
Sanctions are more a nuisance than an impediment—witness
the 5 percent growth rate of the Sudanese economy in 2010,
despite the global recession. The unintended consequence of
this eastward movement of business has been economic
monopolies and environmental damage. Sudan became the
guinea pig for Chinese and Indian oil companies undertaking
their first drilling and pumping activities abroad without the
environmental safeguards and the more advanced technology
used by Western oil companies, but poor technology has not
slowed resource extraction. The sanctions do not appear to
have changed Khartoum's political calculations or military
strategy in Darfur and, ultimately, have not diminished
foreign investment in the country.

What are the prospects for the North?

Despite its success in maintaining power, the NCP is losing
control of the North. Neighboring countries are quietly preparing for the potential dissolution of what remains of the
Sudanese state by bolstering their border security. The Bashir
government is now the weakest of any since Sudan's

independence in terms of its ability to exercise legitimate authority over the remaining regions of the country. Under the NCP, Sudan is becoming a failed state, despite Khartoum's earlier rearmament campaign, skillful use of oil revenues, now in steep decline, and use of repression and brutality to intimidate or murder its opponents.

One event clearly shows this growing weakness. In April 2008, Darfuri rebel leader Khalil Ibrahim decided to mobilize his JEM militia for an assault on Khartoum to depose the national government (likely with weapons provided by the Chadian and Libyan governments). Astonishingly, 130 trucks mounted with heavy automatic weapons and between 1,000 and 2,000 rebel soldiers traveled nearly 900 miles from the Chadian-Darfuri border to Omdurman, a suburb of Khartoum, without being stopped by the Sudanese military. The rebels fought their way through Omdurman to the bridge over the Nile near the Presidential Palace before they were finally stopped. One explanation for why the Sudanese military, exhausted and demoralized by the continuous state of warfare in the country, did not intervene to stop the rebel army was that the Bashir government feared that the SAF presence in the city might turn into a coup against the NCP. Instead, the NISS saved the regime when it mobilized its own internal forces, drove the rebel invasion back, and reclaimed the city. This was the first time in three decades that there was street fighting in Khartoum.

Many in the Three Tribes asked how Ibrahim was able to launch an attack that nearly reached the Presidential Palace in the middle of Khartoum. Khalil Ibrahim has often referred to Hassan al-Turabi as his political "godfather" and role model, and they were closely allied for many years. In fact, there is substantial evidence that the two men plotted the JEM attack on Khartoum together: the route through Omdurman that JEM took to get to the Nile River ran directly through neighborhoods known as Turabi's Islamist strongholds. Bashir ordered Turabi's arrest and imprisonment following the attack. In the 1990s, while Turabi was in power, he personally recruited new officers to the SAF on the basis of their personal loyalty to him and his Islamist revolution. By 1998, half of the SAF officer corps had been chosen by Turabi, and by 2010 they had risen in the ranks to become senior officers. Following the abortive rebel attack, Bashir purged dozens of mid-ranking SAF officers whose loyalty to the NCP he believed was questionable. This further weakened the already demoralized Sudanese military, as they lost many senior officers. After the rebel attack the SAF was placed under the operational command of the NISS, so the secret police controled the military.

No group had come so close to unseating the Bashir government since it had taken power in 1989, and the NCP leadership took action to prevent a repetition of this security breach. They arrested and shot as many Zaghawa men as they could find in Darfur who, according to their intelligence, had participated in the invasion. Fearful of a coup attempt, they hired a South African security company in 2007 to advise them on securing Khartoum from an attack. Based on their advice, the NISS constructed a chain of underground weapons arsenals and fortifications so the city could be defended street by street should another invasion occur. Most army troops were withdrawn from the city; only 4,000 of the regime's most trusted elite troops remained stationed in the capital.

All this shows just how tenuous the Bashir government's control had become. For twenty years, the basis of the Bashir government's power was the party apparatus, NISS, and the military. One of those three pillars—the military—proved utility in protecting the NCP in a crisis, and the other two pillars will begin to crumble as the regime cannot pay employees given the loss of oil revenues.

In addition to losing control in the North, the NCP faced the prospect of a determined opponent to its south deeply hostile to having an Islamist state on its northern border. The NCP has always feared that if the South gained independence, Western donors would support the creation of a strong southern state, including its military, and this seems to be the case. The Bashir government has divided its opponents both at home and abroad and renegotiated every agreement over and over again in order to obtain better terms (so that no agreement is ever truly finalized, and as a result, no one who negotiates with the regime trusts them to honor what they sign). The NCP leaders use the media and propaganda effectively, making themselves look more formidable than they are, and they have methodically and systematically stonewalled their foreign opponents in the belief that they can outlast their adversaries and enemies, who will lose interest in Sudan and move on to other issues. They believe that time is on their side. While these tactics have worked for two decades, they are increasingly ineffective. Time is now on the side of the enemies of the NCP, at least within Sudan.

As a result of these forces at work, Khartoum has developed a siege mentality. Bashir privately told visitors in 2007 he might be the last Arab (implicitly from the Three Tribes) president of Sudan and saw the African population of Sudan closing in on Khartoum. However badly the Three Tribes have governed, however parochial their policies and egregious their crimes, they do have legitimate interests, and ignoring them will only guarantee that all the voices of moderation in the North will be drowned out by Arab supremacist and Islamist extremists—which may now be taking place.

The likely beneficiary of the NCP's possible demise is Hassan al-Turabi or one of his younger Islamist acolytes, as he is the only opposition figure with an organized and dedicated following, particularly in the armed forces and thus able to orchestrate a government takeover. A Turabi-dominated government would bring to power the most intransigent, obstructionist, and reactionary elements of the Sudanese political system. Turabi organized the coup that deposed his brother-in-law Sadiq al-Mahdi in order to kill the peace process of 1989. In January 2011, after the referendum had been approved and the democratic revolution was sweeping across the Arab world, Turabi warned that Sudan would likely experience an armed uprising like the one that ousted the Tunisian government in January. He added that it was likely to originate in Darfur (suggesting that he was anticipating another attack by Khalil Ibrahim).

It may not matter much who takes over the Sudanese state should the NCP be deposed. The centrifugal forces pulling the country apart over the past half century, from independence to the present day, have accelerated over the past twenty years and may soon enough result in the dissolution of an entity governed from Khartoum (irrespective of the secession of the South). Sudan's neighbors and the Western powers may either slow down or accelerate this process, but their influence will not be decisive. The centrifugal forces may already be too strong to reverse, even were the people of the North to replace Bashir with more enlightened leadership.

The risk of a takeover by Turabi's allies increased in 2011 with the Arab revolution to Sudan's north. Khartoum saw itself for twenty years surrounded by states hostile to its radical Islamist agenda, but that changed as the populist revolution spread. Now in the three Arab states to Sudan's north—Egypt, Tunisia, and Libya—the prospect of a future takeover through democratic means by the Muslim Brotherhood is not as far-fetched as it had once been. It may not be immediate, but the Brotherhood's stock is now rising, and it is no longer facing brutal secular security forces suppressing it. In the Egyptian elections in December 2011 the Muslim Brotherhood and its allies took 60 percent of the seats in the new Parliament. In the Tunisian elections in October 2011 the Islamist Ennahdha party took 42 percent of the vote—three times the size of the next highest party. In October 2011 the new government of

Libya announced Sharia law would be the basis of their new legal code—a central tenet of the Muslim Brotherhood platform. While the external political environment facing Khartoum has radically changed in a remarkably short period of time, it faces a rising tide of internal opposition and dissolution.

At the 2007 Darfur peace talks in Sirte, a young lawyer stood up in a plenary session and announced that Sudan ceased to exist as a state and that the country was breaking into four parts: the South; the Arab Triangle in the center of the country, including Khartoum, North Khartoum, and Omdurman; the Darfur and Kordofan regions to the west (much of which were no longer under the control of the central government); and last, the east, which is composed of the Blue Nile, Kassala, Gezira, and Red Sea regions that border Ethiopia, Eritrea, and the Red Sea (where Arabs are a minority). The lawyer's comments marked the only time during the Sirte conference that the NCP delegation became visibly angry; one member made a veiled threat against the lawyer.

In June 2011, Bashir ordered the SAF to bomb, invade, and occupy the disputed Abyei territory, displacing hundreds of thousands of Dinka people, when he was required under the CPA to hold a referendum to let the people determine the status of the region (to join the North or the South). Khartoum has long seen the 38,000 SPLA (North) troops in the Nuba Mountains under the command of Abdel Azziz al-Hilu, who had been a senior commander of the SPLA, as the greatest threat to its autocratic control. In June 2011, weeks before southern independence day celebration, Bashir ordered Abdul Azziz al-Hilu's army to surrender its weapons to the SAF; he refused because Bashir refused to implement the provisions of the CPA for Abyei and the Nuba Mountains. Bashir then attempted to take Nuba by force, arrested civilian political and religious leaders who have disappeared and may have been executed, and began aerial bombardment of civilian areas. The UN reports that 175,000 people have been displaced by the bombing. The SAF ground troops feared entering the Nuba Mountains on the ground, as al-Hilu's troops were so well dug in and armed, so they expelled all humanitarian organizations and prevented the delivery of food to the displaced. The charismatic SPLM commander Malik Agar was elected governor of Blue Nile State (which is in the North) in June 2010 with 56 percent of the vote. Agar has 10,000 troops under his command. In August 2011, Bashir announced he was firing Agar and replacing him with a military governor he appointed. He ordered his troops to bombard the governor's office in the state capital with hopes he would kill Agar; instead his soldiers killed dozens of innocent civilians, and Agar was untouched. In both the Nuba Mountains and Blue Nile, the CPA required a "popular consultation," such that the government was required to hold formal negotiations with local political leaders and civil society about the future of the two regions. While the public had been consulted in these areas to varying degrees, negotiations with Khartoum based on these consultations had not taken place, and before they could Bashir ordered the bombing of both South Kordofan and Blue Nile states. These SPLA North commanders refuse to demobilize until Khartoum allows some measure of control of the people in these areas over their government, which it had refused to do. The Red Sea region—home, as we've seen, to the Beja tribe, who are ethnically related to the neighboring Eritreans—revolted against Khartoum, and despite the eventual signing of a peace agreement, only a tenuous peace now holds there. The Beja Congress, which led the rebellion, regularly sends delegates to SPLM council meetings in Juba, where they have been outspoken about Khartoum failing to uphold the peace agreement and its negligence in developing the Beja region. As for Darfur, talk of self-determination and even secession is common now. In January 2011, Ngok Dinka leaders warned that if Khartoum stonewalled a settlement on

Abyei they would storm Khartoum. Thus an anti-Bashir, anti-NCP coalition is forming along the periphery, potentially initiating the dissolution of what is left of the North; Bashir's military attacks were an attempt to forestall this alliance.

Anticipating the breakup, Khartoum began consolidating its control over the Arab Triangle. A few years early, at an NCP leaders' conference in 2008, former finance minister Abdel Rahim Hamdi argued that Darfur and southern Sudan were no longer viable components of a Sudanese state and that the government should focus on the Arab Triangle and Kordofan. Khartoum seems to have taken Hamdi's advice. In 2010 it canceled two large development projects south of Khartoum—in Kassala and Gezira—that would have resuscitated the vast, but increasingly decrepit, irrigation system and railroad network that transports the region's agricultural production to Port Sudan. Kassala and Gezira have been dominated by secular, Socialist-led labor unions and to this day are militantly hostile to NCP-style Islamists. To make matters worse for Khartoum, a million Fur and Masalit tribespeople live there, mostly descendants of farmers who migrated from Darfur in the 1920s to farm lands served by the Gezira irrigation project. It was their tribal brothers and sisters in Darfur who were murdered and raped by Khartoum in 2003 and 2004, so the NCP is not particularly popular there. As Khartoum triages Kassala, Sennar, and Gezira in order to solidify its control over the Arab Triangle in the center, dissenting voices from the periphery will grow louder with time.

The NCP fears the breakup of the Sudanese state more than nearly anything else: more than ICC war crimes trials, more than renewed war with the South, more than UN resolutions condemning their atrocities, and more than U.S. economic sanctions. It was this fear that led to the terrible atrocities in Darfur. Even as they were negotiating the CPA with the South, the NCP tried to crush the rebellion there before it spread. And it was the same fears that drove the atrocities against civilian opponents of the Bashir government in the Nuba Mountains and Blue Nile State in June, July, and August 2011. The Bashir government properly fears that if it loses control and is deposed from power, its members will be at risk of retributive violence from the very tribes and families they have victimized and brutalized. Unless Bashir and his party are given a safe way out of power, they will cling to it with ruthless brutality as the country falls into chaos around them.

In the end, Arabization and Islamization of the country have done the opposite of what the Three Tribes intended; instead of uniting the country, the strategy has torn it apart. Outside the Arab Triangle, the four regions of historic Sudan are all home to centuries-old, non-Arab kingdoms: the Fur sultanate to the west, the Shilluk kingdom in the center, the Azande kingdom in the south, and the Funj sultanate to the east. These ancient kingdoms and sultanates functioned independently for centuries before the Sudanese state was created in 1956. They may simply be reconstituting themselves in a different and more modern form, returning Sudan to its pre-Egyptian colonial past. Sudan's future will be determined by whether the Arab supremacist and ultranationalist elites destroy the country or render it ungovernable before they are driven from power.

Will South Sudan become a failed state?

Like northern Sudan, South Sudan is a fragile state, but it is unlikely to become a failed state, unless Juba's leadership makes imprudent decisions or mismanages its wealth. Oil revenues have been both a curse and a blessing. Natural resources used wisely can build a private market economy, public infrastructure, and public services. Used unwisely, particularly in a young country with weak institutions, these riches can corrupt its values and culture, squander resources, and despoil the environment. The government in Juba has already suffered costly scandals in which two finance ministers have been forced to resign—one involving misuse of a $500 million reserve fund in 2006, the other involving $2.5

billion in food contracts in 2009. Some ministers are simply diverting funds for their own use; others are engaged in corrupt procurement practices.

The combination of peace and oil revenue, coupled with low taxes and minimum business regulation, has transformed, however unevenly, the face of the new state. The population of Juba, which was inhabited by 100,000 people at the end of the war, soared to an estimated 1.1 million people by the end of 2010. The infrastructure of this capital city has evolved rapidly: major roads have been paved; a new electric line distribution system is slowly being built; new ministry buildings have been erected or renovated; and seven commercial banks, restaurants, 175 small hotels, foreign consulates, and development agency offices have all cropped up between 2006 and 2011. In provincial cities, fired brick houses with corrugated steel roofs are replacing traditional circular grass-roofed, mud-brick *tukuls*. Seven new water-bottling plants and a brewery have been built. With oil money flowing and infrastructure contracts anticipated in the near future, private companies are establishing a presence in Juba. The southern economy is booming.

Daily bus and air flight service now connect Juba and southern provincial cities, isolated for decades by the war, with Nairobi and Kampala. Juba Airport has twice the number of daily flights as Kampala, the largest city and capital of Uganda. Nearly one million southerners have cell phones when in 2005 few people had them.

Since 2005, more than 12,000 companies, of which one third are construction-related businesses, have officially registered. In addition to the traditional open-air markets run by the Arabs, there is a proliferation of new stores, business offices, and construction companies from a new class of merchants, entrepreneurs, and managers, many from Uganda, Kenya, Ethiopia, and Eritrea. These merchants call South Sudan the new frontier, where markets are freer and starting a new business is much easier than in their home countries (though some complain that profits have been decreasing recently as competition increases). Their presence is causing some tensions with southerners, given that these East African businessmen are bringing skilled workers from their home countries—some 100,000 have immigrated in five years—who are much more experienced in starting and managing profit-making businesses, skills to which southerners are only now gaining exposure. Entrepreneurial instincts are not inherent to the tribal culture of the South, in part because of the forty-five years of war on their soil. With few private sector jobs available to southerners, young people gravitate to the patrimonial jobs in the less productive public sector. These tendencies privately worry southern leaders.

The rural areas in the South lag far behind. The schools and health clinics built by donor aid agencies, state governors, church groups, and NGOs are scattered and sparse. Rural people increasingly resent the rapid development of Juba, juxtaposed with their own underdevelopment and poverty. While it is understandable that Juba has focused on setting up the infrastructure of the new government since the signing of the CPA, the rural poor are waiting for their share of the peace dividend.

Officials in Juba have other things to worry about apart from restive rural areas. In the first six months of 2009, more than 2,000 southerners died in localized tribal conflicts, mostly in the Jonglei region, which led some outside analysts to predict that the South would destabilize from ethnic wars after independence. Two circumstances caused this unrest: severe food shortages and the suspension of Khartoum's oil payments to the GOSS treasury, with the subsequent suspension of wages to civil servants and soldiers. Four of six harvests failed over a two-year period because of poor rains, and the UN and aid agencies prematurely phased out their humanitarian food aid programs, leaving people with no fallback source of food when crops failed. When world oil prices collapsed after the worldwide 2008 economic meltdown, payments to Juba by Khartoum were suspended for a few months; GOSS employees and former militia soldiers went unpaid. Some soldiers looked for their livelihoods at the end of an AK-47 barrel and through cattle rustling. Unlike other developing countries, in which political leaders stoke tribal rivalries to maintain control, leaders in South Sudan have sought to maintain ethnic balance in public appointments. Whenever Dinka-Nuer fighting has broken out in the South, Salva Kiir (the highest ranking Dinka) and Riak Machar (the highest ranking Nuer)—despite their personal rivalries— have created a united front to calm the situation down.

Juba spends on average a third of its budget on its military—$1 billion in 2009—of which 89 percent is paid in salaries to 300,000 SPLA soldiers (125,000 regular SPLA soldiers and 175,000 irregulars absorbed after 2005 into the SPLA from militias that had been organized and armed by Khartoum to foment tribal strife in the South during the war). An additional 100,000 civil service employees are on the public payroll as well. Thus, Juba employs a sizeable portion of the adult population of 3.9 million people. This figure represents a comparatively enormous number of people on the public payrolls, particularly in a government that is only five years old, as well as a burden inherited by the South. To keep the population in cities pacified during the Second Civil War Khartoum bought the loyalty of more than 100,000 city dwellers by putting them on its public payroll. Most of these employees had no skills, many were illiterate, and they typically had no real duties to perform. But they caused no trouble as long as their salaries were paid. These patrimonial jobs hindered the development of a work ethic and entrepreneurial spirit among city dwellers. In addition, free NGO, UN, and donor food aid during the Second Civil War to prevent mass starvation conditioned the public to expect free food, thus accelerating the deterioration of their work ethic. The oil companies also contribute to this pathology when they pay off village chiefs and hire local staff when no work is expected.

Juba attempted to reduce these bloated payrolls so that teachers, police, and construction workers could be hired instead. However, this caused widespread demonstrations and unrest, so the layoffs had to be postponed. Unifying all militias under the authority of the SPLA was essential to civil peace, but it has also proven very expensive. Kuol Mangyang, elected governor of Jonglei State in 2010, became so disgusted with the situation that he announced that those on the public payroll would only get paid if they actually reported to work on a regular basis at a particular government building. Once people came to collect their checks, he locked the gates and compared the payroll on paper to the number of people who actually showed up for work. Some were soldiers collecting two paychecks; some were ghost employees who did not exist but whose check went to someone else; and some were cows (all cows in southern Sudan have names). He promptly cleaned up these payrolls, creating some political unrest.

Having 400,000 salaried public employees and soldiers has led to the dispersal of oil revenues to a new class of GOSS state employees. The unintended consequence of this large public payroll has been the democratization of oil revenues, involving perhaps a quarter to a third of the families in the South. This in turn has fueled the growing consumer economy, particularly in the rapidly growing urban areas like Juba. Such economic growth has not materialized in rural areas, which are not much better off than they were during the rebellions, except that now they can farm and herd their animals in relative peace.

Waste is rampant, given that there are only very limited financial accountability systems to ensure that the lower-level soldiers and civil servants actually receive their proper pay regularly. Payments are made in cash by supervisors— the banking system remains weak and underdeveloped. The Kenya Commercial Banks and other banks are opening regional offices in the provincial cities, and this may improve the situation, and in some areas payment is being made through cell phones, reducing the level of diversion.

Man with tractor in Al Wahdah, Unity State, South Sudan. (Henrik Stabell/NPA)

Most soldiers and civil servants see their jobs as the fruits of peace under the CPA rather than as duties to be performed and public services to be delivered to the people. Again, this represents one of the legacies of Sadiq al-Mahdi's strategy carried out by the Bashir government for winning the war in the South: using patronage jobs, money, and guns to turn the South against itself. Next to the enormous loss of life and mass population displacement and the destruction of their culture during the first and second civil wars, this bloated public payroll is the sorriest of the North's legacies in the South.

Moreover, given that the oil sector satisfies its revenue needs, the government in Juba encourages private sector investment and imposes no taxes to speak of. Some companies have signed mineral exploration contracts with the Juba government, which plans to diversify its future sources of revenue. Nonetheless, no exports of any significant volume have yet resulted from this exploration. Because they are almost completely dependent on oil revenues to function (98 percent of its revenue was from oil, as of 2011), the southern government and economy remain vulnerable to disruption from price shocks, production problems, or Khartoum's shutting down the pipeline. The overreliance on extractive industry revenues instead of taxes to pay for government services has made the Juba government less accountable for its management of public resources—if tax revenues were misused, it would create a much bigger outcry from those paying them. Average citizens feel no connection to oil company revenues when they are misspent by Juba and thus do not demand accountability.

Why did the referendum on secession become so controversial?

The South's response to the North's pressure during the final CPA negotiations was to organize the rebel movements of the northern periphery—an alliance similar to the one they created in late 2007 when the NCP was obstructing CPA implementation. Salva Kiir has told Khartoum that it should now begin a peaceful process of political and economic reform in the North that would decentralize power and wealth equally to the periphery. The South has implied that should the North resist the reform movement, it would seek alternatives, which is a polite way of threatening the use of military force. Bashir, in a surprise move, visited Juba on January 4, 2011—five days before the referendum—and offered assistance and economic cooperation to the South should it vote for secession. He repeated the offer of cooperation in his speech at the July 9, 2011, independence celebration in Juba. He maintained that while he would be sad to see the South leave, the North would keep its word and implement whatever the southern voters decided. His offer may not have been purely rhetorical but instead a realistic reassessment of the NCP's traditional alliance with neighboring Arab states (which were angry over the splitting of the Sudanese state) and a sign that the new North might consider an economic alliance with the South.

In the negotiations, all major issues remained unresolved as of the end of 2011. The North wanted a firm agreement on the exact length of time and percentage of oil revenues it would receive from the South, which will be payment for the use of the oil pipeline to northern refineries and then onto Port Sudan for shipment to international markets. The North borrowed billions to finance this oil infrastructure, and it wanted the South to assume a portion of this debt. Other complex issues remained that needed to be resolved, including the citizenship status of southerners living in the North and northerners living in the South; the seasonal use of southern pasture lands by northern Arab nomads; the continued use of the northern currency in economy of the South; the status of the highly contested and occupied Abyei region; and the demarcation of the border. Khartoum slowed the referendum's preparation in order to pressure the South to resolve the terms of the secession before the vote.

Southerners, on the other hand, demanded that the referendum be held first and these issues be negotiated afterward. From past experience, they knew that northerners would try to renegotiate the terms of the referendum—a tactic they have employed on every important provision of the CPA—and hold it hostage until they were satisfied that the divorce settlement will protect their vital interests. Bashir, as we've seen, repeatedly promised in public that the referendum would be held, while in private the NCP negotiated every minute detail in order to slow the process to a crawl.

Beginning in mid-2010, Khartoum massed heavy weaponry and its best-trained military units on the border with the South, particularly near the oil fields. The SPLA reciprocated by positioning their best-trained troops to face them. After Garang and Bashir had signed the CPA in January 2005, the SAF troops in the region exchanged their uniforms for the civilian suits of oil workers and security guards; they had hidden stocks of weapons in the oil fields as insurance, in case they failed to stop the referendum or didn't get the settlement they wanted. In August 2010, in Upper Nile State, SAF units advanced southward across the boundary (which is informal), only to be turned back by SPLA units—without any shots being fired. The GOSS officials concluded from these deployments—and given other ambiguous evidence—that Khartoum was plotting to attack, reoccupy the oil fields, and abrogate the referendum (or at least undermine it), precipitating a crisis that they intended to resolve by force. None of these fears were realized, at least as of the beginning of 2012.

They were right to be concerned, however. A hard-line faction within the NCP never supported the CPA and continues to undermine its provisions. Bashir and Ali Osman Taha, the leaders of the pro-CPA faction, kept control of the debate. The NCP cabinet put in place after the 2010 national elections—in which Bashir was reelected with 68 percent of the vote (though the elections were neither free nor fair)—represents the most intractable and reactionary cabinet of leaders since Sudan's independence in 1956. Bashir has argued privately that the North has no choice but to allow the referendum and the South's independence, given the increasingly well-armed and -trained SPLA. Turabi's allies in the Khartoum press corps wrote inflammatory opinion pieces attacking the secession movement, which they continued to oppose. They asked what the North was getting in return for its surrender through secession of the 80 percent of its resources—oil, minerals, water, animal herds, and farmland—that were in the South.

In mid-2010, shortly before the referendum, Bashir closed three of these newspapers in Khartoum (including one run by his uncle) and gave orders for all sermons at Friday mosque prayers to be reviewed and approved by state censors before being given. This did not prevent the foreign minister, Ali Kharti (one of the leaders of the PDF in the 1990s and one of the key organizers of the Janjawiid militia in Darfur), from warning that southerners in Khartoum would not be treated at hospitals, employed, or able to buy food should they vote for independence. The minister of information made equally inflammatory public statements. In late 2010, disputes within the NCP spilled into public view when Bashir contradicted his own ministers and pledged that he would protect southerners living in the North, their right to move freely, and their economic and property rights. He also reaffirmed his insistence that the referendum be held.

The referendum vote finally took place over seven days, beginning on January 9, 2011. Except for a few scattered incidents among the Misiriyya in Abyei, there was no violence or disruptions. Five hundred international monitors reported no interference or intimidation by any government—either Khartoum's or Juba's—and heavy turnout. Reports from Sudanese embassies around the world and in the IDP settlements outside Khartoum indicated that southerners voting outside the South were able to do so without interference or incident. The AU was quick to affirm the 98.5 percent vote in favor of secession. Other countries followed with announcements that they would establish diplomatic relations with the new Republic of South Sudan after July 9, 2011. The Obama administration had offered the Bashir government a plan to normalize relations with the United States—including eliminating economic sanctions, establishing full diplomatic recognition, and taking Sudan off the list of countries that sponsor terrorist groups—should Khartoum refrain from interfering. On January 13, 2011, the U.S. State Department issued an unusual press statement complimenting Bashir on his cooperation.

South Sudan police march in the Independence Day celebration in
Juba on July 9, 2011. (Henrik Stabell/NPA)

The July 9 independence celebration in Juba formally
ended fifty-five years of struggle by the southern people and
launched the birth of a new nation. Thirty heads of state, UN
secretary general Ban Ki-moon, the crown prince of Norway,
and the major northern political leaders—Omar al-Bashir,
Nafie ali Nafie, Hassan al-Turabi, and Sadiq al-Mahdi—attended the celebration. I asked the southern leaders how difficult it was for them to have these men in Juba, given what
they had done to the southern people. Their reply illustrated
how politically shrewd and calculating they had become:
"The presence of these men, whatever the past had brought,
was an implicit acceptance of the independence of the South
and the legitimacy of the Republic of South Sudan." Many of
the countries at the ceremony announced the establishment
of formal diplomatic relations with Juba. Within two weeks
of the ceremony, Salva Kiir traveled to the UN as the new
republic became its 193nd member state. The AU accepted
the South as a member, as did dozens of other countries.
The war for independence was over, and now the battle

to keep the peace and extend development would be the central priority. International acceptance of Southern independence and sovereignty could not have occurred without Khartoum's full assent and cooperation, which in turn could not have taken place if Western military force or more economic sanctions were used to intimate them. Khartoum needed to voluntarily allow the South to become independent—which it finally did do.

Will the North and South return to war?

More than any other single factor, the balance of military power between the North and the South—now two sovereign states with large armies—will determine whether or not the peace will hold. The North has air superiority, particularly because of its recent purchases of advanced aircraft and weapons from the Russians and Chinese and its hiring of mercenary pilots to operate them. It would likely bomb the South but be unable to execute a ground invasion. The soldiers of the SAF were demoralized by the Darfur civil war and would be again if ordered into combat in the South. The units manned by soldiers originally recruited in the South were kept away from the North–South border in 2010 and 2011 because Khartoum remained unsure of their loyalty. In late 2011 Khartoum demobilized and returned to South Sudan 30,000 SAF soldiers who were ethnic Southerners (a third of its army) whose loyalty it distrusted. (When Khartoum ordered the Fourteenth Division of the SAF, most of whom are Nubans, to disarm Abdul Azziz's forces in the Nuba Mountains in June 2011, many units refused to carry out their orders; 400 troops mutinied and joined his forces. In the ensuing battle Abdul Azziz's forces took control of 76 of 79 SAF garrisons in the Nuba Mountains, leaving Khartoum with three garrisons—an extraordinary defeat for the SAF.) In July 2011, fearing more troop desertions, Khartoum formally legitimized the Arab militias—which, as we've seen, it had subsidized and secretly commanded in the past (and then denied knowledge of their atrocities)—by absorbing them into the SAF and the military command structure. Khartoum deployed Janjiwiid troops from Darfur—now formally absorbed into the SAF—in the battle against Malak Agar's forces in Blue Nile State in late 2011, because it could not trust regular SAF troops to carry out their orders.

The SPLA makes up for its relative weakness in weapons systems with a higher level of morale, which supported SPLA victories in the late 1990s and early 2000s, and a larger land army than the North. The South has also began arming itself using oil revenues with modern weapons systems, purchasing 300 new T-72 tanks from Ukraine (one shipment of which was looted by Somali pirates), which can outgun the SAF's older tank arsenal. The SPLA general staff has worked during the years since the CPA's passage to convert their guerrilla army into a conventional force, an effort that will take a generation to complete. Both the SAF and the SPLA have command-and-control challenges because their soldiers' various ethnic and tribal loyalties can conflict with the orders of their senior officers and political leadership. It is unclear whether all SPLA and SAF units would follow orders into combat should the North and South return to war, though the SAF has a much larger problem because their recruiting grounds—Darfur, the Nuba Mountains, Blue Nile, and southern Sudan—have been brutalized by Khartoum over the years. Should a new war erupt, it will be of a conventional type, with heavy military casualties, and likely be fought in the North, given that the South's northern allies (the Darfuri rebels and the Beja, Blue Nile, and Nuba Mountain forces) would take the battle to Khartoum.

Perhaps a third of my time as the U.S. Envoy I spent quietly putting in place a continuing U.S. government military assistance program to modernize the SPLA and linking up SPLA commanders with the U.S. military command structure. President Bush, Secretary Rice, and I all agreed in our first meeting on Sudan in the Oval Office that a strong military deterrent in the South was the only way to limit effectively Northern adventurism and intimidation. The U.S. government program had bipartisan support in Congress, amounted to more than $30 million a year, and focused on training, institution building, building construction, and technical assistance, but involved no weapons system transfers.

A slow-moving, relatively invisible internal military coup may have taken place in Khartoum in June 2011, displacing the civilian NCP leadership and replacing it with military officers loyal to President Bashir. Seasoned UN officials have noticed that for the first time, senior SAF officers are attending official Sudanese government meetings with international organizations and other foreign diplomats. Bashir may have decided that he was increasingly at risk of being deposed by a coup of Islamist officers angry with the gradual dissolution of the Sudanese state, widespread corruption in the Bashir government, the loss of the South and its resources, the presence of 26,000 UN/AU peacekeeping troops in Darfur and 10,000 in South Sudan (which has outraged Islamist officers), and the shrinking power and influence of Khartoum in governing what remained of the country. Instead of negotiating political agreements to resolve long-standing political disputes in the Darfur, Abyei, Nuba Mountains, and Blue Nile states, President Bashir appears to have decided on the military option: trying to crush all opposition by arresting or killing them, stop all political negotiations, and consolidate all political power in his own hands. By allying himself with the generals, he reduced the risk of a coup but increased the risk of a dissolution of the northern Sudanese state, as none of the legitimate grievances of the regions and tribes in the North will be addressed through more bloodshed. Should these generals persuade Bashir to launch a military attack against the South and roll back the last decade of political negotiations that led to southern independence, it would plunge the country into the worst kind of bloodshed seen in the last century. And since the Republic of South Sudan is now a sovereign, independent state, such aggression would be an international war with serious political implications.

What are the South's prospects?

The one region of the country that may be the most stable and prosperous a decade from now is the same region that has been the most brutalized by Sudan's bloody history. The South may still have the brightest hope for a prosperous future. It is unified both by its animosity toward the North and its determination to make itself an economic and political success. Some scholars believe that South Korea, Taiwan, Thailand, Hong Kong, Malaysia, and Singapore—the so-called East Asia economic tigers—broke out of their cycles of grinding poverty and established prospering democracies between 1960 and 1990 because their elites undertook economic and political reforms as they feared insurgencies supported by Mao's China. The South is in a similar position relative to the North, making the new government in Juba determined to speed development, distribute wealth more equitably, clean up corruption, and avoid the failed economic policies of other African states following their liberation struggles from the colonial powers. Thus the existence of a hostile and belligerent North looming across the 1,240-mile border between the two countries may be the unifying cement that holds the South together while it constructs its new society, government, and economy. The risk is that these deep suspicions between the two countries will draw them into another war.

Unless the North and South are able to put the last two bloody centuries behind them and normalize their commercial and political relationships, it is unlikely that they will be able to encourage investment, development, and the expansion of oil and mineral exploration. More than anything else, the South's future will be determined by how rapidly it can build government capacity and extend the rule of law, establish public order, encourage private business investment, and avoid a new conventional war with the North. The South has been remarkably restrained in dealing with the provocations of the Khartoum government in mid-2011. Whether it can continue this restraint long enough to build its internal institutions to withstand northern pressure remains to be seen.

One of the South's greatest challenges remains the rising expectations of younger people who believe Eden lies before them and that the only thing keeping them from it had been the North. It will soon become evident that this is only half the problem; stabilization and development are long and complex processes. The South Korean and Taiwanese miracles took thirty years to unfold and mature. Institutions cannot be put in place, roads and bridges constructed, and public services created overnight. A safe and prosperous southern Sudan will take many decades to materialize. Critics question whether the South has a generation to achieve these goals.

Mundari lady, Central Equatorial State, South Sudan. (Henrik Stabell/NPA)

The second major challenge for the South will be managing tribal tensions, which are always simmering beneath the surface even in relatively stable areas. Some evidence exists that the North has been arming and equipping several anti-Juba militias in the oil-producing areas to foment intertribal conflict. Juba believes that Khartoum is attempting to use these militias to take control of the oil areas and declare a rump republic that it would control along with the oil fields. Deep resentment exists among those southern tribes, which have few if any officials representing them in the government to protect their interests; the Equatorian tribes resent the domination of the Republic by the Nilotic tribes, particularly the Dinkas; and the traditional Dinka-Nuer rivalry remains poisonous. While the Dinkas make up at least 35–40 percent of the southern population, in some areas 60 percent of the prized senior public sector jobs have gone to them. The South's ethnic imbalance is not comparable to the dominance of the Three Tribes in the North, which control 70 percent of senior-level jobs while they represent less than 6 percent of the country's historic population. The third serious challenge facing the South is the lack of an educated population capable of running a modern state and economy. In some areas illiteracy rates are 70–80 percent, and the number of people with college degrees and management experience is much more modest. Juba is now trying to bring back the educated southern diaspora with degrees and management experience to run the new government.

As of this writing, the three most functional indigenous institutions are the Christian churches (Roman Catholic, Anglican, Presbyterian, and Pentecostal), the SPLM, and the SPLA. Of these, the most powerful by far are the churches. The values the churches inculcate, and the extent to which they use their influence to pursue the public good, will determine the South's future. The role of the churches should not be compared to that of the Christian churches in the current day West, where churches—however influential—

make up only one of many institutions that guide the building of a modern civil society. In South Sudan, Christian churches are *the* central private institution, exercising a powerful influence in the development of the emerging social order.

The North and the South have seen tangible benefits from peace, however unevenly distributed among the people. As we've seen, both economies boomed after the CPA was signed, and oil revenues have continued to pour into their treasuries. Juba and Khartoum have a great deal to lose should they be drawn into war. One of the unintended consequences of the development of the southern oil fields and the related infrastructure supporting it—the pipeline, refineries, and port in the North—has been the integration of the two economies. Both sides are now dependent on each other for their survival. Without oil, Sudan—North and South—faces instability, and the reality is that the production from the oil field may start declining by 2020. Absent new discoveries, both governments will be at risk of falling, and Sudan will be at risk of returning to a state in which "it will be all against all," as Thomas Hobbes put it. The cities will be depopulated, people will return to the bush, men with guns will rule, and chaos will ensue. Should the remaining oil revenues be wisely invested in development projects—particularly education and infrastructure—speeding economic growth, and producing private sector jobs, that day may never come. Which of these two scenarios unfolds is an open question only time will answer.

Appendix: Facts about Historic Sudan

Population

Historic Sudan

- 45,047,502

South Sudan

- 8,260,000[1]

Geography in square miles and square kilometers

Historic Sudan

- 1,861,484 square kilometers
- 718,722.99 square miles

South Sudan

- 644,329 square kilometers
- 248,776.817 square miles

Major languages[2]

Historic Sudan

- Arabic (official), English (official), Nubian, Ta Bedawie, Dinka, Fur, and more than seventy major tribal languages, several of which are spoken by more than 100,000 people

South Sudan

- English (official), Arabic (official)—including Juba Arabic, a local dialect—and regional languages, including Dinka, Nuer, Bari, Zande, and Shilluk

Ethnic groups or tribes[3]

Historic Sudan

- Sudanese Arab (approximately 70%)
- The largest non-Arab groups are Fur, Beja, Nuba, and Fallata

South Sudan

- Dinka, Kakwa, Bari, Azande, Shilluk, Kuku, Murle, Mandari, Didinga, Ndogo, Bviri, Lndi, Anuak, Bongo, Lango, Dungotona, and Acholi

Religions

Historic Sudan

- Sunni Muslim 70%
- Christian 20%
- Traditional religion 10%[4]

National sovereign debt

Historic Sudan

- Public debt: 92.6% of GDP (2010 est.)
- External debt: $37.73 billion (December 31, 2010, est.)

South Sudan

- No large external debt or structural trade deficits

Currency (North and South)[5]

- Exchange rate for the Sudanese pound: 1.00 SDG = 0.373483 USD.

Trade

Historic Sudan

- $10.29 billion (2010 est.)
- Commodities: oil and petroleum products, cotton, sesame, livestock, groundnuts, gum arabic, sugar
- Partners: China 60.3%, Japan 14%, Indonesia 8.6%, India 4.9% (2009)

Economic growth rates

Historic Sudan

Real GDP (after inflation) in 2010: 5.2%; 2009: 4.2%; 2006 and 2007: 10%
Agriculture employs 80% of the workforce and represents a third of GDP

Natural resources

Historic Sudan

- Petroleum; small reserves of iron ore, copper, chromium ore, zinc, tungsten, mica, silver, gold; hydropower

South Sudan

- Hydropower, fertile agricultural land, gold, diamonds, petroleum, hardwoods, limestone, iron ore, copper, chromium ore, zinc, coltan (Columbite-tantalite), tungsten, mica, silver

Total GDP and per capita GDP

Historic Sudan

- GDP (purchasing power parity): $100 billion (2010 est.)[6]
- Per capita income: $2,300 (2010 est.)

South Sudan

- GDP in 2010: 30 billion Sudanese pounds, equivalent to $13 billion

- GDP per capita income in 2010: 3,564 Sudanese pounds, equivalent to $1,546

International performance index ranks: UNDP Human Development Index

Historic Sudan

- 2010: 154 out of 169 countries[7] (169 is lowest level)

Transparency International—Corruption Index

Historic Sudan

- Corruption ranking: 172 out of 178 countries[8] (178 is most corrupt)

Freedom House—Democracy Index

Historic Sudan

- Political Rights Score: 7 (7 is lowest)
- Civil Liberties Score: 7 (7 is lowest)
- Status: Not free[9]

World Bank Doing Business Report

Historic Sudan

- 2011: Ease of doing business ranking: 154 out of 183 countries (183 is the worst)

Notes

1. Republic of South Sudan National Bureau of Statistics, http://ssnbs.org/.

2. For more information about languages in Sudan, see http://countrystudies.us/sudan/36.htm and www.ethnologue.com/show_country.asp?name=sd.

3. For more information about ethnic groups, see www.joshuaproject.net/countries.php?rog3=SU.

4. www.cia.gov/library/publications/the-world-factbook/geos/ su.html.

5. See more information about currency at http://af.reuters.com/ article/topNews/idAFJOE7770PW20110808.

6. www.cia.gov/library/publications/the-world-factbook/geos/ su.html.

7. http://hdr.undp.org/en/statistics/.

8. www.transparency.org/policy_research/surveys_indices/ cpi/2010/results.

9. www.freedomhouse.org/uploads/fiw11/CombinedAverage Ratings(IndependentCountries)FIW2011.pdf.

BIBLIOGRAPHY

Ashworth, John. *CPA Alert: The State of Sudan's Comprehensive Peace Agreement*. Alert no. 2. Utrecht: IKV Pax Christi / Horn of Africa Programme, 2010.

Burr, Millard J., and Robert O. Collins. *Darfur: The Long Road to Disaster*. Rev. ed. Princeton, N.J.: Markus Wiener, 2006.

Burr, Millard J., and Robert O. Collins. *Requiem for the Sudan: War, Drought, and Disaster Relief on the Nile*. Boulder, Colo.: Westview Press, 1995.

Burr, Millard J., and Robert O. Collins. *Sudan in Turmoil: Hasan al-Turabi and the Islamist State, 1989–2003*. Rev. ed. Princeton, N.J.: Markus Wiener, 2010.

Collins, Robert O. *A History of Modern Sudan*. Cambridge: Cambridge University Press, 2008.

Collins, Robert O. *The Southern Sudan in Historical Perspective*. New Brunswick, N.J.: Transaction, 2006.

Crilly, Rob. *Saving Darfur: Everyone's Favourite African War*. London: Reportage Press, 2010.

De Waal, Alex. *Famine Crimes: Politics and the Disaster Relief Industry in Africa*. African Issues. Bloomington: Indiana University Press/ African Rights and the International African Institute, 1997.

De Waal, Alex. *Famine That Kills: Darfur, Sudan*. Rev. ed. Edited by John D. Hargreaves, Michael Twaddle, and Terence Ranger. Oxford: Oxford University Press, 2005.

De Waal, Alex, ed. *Islamism and Its Enemies in the Horn of Africa*. Bloomington: Indiana University Press, 2004.

De Waal, Alex, ed. *War in Darfur and the Search for Peace*. Boston: Harvard University Press/Global Equity Initiative, 2007.

Deng, Francis M. *The Dinka of Sudan*. Long Grove, Ill.: Waveland Press, 1984.

Deng, Francis M. *Sudan at the Brink: Self-Determination and National Unity*. Edited by Kevin M. Cahill, M.D. New York: Fordham University Press and the Institute for International Humanitarian Affairs, 2010.

Deng, Francis M. *War of Visions: Conflict of Identities in the Sudan*. Washington, D.C.: Brookings Institute, 1995.

Eggers, Dave. *What Is the What: The Autobiography of Valentino Achak Deng*. San Francisco: McSweeney's Books, 2006.

El Mahdi, Mandour. *A Short History of the Sudan*. Oxford: Oxford University Press, 1965.

Evans-Pritchard, E. E. *The Azande: History and Political Institutions*. London: Oxford University Press, 1971.

Flint, Julie, and Alex de Waal. *Darfur: A New History of a Long War*. African Arguments. London: Zed Books/International African Institute, 2008.

Flint, Julie, and Alex de Waal. *Darfur: A Short History of a Long War*. African Arguments. London: Zed Books/International African Institute, 2005.

Genser, Jared, and Irwin Colter, eds. *The Responsibility to Protect: The Promise of Stopping Mass Atrocities in Our Times*. Chapter on Darfur by Andrew Natsios and Zachary Scott. New York: Oxford University Press, 2011.

Government of Southern Sudan. *Laws of Southern Sudan: The Interim Constitution of Southern Sudan, 2005*. Juba, Sudan: Government of Southern Sudan/Ministry of Legal Affairs and Constitutional Development, 2005.

Hamdi, Mohamed Elhachmi. *The Making of an Islamic Political Leader: Conversations with Hasan al-Turabi*. Translated by Ashur A. Shamis. Boulder, Colo.: Westview Press, 1998.

Hamilton, Rebecca. *Fighting for Darfur: Public Action and the Struggle to Stop Genocide*. New York: Palgrave Macmillan / St. Martin's Press, 2011.

Hoile, Dr. David. *Darfur in Perspective*. 2nd ed. London: European-Sudanese Public Affairs Council, 2006.

Johnson, Douglas H. *The Root Causes of Sudan's Civil War*. African Issues. Bloomington: Indiana University Press/International African Institute, 2003.

Jok, Jok Madut. *Sudan: Race, Religion, and Violence*. Oxford: Oneworld, 2007.

Lagu, Joseph, Lt. Gen. (Retired), and Hon. D. Letts. *Sudan: Odyssey through a State: From Ruin to Hope*. Omdurman, Sudan: Omdurman Ahlia University/MOB Center for Sudanese Studies, 2006.

Lowrie, Arthur L., ed. *Islam, Democracy, the State and the West: A Round Table with Dr. Hasan Turabi*. Tampa, Fla.: World and Islam Studies Enterprise and University of South Florida, Committee for Middle Eastern Studies, 1993.

Mamdani, Mahmood. *Saviors and Survivors: Darfur, Politics, and the War on Terror*. New York: Pantheon Books, 2009.

Minear, Larry, et al. *Humanitarianism under Siege: A Critical Review of Operation Lifeline Sudan*. Trenton, N.J.: Red Sea Press, and Washington, D.C.: Institute on Hunger and Development/Bread for the World, 1991.

Moorehead, Alan. *The Blue Nile*. New York: Harper and Row, 1962.

Moorehead, Alan. *The White Nile*. New York: Harper, 1960.

O'Fahey, R. S. *State and Society in Dar Fur*. London: C. Hurst, 1980.

O'Fahey, R. S., and J. L. Spaulding. *Kingdoms of the Sudan*. London: Methuen, 1974.

Salih, Tayeb. *Season of Migration to the North*. Edited by Chinua Achebe. Translated by Denys Johnson-Davies. African Series Writers. London: Heinemann Educational Books, 1970.

Scroggins, Deborah. *Emma's War*. New York: Vintage Books, 2004.

Thesiger, Wilfred. *The Life of My Choice*. London: Flamingo, 1992.

Totten, Samuel, and Eric Markusen, eds. *Genocide in Darfur: Investigating the Atrocities in the Sudan*. New York: Routledge, 2006.

Walzer, Craig, et al. *Out of Exile: Narratives from the Abducted and Displaced People of Sudan*. San Francisco: McSweeney's Books, 2008.

Wright, Lawrence. *The Looming Tower: Al-Qaeda and the Road to 9/11*. New York: Vintage Books, 2007.

INDEX

246 Index

Rizaiqat tribe, 9–10, 96
Roosevelt, Theodore, 33

el-Sadat, Anwar
attempts and assassination
of, 56, 93, 122
support from, 48, 55–56
Sadiq al-Mahdi, Sadek (Mahdi's
great-grandson)
arrest of, 48, 80
background of, xix, 26
exile of, 53
Islamism and, 54, 55
policies of, xxi, 72–74, 76, 77,
183, 214
removal of, 82, 130, 199–200
Second Civil War and,
72–74
SAF. *See* Sudanese Armed
Forces
Sahara Desert, 8
movement of, 54, 118
Salafism, xxi
Salim, Mamdouh, 94
Salim, Salim, 188
Sambeyo, Lazarus, 168
Sand War, 122
al-Sanoussi, Ibrahim, 88
Saudi Arabia, 89–90, 102
Save Darfur Coalition, 151, 158
schools, 32, 38, 43
Schultz, George, 76
Second Civil War, xvi–xvii, xix
beginning of, 57–58, 65
Bush's, G.W., focus on end
to, 166–69
Darfur rebellions
and, 128–29

economy impacted by, 96,
111–12
employment during, 207
event precipitating, 59–61
fatalities during, 73, 77–79
Garang, John, and, 65–66,
97–100, 129
negotiation of end to, 163–66
roots of, 54
Sadiq and, 72–74
southerners attacking
southerners in, 73, 79, 98
Selassie, Haile (Ethiopian
emperor), 50, 68
Sennar Dam, 33, 99
September Laws, 60–61
Shaiqiyya, 17, 21, 111. *See also*
The Three Tribes
Sharia law
imposition of, 61, 92, 103,
171, 201
repeal of, 73
al-Turabi and, 55, 86, 89
Shaykan, battle of, 21–22
shed boys, 75
sheikh, xvii
Shell Oil, 58
Shi'a, 92
Shifa pharmaceutical plant,
bombing of, 113, 165
Shilluk Kingdom, 16, 204
Shilluk tribe, xvii. *See also*
Nilotic Tribes
al-Shingeiti, Muhammad
Salih, 38
Sirte Peace Conference
(2007), 123, 189, 201
slave trade, 18, 19, 21, 31, 44